THE WHITE BIRD

THE WHITE BIRD
Writings by John Berger

———

Edited and with an introduction by

LLOYD SPENCER

A TIGERSTRIPE BOOK

Chatto & Windus
LONDON

A TIGERSTRIPE BOOK

Published in 1985 by
Chatto & Windus
40 William IV Street, London WC2N 4DF

British Library Cataloguing in Publication Data

Berger, John
The white bird: writings by John Berger. –
(A Tigerstripe book)
I. Title   II. Spencer, Lloyd
082   PR6052.E564

ISBN 0-7011-3006-7

Photoset by Rowland Phototypesetting Ltd
Bury St Edmunds, Suffolk
Printed in Great Britain by
Redwood Burn Ltd,
Trowbridge, Wiltshire

Contents

List of Illustrations   page ix
Introduction by Lloyd Spencer   xi

1 THE WHITE BIRD
Rembrandt self-portrait   3
Self-portrait 1914–18   4
The white bird   5

2 LEAVING HOME
The storyteller   13
On the edge of a foreign city   19
The eaters and the eaten   27
Dürer: a portrait of the artist   33
One night in Strasbourg   41
On the banks of the Sava   45
Four postcard poems   50
On the Bosphorus   52
Manhattan   61
The theatre of indifference   68

3 TWO DREAMS
The city of Sodom   77
The deluge   79

4 LOVE'S ABC
Kerchief   85

Goya: the Maja, dressed and undressed   86
Bonnard   92
Modigliani's alphabet of love   99
The Hals mystery   106

5 THE LAST PICTURES
In a Moscow cemetery   121
Ernst Fischer: a philosopher and death   126
François, Georges and Amélie: a requiem in three parts   139
Drawn to that moment   146
The unsaid   152

6 THE 'WORK' OF ART
On a Degas bronze of a dancer   157
The moment of Cubism   159
The eyes of Claude Monet   189
The *work* of art   197
Painting and time   205
The place of painting   212
On visibility   219

7 THE UNMADE ROAD
Redder every day   225
Mayakovsky: his language and his death [*with Anya Bostock*]   226
The secretary of Death   238
The hour of poetry   243
The screen and *The Spike*   253
Sicilian lives   261
Leopardi   269
The production of the world   276
Mother tongue   282

8 THE SIXTH OF AUGUST 1945
Hiroshima   287
Of all the colours   296

Sources and acknowledgments   299

To the memory of Howe Bancroft

List of Illustrations

Rembrandt van Rijn, The Polish Rider (Frick Collection, New York) *page* 2

Albrecht Dürer, Self-portrait (Alte Pinakothek, Munich) 38

Albrecht Dürer, Self-portrait (Prado, Madrid) 39

Lucas van Leyden, Lot and His Daughters (Louvre, Paris) 78

Albrecht Dürer, The Deluge (Kunsthistorisches Museum, Vienna) 80

Edouard Manet, Olympia (Musée d'Orsay, Paris) 109

Rembrandt van Rijn, Bathsheba (Louvre, Paris) 111

Franz Hals, The Gipsy Girl (Louvre, Paris) 114

Hiroshima: paintings by survivors (*Unforgettable Fire*, NHK, Tokyo, 1977) 289, 290

ix

Introduction

In the nineteenth century there was a tradition whereby novelists, storytellers and even poets offered the public an historical explanation of their work, often in the form of a preface. Inevitably a poem or a story deals with a particular experience: how this experience relates to developments on a world scale can and should be implied within the writing itself – this is precisely the challenge posed by the resonance of a language (in one sense any language, like a mother, knows all); nevertheless it is not usually possible in a poem or a story to make the relation between particular and universal fully explicit. Those who try to do so end up writing parables. Hence the writer's desire to write an explanation *around* the work he is offering to the reader. The tradition became established in the nineteenth century exactly because it was a century of revolutionary change in which the relation between the individual and history was becoming a conscious one. The scale and rate of change in our own century is even greater.

Thus wrote John Berger at the beginning of the 'Historical Afterword' to his collection of stories of peasant experience, *Pig Earth*, the first part of the trilogy *Into Their Labours* on which he is still engaged.

Today John Berger is well known for his novels and stories as well as for his works of non-fiction, including several volumes of art criticism and his work with the photographer Jean Mohr. Throughout his career John Berger has also been active as an essayist, writing regularly for a wide audience. It is this aspect of his writing in particular which this volume presents.

This is his fifth volume collection of essays and it is the most comprehensive in the period of time it embraces, in the range of types of writing and in the issues it addresses. Anchored in the concerns of his most recent work, it allows one a sense of the development of his writings. Representative of John Berger the essayist, it throws light on the impulses behind much of his work in other media and genres. Love and passion, death, power, labour, the experience of time and the nature of our present history: the many themes that run through this volume are important not only as foci for John Berger's work but are also urgent contemporary concerns. Selecting and arranging the material was relatively simple. Introducing it is less so.

I remember well my surprise when I first sat down to work with John Berger. I had been invited by him to spend a week talking about photographs and about his long essay on photography ('Appearances', in *Another Way of Telling*). I had come armed with detailed comments on the first draft of the essay. I found I could refer easily and confidently not only to writers such as Walter Benjamin and Susan Sontag who had clearly influenced the essay, but also to John Berger's own previous writings on photography.

What came as a surprise was just how unhelpful this academic and essentially linguistic facility turned out to be, for the nature and intensity of John Berger's concentration astounded me and provided a kind of instantaneous instruction. Almost at once I realized that where I had approached the whole exercise as if the problem were to make these various statements and analyses (which had already proved for me their power of illumination and explanation) merely consistent with one another and to push the argument along, for John Berger, even at such a late stage in the process of writing, what mattered was what could be *seen*, what could be read from appearances themselves, almost to the exclusion of the familiar words and formulations. These he had clearly put aside – even the phrases in the essay on which we were working were almost forgotten. The words which mattered were those called forth by what we could see. The focus was entirely on images and appearances, on the photographs on the desk and occasionally on the worlds that appeared through the open window.

The affinity between this discipline, which is clearly now habitual and largely unconscious in John Berger, and the philosophic methods of the early phenomenologists is not an accidental one; there are many traces of the influence of that tradition in European philosophy in Berger's writings. But Berger clearly owes less to any philosophic training than to his own early passion for painting and drawing and his life-long involvement with the visual arts. It is appropriate to borrow his own shorthand and to say that with John Berger seeing really does come first. And despite the career he has made in writing, and despite the levels of complexity and abstraction present in his writing, there is a sense in which *seeing*, perceiving and imagining, has retained its primacy as a way of understanding the world.

John Berger was born in London on 5th November 1926. A kind of inner exile and emigration began for him when he was sent away to a school he loathed. It could only be reinforced by his precocious reading of the anarchist classics. At sixteen, and very much against the wishes of his family, he left school in order to be an artist. His studies at the Central School of Art were interrupted by the war. He refused the commission to which he was expected to accede and spent the war as a private and then a lance corporal. That meant living with working-class men in a kind of proximity not normally possible for anyone of his background. It proved to be a decisive influence. When he left the army he enrolled at the Chelsea Art School and began to involve himself in current politics.

Exploring relationships between visual and verbal meaning, between words and images has been a recurring preoccupation of John Berger's work. But before he began to explore their interrelation he experienced a kind of divided loyalty. As a boy he painted pictures and wrote poems and stories in equal numbers. While still at school this lent his painting a literary, anecdotal quality and invested his writings with a preoccupation with visual description. His painting continued after he left school and he had a series of successful exhibitions. Even today he still draws. But he began earning a living by talking about art and later by writing art criticism. Writing became his main vehicle, his own means of communication, but in a sense his primary reality and his constant concerns were visual.

In 1952 he began ten years as the art critic of the *New Statesman*. With his outspoken politics and his sensitivity to the actual processes of painting he soon established himself as one of the best-known and most controversial critics. At the end of a decade as the only Marxist art critic in Britain writing regularly for a wide audience, Berger left Britain for good. At more or less the same time he escaped finally from having to express everything he thought or felt in terms of art criticism.

Art, politics and exile are the key elements in his first novel, *Painter of Our Time* (1958), which drew on the several friendships he had formed with emigré artists living in London, most of them in exile from Eastern and Central Europe. Janos Lavin, the main character of the novel, is a deeply political painter, living and dreaming the legacy of Modernism and meditating on the imperatives of a new and critical realism needed in socialist art and thinking. At the end of the novel he disappears from London, drawn back to his native Hungary by the events of 1956, leaving even those who know him most intimately (his wife, the writer of the novel, and its readers) utterly uncertain about what course of action he might have followed or what might become of him. A novel which demonstrated so compellingly the intractable complexity of political realities was unlikely to find a welcome in the polarized Cold War climate just two years after the invasion of Hungary. So fierce were the attacks on the book from right and left that it was discreetly withdrawn by its publishers after only a few weeks. Today few would question its wisdom and integrity.

The struggle to consolidate the legacy of Modernism in new social and political contexts is at the heart of two major studies of individual artists, one under communism, the other under capitalism, which followed; *The Success and Failure of Picasso* (1965) and *Art and Revolution. Ernst Neizvestny and the role of the artist in the U.S.S.R.* (1969). From this period and exemplifying the flexible and far-reaching Marxist approach the seminal essay, 'The Moment of

Cubism' (1966–8), is reprinted here as the centrepiece of the section on 'The *work* of art'.

But the work of Berger's which undoubtedly had the most wide-spread impact on the study of the visual arts was the BBC TV series and the book which resulted, *Ways of Seeing* (1972). As a crucial milestone in the dissemination of a historical and materialist approach to art *Ways of Seeing* appears on a great many reading lists. It remains one of the most succinct and challenging statements on the social role of the dominant traditions in Western art, and on the ideological and technological conditioning of our ways of seeing both art and the world.

As a polemical masterpiece *Ways of Seeing* lends itself to superficial misreading, and even some of the people it has influenced most have found it difficult to reconcile its forceful argument with John Berger's approach in his many essays on individual masters and particular paintings. When he examines the work of Rembrandt or Hals, of Monet or van Gogh (as he does in essays in this collection) he is not concerned to root out elements of class ideology and historical limitation. Precise historical and biographical information is often used, but the intent is to learn from the paintings themselves.

One chapter in *Ways of Seeing* is about women as visual objects. Its argument became a milestone in feminist analysis of art and the media. The earlier books on Picasso and on Neizvestny both contained important passages on the force of sexual passion, its elemental nature and its liberatory possibilities. These two perspectives were brought into tension in the novel *G* (1972), which narrates, amongst other things, the sexual obsession of its protagonist, G. In this volume the essays in the section entitled 'Love's ABC' explore the particular experiences of love and passion of a series of artists, and the essay 'One night in Strasbourg' records thoughts on passion set down while Berger was at work on the film script *Le Milieu du Monde*.

G ends in Trieste, described as the nodal point at which developed and underdeveloped regions meet. Among the many prizes awarded for the novel was Britain's premier literary prize, the Booker McConnell. In his acceptance speech Berger denounced the Booker McConnell Corporation with its sugar plantations and gave half his prize money to West Indian revolutionary groups opposed to the neo-colonialism of which the Booker corporation was part. The other half of the prize went to finance *A Seventh Man* (1975), a book about the experience of 11 million migrant workers in Europe and about the economic mechanisms which fed off their personal aspirations and ensured Europe's continued active underdevelopment of the states on its periphery.

By exposing in comprehensive and graphic terms the nature of the exploitation of Europe's migrant workers *A Seventh Man* posed important problems for the official Marxist ideologies or sectional politics of particular opposition parties and small groups. It reminded Marxism of its claims to be a universal outlook invested with the hopes of all mankind, and not simply a weapon and a set of tactics by which particular groups (albeit not the most advantaged) could further their own particular interests.

Since then Berger has presented another issue which is a troubling reminder: the vexed problem of peasants as a social class. He has done this at a time when all over the world the traditional peasant way of life is being rapidly and often violently transformed.

Today John Berger lives and works in a tiny peasant village in the French Alps. He is accepted as a welcome stranger in the community and to many he has become a particularly well-loved friend. His gift as a storyteller is recognized and appreciated and, over the past decade, it has developed greatly.

In 1935 Walter Benjamin wrote a very great essay entitled 'The Storyteller,' which has clearly influenced John Berger's work. Benjamin distinguishes two traditional types of storyteller: the resident tiller of the soil and the traveller, someone who has come from afar. On several occasions with John Berger at his Alpine home I have seen representatives of both types at table together.

It is not possible to formulate all the ways in which Berger's own development has led to and been influenced by the peasant experience. To isolate just one important aspect: the peasantry have preserved a sense of history, and an experience of *time*, opposed to that propagated by industrial capitalism. In Berger's terms it is not the Marxian or proletarian revolution which plays the role of destroying history, but capitalism itself, which has an interest in severing every link with the past and orientating all effort and imagination toward that which is yet to take place.

Peasants are no strangers to exploitation or alienation but they are less susceptible to certain kinds of self-deception. Like the slave in Hegel's well-known master–slave dialectic, they remain in more immediate contact with death and with the elemental processes and rhythms of the world. By the labour of their own hands they produce and order their world. In their anecdotes and stories, even in gossip, they weave their own history according to the laws of remembrance. They know who it is that benefits by progress and they keep alive a dream, sometimes silent or secret, of a totally different world. John Berger has demonstrated what it is to learn from them.

The storyteller lends his voice to the experience of others. The essayist lends himself to the specific occasion, or issue about which he writes. John Berger's own career and development form one context in which the writings offered here can be understood. But the point of learning more *about* John Berger is in order more effectively to learn *from* him, to learn more about the various urgent issues and the many difficult questions he raises.

As with most such collections of writings this volume owes a part of its content to accident and circumstance. When considering material for inclusion in this book I had to respect quite incidental and external constraints: for example, very few of the pieces included have appeared in previous collections. Nevertheless the writings selected organized themselves fairly straightforwardly into a simple arrangement under a handful of headings: travel and emigration, dreaming, love and passion, death, art as activity and artifact, and the relation between work in language and the physical labour which produces and reproduces the world. These simple groupings had the advantage of allowing me to place alongside one another writings of a more general and far-reaching nature and pieces which are very specific and limited in the immediate objects or issues they address. Thus the arrangement of writings in the body of this collection ignores chronology (dates can be checked in the list of sources on page 299).

The concern with works of art, with the work art *does*, and the work by which art is produced, provide a natural focus for any collection of John Berger's writings. The concern with storytelling, and with language, is a concern more all-embracing and more diffuse in John Berger's life and hence in this work. The section entitled 'Leaving Home' introduces the themes of travel, exile and emigration; 'The Unmade Road' towards the end of this collection continues these reflections. All the pieces in 'Love's ABC' show John Berger attentive to works of art, and to paintings in particular. Different media and very different circumstances come together in the four essays on death, the 'Last pictures'; in each it is clear that the dead belong not only to the past – it is never the dead who bury the dead – but also to the present and to the future.

In putting this book together it has occurred to me that it too can be read as a story, or, rather, that it can function, as a whole text, like a story.

Berger once wrote:

'The story does not ultimately depend upon what is said, upon what we, projecting onto the world something of our own cultural paranoia, call its *plot*. The story does not depend upon any fixed repertoire of ideas and habits: it depends on its stride over spaces. In these spaces lies the meaning it bestows on events. Most of this meaning comes from the common aspirations of both characters and reader.

The task of the story teller is to know these aspirations and to turn them into the very strides of his own story. If he does this, the story can continue to play an important role wherever the harshness of life is such that people come together to try to change it. Then in the silent spaces of his story both past and future will combine to indict the present.'

Lloyd Spencer
Manchester 1985

I

THE WHITE BIRD

———

Rembrandt: *The Polish Rider*

Rembrandt self-portrait

———

The eyes from the face
two nights looking at the day
the universe of his mind
doubled by pity
nothing else can suffice.
Before a mirror
silent as a horseless road
he envisaged us
deaf dumb
returning overland
to look at him
in the dark.

1985

3

Self-portrait
1914–18

———

It seems now that I was so near to that war.
I was born eight years after it ended
When the General Strike had been defeated.

Yet I was born by Very light and shrapnel
On duck boards
Among limbs without bodies.

I was born of the look of the dead
Swaddled in mustard gas
And fed in a dugout.

I was the groundless hope of survival
With mud between finger and thumb
Born near Abbeville.

I lived the first year of my life
Between the leaves of a pocket bible
Stuffed in a khaki haversack.

I lived the second year of my life
With three photos of a woman
Kept in a standard issue army paybook.

In the third year of my life
At 11 am on November 11th 1918
I became all that was conceivable.

Before I could see
Before I could cry out
Before I could go hungry

I was the world fit for heroes to live in.

1985

4

The white bird

From time to time I have been invited by institutions – mostly American – to speak about aesthetics. On one occasion I considered accepting and I thought of taking with me a bird made of white wood. But I didn't go. The problem is that you can't talk about aesthetics without talking about the principle of hope and the existence of evil. During the long winters the peasants in certain parts of the Haute Savoie used to make wooden birds to hang in their kitchens and perhaps also in their chapels. Friends who are travellers have told me that they have seen similar birds, made according to the same principle, in certain regions of Czechoslovakia, Russia and the Baltic countries. The tradition may be more wide-spread.

The principle of the construction of these birds is simple enough, although to make a fine bird demands considerable skill. You take two bars of pine wood, about six inches in length, a little less than one inch in height and the same in width. You soak them in water so that the wood has the maximum pliability, then you carve them. One piece will be the head and body with a fan tail, the second piece will represent the wings. The art principally concerns the making of the wing and tail feathers. The whole block of each wing is carved according to the silhouette of a single feather. Then the block is sliced into thirteen thin layers and these are gently opened out, one by one, to make a fan shape. Likewise for the second wing and for the tail feathers. The two pieces of wood are joined together to form a cross and the bird is complete. No glue is used and there is only one nail where the two pieces of wood cross. Very light, weighing only two or three ounces, the birds are usually hung on a thread from an overhanging mantlepiece or beam so that they move with the air currents.

It would be absurd to compare one of these birds to a van Gogh self-portrait or a Rembrandt crucifixion. They are simple, home-made objects, worked according to a traditional pattern. Yet, by their very simplicity, they allow one to categorize the qualities which make them pleasing and mysterious to everyone who sees them.

First there is a figurative representation – one is looking at a bird, more precisely a dove, apparently hanging in mid-air. Thus, there is a reference to the surrounding world of nature. Secondly, the choice of subject (a flying bird) and the context in which it is placed (indoors where live birds are unlikely) render the object symbolic. This primary symbolism then joins a more general, cultural one. Birds, and doves in particular, have been credited with symbolic meanings in a very wide variety of cultures.

Thirdly, there is a respect for the material used. The wood has been fashioned according to its own qualities of lightness, pliability and texture. Looking at it, one is surprised by how well wood becomes bird. Fourthly, there is a formal unity and economy. Despite the object's apparent complexity, the grammar of its making is simple, even austere. Its richness is the result of repetitions which are also variations. Fifthly, this man-made object provokes a kind of astonishment: how on earth was it made? I have given rough indications above, but anyone unfamiliar with the technique wants to take the dove in his hands and examine it closely to discover the secret which lies behind its making.

These five qualities, when undifferentiated and perceived as a whole, provoke at least a momentary sense of being before a mystery. One is looking at a piece of wood that has become a bird. One is looking at a bird that is somehow more than a bird. One is looking at something that has been worked with a mysterious skill and a kind of love.

Thus far I have tried to isolate the qualities of the white bird which provoke an aesthetic emotion. (The word "emotion", although designating a motion of the heart and of the imagination, is some-what confusing for we are considering an emotion that has little to do with the others we experience, notably because the self here is in a far greater degree of abeyance.) Yet my definitions beg the essential question. They reduce aesthetics to art. They say nothing about the relation between art and nature, art and the world.

Before a mountain, a desert just after the sun has gone down, or a fruit tree, one can also experience aesthetic emotion. Consequently we are forced to begin again – not this time with a man-made object but with the nature into which we are born.

Urban living has always tended to produce a sentimental view of nature. Nature is thought of as a garden, or a view framed by a window, or as an arena of freedom. Peasants, sailors, nomads have known better. Nature is energy and struggle. It is what exists without any promise. If it can be thought of by man as an arena, a setting, it has to be thought of as one which lends itself as much to evil as to good. Its energy is fearsomely indifferent. The first necessity of life is shelter. Shelter against nature. The first prayer is for protection. The first sign of life is pain. If the Creation was purposeful, its purpose is a hidden one which can only be discovered intangibly within signs, never by the evidence of what happens.

It is within this bleak natural context that beauty is encountered, and the encounter is by its nature sudden and unpredictable. The gale blows itself out, the sea changes from the colour of grey shit to aquamarine. Under the fallen boulder of an avalanche a flower grows. Over the shanty town the moon rises. I offer dramatic examples so as to insist upon the bleakness of the context. Reflect upon more everyday examples. However it is encountered, beauty is always an exception, always *in despite of*. This is why it moves us.

It can be argued that the origin of the way we are moved by natural beauty was functional. Flowers are a promise of fertility, a sunset is a reminder of fire and warmth, moonlight makes the night less dark, the bright colours of a bird's plumage are (atavistically even for us) a sexual stimulus. Yet such an argument is too reductionist, I believe. Snow is useless. A butterfly offers us very little.

Of course the range of what a given community finds beautiful in nature will depend upon its means of survival, its economy, its geography. What Eskimos find beautiful is unlikely to be the same as what the Ashanti found beautiful. Within modern class societies there are complex ideological determinations: we know, for instance, that the British ruling class in the eighteenth century disliked the sight of the sea. Equally, the social use to which an aesthetic emotion may be put changes according to the historical moment: the silhouette of a mountain can represent the home of the dead or a challenge to the initiative of the living. Anthropology, comparative studies of religion, political economy and Marxism have made all this clear.

Yet there seem to be certain constants which all cultures have found 'beautiful': among them – certain flowers, trees, forms of rock, birds, animals, the moon, running water . . .

One is obliged to acknowledge a coincidence or perhaps a congruence. The evolution of natural forms and the evolution of human perception have coincided to produce the phenomenon of a potential recognition: what *is* and what we can see (and by seeing also feel) sometimes meet at a point of affirmation. This point, this coincidence, is two-faced: what has been seen is recognized and affirmed and, at the same time, the seer is affirmed by what he sees. For a brief moment one finds oneself – without the pretensions of a creator – in the position of God in the first chapter of Genesis . . . And he saw that *it was* good. The aesthetic emotion before nature derives, I believe, from this double affirmation.

Yet we do not live in the first chapter of Genesis. We live – if one follows the biblical sequence of events – after the Fall. In any case, we live in a world of suffering in which evil is rampant, a world whose events do not confirm our Being, a world that has to be resisted. It is in this situation that the aesthetic moment offers hope. That we find a crystal or a poppy beautiful means that we are less alone, that we are more deeply inserted into existence than the course of a single life would lead us to believe. I try to describe as accurately as possible the experience in question; my starting point is phenomenological, not deductive; its form, perceived as such, becomes a message that one receives but cannot translate because, in it, all is instantaneous. For an instant, the energy of one's perception becomes inseparable from the energy of the creation.

The aesthetic emotion we feel before a man-made object – such as the white bird with which I started – is a derivative of the emotion we feel before nature. The white bird is an attempt to translate a message received from a real bird. All the languages of art have been developed as an attempt to transform the instantaneous into the permanent. Art supposes that beauty is not an exception – is not *in despite of* – but is the basis for an order.

Several years ago, when considering the historical face of art, I wrote that I judged a work according to whether or not it helped men in the modern world claim their social rights. I hold to that. Art's other, transcendental face raises the question of man's ontological right.

The notion that art is the mirror of nature is one that only appeals in periods of scepticism. Art does not imitate nature, it imitates a creation, sometimes to propose an alternative world, sometimes simply to amplify, to confirm, to make social the brief hope offered by nature. Art is an organized response to what nature allows us to glimpse occasionally. Art sets out to transform the potential recognition into an unceasing one. It proclaims man in the hope of receiving a surer reply . . . the transcendental face of art is always a form of prayer.

The white wooden bird is wafted by the warm air rising from the stove in the kitchen where the neighbours are drinking. Outside, in minus 25°C, the real birds are freezing to death!

1985

2

LEAVING HOME

———

The storyteller

———

Now that he has gone down, I can hear his voice in the silence. It carries from one side of the valley to the other. He produces it effortlessly, and, like a yodel, it travels like a lasso. It turns to come back after it has attached the hearer to the shouter. It places the shouter at the centre. His cows respond to it as well as his dog. One evening two cows were missing after we had chained them all in the stable. He went and called. The second time he called the two cows answered from deep in the forest, and a few minutes later they were at the stable door, just as night fell.

The day before he went down, he brought the whole herd back from the valley at about two in the afternoon – shouting at the cows, and at me to open the stable doors. Muguet was about to calve – the two forefeet were already out. The only way to bring her back was to bring the whole herd back. His hands were trembling as he tied the rope round the forefeet. Two minutes pulling and the calf was out. He gave it to Muguet to lick. She mooed, making a sound a cow never makes on other occasions – not even when in pain. A high, penetrating, mad sound. A sound stronger than complaint, and more urgent than greeting. A little like an elephant trumpeting. He fetched the straw to bed the calf on. For him these moments are moments of triumph: moments of true gain: moments which unite the foxy, ambitious, hard, indefatigable, seventy-year-old cattle-raiser with the universe which surrounds him.

After working each morning we used to drink coffee together and he would talk about the village. He remembered the date and the day of the week of every disaster. He remembered the month of every marriage of which he had a story to tell. He could trace the family

13

relations of his protagonists to their second cousins by marriage. From time to time I caught an expression in his eyes, a certain look of complicity. About what? About something we share despite the obvious differences. Something that joins us together but is never directly referred to. Certainly not the little work I do for him. For a long time I puzzled over this. And suddenly I realized what it was. It was his recognition of our equal intelligence; we are both historians of our time. We both see how events fit together.

In that knowledge there is – for us – both pride and sadness. Which is why the expression I caught in his eyes was both bright and consoling. It was the look of one storyteller to another. I am writing on pages like these which he will not read. He sits in the corner of his kitchen, his dog fed, and sometimes he talks before he goes to bed. He goes to bed early after drinking his last cup of coffee for the day. I am seldom there and unless he were personally telling me the stories I wouldn't understand them because he speaks in patois. The complicity remains however.

I have never thought of writing as a profession. It is a solitary independent activity in which practice can never bestow seniority. Fortunately anyone can take up the activity. Whatever the motives, political or personal, which have led me to undertake to write something, the writing becomes, as soon as I begin, a struggle to give meaning to experience. Every profession has limits to its competence, but also its own territory. Writing, as I know it, has no territory of its own. The act of writing is nothing except the act of approaching the experience written about; just as, hopefully, the act of reading the written text is a comparable act of approach.

To approach experience, however, is not like approaching a house. Experience is indivisible and continuous, at least within a single lifetime and perhaps over many lifetimes. I never have the impression that my experience is entirely my own, and it often seems to me that it preceded me. In any case experience folds upon itself, refers backwards and forwards to itself through the referents of hope and fear; and, by the use of metaphor which is at the origin of language, it is continually comparing like with unlike, what is small with what is large, what is near with what is distant. And so the act of approaching a given moment of experience involves both scrutiny (closeness) and the capacity to connect (distance). The movement of writing resembles that of a shuttlecock: repeatedly it approaches and withdraws, closes in and takes its distance. Unlike a shuttlecock, however, it is not fixed to a static frame. As the movement of writing repeats itself, its nearness to, its intimacy with the experience increases. Finally, if one is fortunate, meaning is the fruit of this intimacy.

For the old man, who talks, the meaning of his stories is more certain but no less mysterious. Indeed the mystery is more openly acknowledged. I will try to explain what I mean by that.

All villages tell stories. Stories of the past, even of the distant past. As I was walking in the mountains with another friend of seventy by the foot of a high cliff, he told me how a young girl had fallen to her death there, whilst hay-making on the alpage above. Was that before the war? I asked. In about 1800 (no misprint), he said. And stories of the very same day. Most of what happens during a day is recounted by somebody before the day ends. The stories are factual, based on observations or on an account given by somebody else. A combination of the sharpest observation of the daily recounting of the day's events and encounters, and of life-long mutual familiarities is what constitutes so-called village *gossip*. Sometimes there is a moral judgment implicit in the story, but this judgment – whether just or unjust – remains a detail: the story *as a whole* is told with some tolerance because it involves those with whom the storyteller and listener are going to go on living.

Very few stories are narrated either to idealize or condemn; rather they testify to the always slightly surprising range of the possible. Although concerned with everyday events, they are mystery stories. How is it that C, who is so punctilious in his work, overturned his haycart? How is it that L is able to fleece her lover J of everything, and how is it that J, who normally gives nothing away to anybody, allows himself to be fleeced?

The story invites comment. Indeed it creates it, for even total silence is taken as a comment. The comments may be spiteful or bigoted, but, if so, they themselves will become a story and thus, in turn, become subject to comment. How is it that F never lets a single chance go by of damning her brother? More usually the comments, which add to the story, are intended and taken as the commentator's personal response – in the light of that story – to the riddle of existence. Each story allows everyone to define himself.

The function of these stories, which are, in fact, close, oral, daily history, is to allow the whole village to define itself. The life of a village, as distinct from its physical and geographical attributes, is the sum of all the social and personal relationships existing within it, plus the social and economic relations – usually oppressive – which link the village to the rest of the world. But one could say something similar about the life of some large town. Even of some cities. What distinguishes the life of a village is that it is also *a living portrait of itself*: a communal portrait, in that everybody is portrayed and everybody portrays; and this is only possible if everybody knows everybody. As with the carvings on the capitals in a Romanesque church, there is an identity of spirit between what is shown and how it is shown – as if the portrayed were also the carvers. A village's portrait of itself is constructed, not out of stone, but out of words, spoken and remembered: out of opinions, stories, eyewitness reports, legends, comments and hearsay. And it is a continuous portrait; work on it never stops.

Until very recently the only material available to a village and its peasants for defining themselves was their own spoken words. The village's portrait of itself was – apart from the physical achievements of their work – the only reflection of the meaning of their existence. Nothing and nobody else acknowledged such a meaning. Without such a portrait – and the 'gossip' which is its raw material – the village would have been forced to doubt its own existence. Every story and every comment on the story which is a proof that the story has been *witnessed* contributes to the portrait, and confirms the existence of the village.

This continuous portrait, unlike most, is highly realistic, informal and unposed. Like everybody else, and perhaps more so, given the insecurity of their lives, peasants have a need for formality and this formality is expressed in ceremony and ritual, but as makers of their own communal portrait they are informal because this informality corresponds closer to the truth: the truth which ceremony and ritual can only partially control. All weddings are similar but every marriage is different. Death comes to everyone but one mourns alone. That is the truth.

In a village, the difference between what is known about a person and what is unknown is slight. There may be a number of well-guarded secrets but, in general, deceit is rare because impossible. Thus there is little inquisitiveness – in the prying sense of the term, for there is no great need for it. Inquisitiveness is the trait of the city *concierge* who can gain a little power or recognition by telling X what he doesn't know about Y. In the village X already knows it. And thus too there is little performing: peasants do not *play roles* as urban characters do.

This is not because they are 'simple' or more honest or without guile, it is simply because the space between what is unknown about a person and what is generally known – and this is the space for all performance – is too small. When peasants play, they play practical jokes. As when four men, one Sunday morning when the village was at mass, fetched all the wheelbarrows used for cleaning out the stables and lined them up outside the church porch so that as each man came out he was obliged to find his barrow and wheel it, he in his Sunday clothes, through the village street! This is why the village's continual portrait of itself is mordant, frank, sometimes exaggerated but seldom idealized or hypocritical. And the significance of this is that hypocrisy and idealization close questions, whereas realism leaves them open.

There are two forms of realism. Professional and traditional. Professional realism, as a method chosen by an artist or a writer like myself, is always consciously political; it aims to shatter an opaque part of the ruling ideology, whereby, normally, some aspect of reality is consistently distorted or denied. Traditional realism, always popular in its origins, is in a sense more scientific than political. Assuming a fund of empirical knowledge and experience, it poses the riddle of the unknown. How is it that . . . ? Unlike science it can live without the answer. But its experience is too great to allow it to ignore the question.

Contrary to what is usually said, peasants are interested in the world beyond the village. Yet it is rare for a peasant to remain a peasant and be able to move. He has no choice of locality. His place was a given at the very moment of his conception. And so if he considers his village the centre of the world, it is not so much a question of parochialism as a phenomenological truth. His world has a centre (mine does not). He believes that what happens in the village is typical of human experience. This belief is only naïve if one interprets it in technological or organizational terms. He interprets it in terms of the species *man*. What fascinates him is the typology of human characters in all their variations, and the common destiny of birth and death, shared by all. Thus the foreground of the village's living portrait of itself is extremely specific whilst the background consists of the most open, general, and never entirely answerable questions. Therein is the acknowledged mystery.

The old man knows that I know this as sharply as he does.

1978

On the edge of a foreign city

—

I

It was called the Café de la Renaissance. It was on the big lorry route, near the level crossing by the railway station. Inside it was not really like a bar at all. Indeed there wasn't a bar. It was just a small front parlour which was called a café. The bottles – only about half a dozen anyway – were kept in a kind of corner medicine cupboard. Three men and a woman were sitting at one of the tables playing cards – belote. The eldest of the men got up to welcome us. He had the face of a fanatic – a Jansenist face: the face of a man who had recognized the vanity of the world and its ways. He showed us to another marble-topped table and wiped it. The whole place was filthy – unswept and untouched for weeks, except at the end where the card players were and where there was a door into the kitchen. There was a certain homeliness there: where we were – four yards away – was like an outhouse, full of the last tenants' junk. On the table next to ours was an open and tattered black umbrella. A bicycle leant against the table. On the wall behind were pinned some postcards and snapshots of a Mediterranean beach. All of them had gone potato yellow. Behind us was a large wooden cupboard: butterflies were pinned to the door of it. The wings of the butterflies were frayed and torn, so that in places you could see through them, as you could see through the umbrella.

We ordered some red wine and got out our bread and sausage to eat. Having brought us the wine, the proprietor with the Jansenist face hurried back to his game. We watched them play. The players consisted of the proprietor, another old man who looked like a brother, a young man and a young woman. They were playing with considerable concentration: their eyes fixed on their cards, occasionally a hand banging a card on the table – with the authority of the hammer that strikes the bell of a public clock. But they were not playing aggressively, with personal ill-feeling. Nor were they drinking. After a while, the brother got up and a woman came in from the kitchen, wiping her hands on her apron, and sat down to take his place. Two young children followed her and started to jump about by the door on to the street. The conversation of the card players was only about the cards. They were playing for chips, not directly for money. As we watched them, we had the sensation more and more strongly that it was like watching the backs of four people bent over the parapet of a bridge and gazing at a river, a boat, a shoal of fish which we could not see. We could in fact see their faces, but they revealed nothing, except their degree of concentration. It was their cards we couldn't see.

An older woman came out of the kitchen and smiled at the players approvingly. When she noticed us, she came over and wished us a good appetite. Then she said: 'It's a good thing to eat sometimes, it's like a recall to order.' She went back and stood for a moment looking down at the cards in the hands of the proprietor. Again she nodded approvingly – as though from the parapet she had seen a golden barque pass by.

On the wall behind the players was a local bus timetable. It was the newest and brightest thing in the room. But there was no clock and when later I asked the proprietor the time he had to go out and ask in another café two doors down the street.

The four went on playing. Each could see what nobody else in the world could see – his own cards. The world didn't care. But the three other players did; they recognized the importance of every particular that with this deal had befallen him. Such interest and such concern amounted to a kind of dependence; each to some degree ruled the others, up to the moment when the hand was finished and the victor declared and at that moment the victor's victory was also terminated.

Thus they established an equity juster than any existing in the world. And thus too they were able to accept the most extreme demands of the cards as a proof of the purity of their actions and intentions. The code to which they submitted, like the code of anarchists, was violent, absolute and closer to their own understanding and longing than any existing in the everyday world. Each card played on the table helped to undermine the authority of this world. It was a conspiracy that we were watching. And one that we might easily have joined.

2

Outside the cathedral of St Jean many cars and two buses are parked: men are in their shirtsleeves. It is Sunday morning when the croissants have more butter in them.

Inside it is crowded. All the chairs are taken and the aisles are full of people standing. It is unusual to see a church so full in this country. But as we make our way forward, towards the priests, the explanation becomes clear. In the centre of the church, surrounded and hidden on three sides by the rest of the congregation and on the fourth side facing the carpeted steps leading up to the high altar, is a square of a hundred girls in white. The white of their long dresses, the white of their gloves and the white of their veils is spotless and uncrumpled. At home a hundred irons must still be warm.

The girls are between eleven and thirteen years old. Against the white their faces look nut-brown. They are caught between the questions and responses which they exchange with the priest and the gaze of their parents and guardians who are in the front ranks of the surrounding congregation and who watch their every move. Caught like this, they seem very still: and, having forgone their freedom of independent movement, very peaceful.

It is somewhat like watching children who are asleep. To the eye of the watcher they acquire a false innocence. In fact if one watches carefully enough, one can distinguish between various degrees of experience. Some are only pretending to sleep and in their white shoes wriggle their toes until they can say what they are dying to say to their companions. Out of the corner of their eyes they have observed the remarkable behaviour of the widow who is watching her niece and constantly smooths down her own black dress over her old hips with thin hands – thirty times a minute.

Some are so aware of what they are wearing, so aware of the white which draws the eyes of all who surround them, that they have begun to dream of getting married.

A few feel impure before the shining purity of the recipient of their vows, and on the faces of these there is a kind of beatitude – as there is in the sight of a white sail so far away that the hull of the ship is invisible.

There is one girl who is a little taller than most of the others and among the nearest to us. She has an aquiline nose and large, dark eyes. Her veil is so crisp that it looks like a linen napkin. Her family are perhaps richer than those of the others. She is proud and self-possessed – as though, if she were sleeping, she would sleep in exactly the position she had decided upon. For her the religious experience which she is now undergoing is part of her private plan for her own development. It is no seduction. It is a long-arranged engagement. But none the less intense. All that will be done unto her will be done in the way that she selects. Always provided that no disaster occurs so that her wishes and decisions become incidental, her life no more than a movement which catches a sniper's eye.

By the west door the man who sells tracts sits behind his table and reads a newspaper.

The girls as they answer sound like doves.

Some of their mothers, pressed right forward to the front rank round the square of girls, have to restrain themselves from putting out a hand and touching their daughters. Their excuse for doing this would be the smoothing of a dress, the straightening of a cuff. But their desire to do so comes from the need to share their memories. They want at this moment to touch their daughters not because their daughters might need their support, but because they want their daughters to know that twenty years ago they too were confirmed in white dresses.

The men stand further back: as though the degree of proximity were inversely related to the degree of scepticism. They watch a ceremony. One or two consult their watches. All are dwarfed by the vast height of the piers. After the ceremony they will go to cafés and restaurants to celebrate. This evening some will play bowls. For many scepticism is mixed with calculation. If their daughters' being received into the church offers in one way or another the possibility of their children being better protected, then indeed they are glad that at last it has come to this – their confirmation. Caution fills their souls.

3

There were three youngish Italians behind the bar, all wearing white shirts – no jackets, for it was hot – and black ties. The boss was called Angelo. Outside in the street you could hear the music of half a dozen different juke boxes. Men, mostly middle-class, were strolling down the street, coming from their shops or offices on their way home. The girls were coming downstairs to begin work and take up their places by the bars. In the shop windows between the cafés were cheap but raffish men's clothes – jeans, leather belts, plastic jackets, cowboy hats. There were also one or two food shops with sausages in their windows – sausages and gherkins and smoked fish. It was all food which was sharp enough to taste even after a lot of drinks or many cigars. And the skins of all these foods were wrinkled.

She sat on a stool by the bar. She was fat, but still pretty in a bursting kind of way. Her face was wide with thick lips. With her was a middle-aged Pakistani businessman in an expensive suit. One of his hands was wedged between her knees. He was drinking too much, and she was trying to dissuade him lest he become incapable. Otherwise they talked of food and of whether beef was better than chicken.

Local clients dropped into the bar, but she steadfastly refused to recognize them and remained apparently absorbed in the man from Karachi. Occasionally she glanced quickly round the bar to keep account. The man from Karachi was wearing a large gold ring, and was beginning to tell her about his children.

Suddenly – and to the clear annoyance of Angelo – a young, very thin man strolled in from the street. He wore white trousers and a leather belt, buckled at the back. He put a hand on her bare, round shoulder. She looked up surprised, and then smiled a message at him. She introduced him to the man from Karachi as her brother. The man from Karachi moved away and offered her brother the stool between them. He accepted, pulling the stool back a little so that the other two could still sit within touching distance of each other. Then he picked up a magazine and began flicking through its pages. From the point of view of the man from Karachi, the young man's face was hidden by the magazine: all he could see were his hands holding the paper, and his stick-like legs between him and the girl.

The man from Karachi observed that surely her brother was married because he wore a ring. She might have let this pass, but couldn't. She explained, no, he wasn't married but he wore the ring because he was a great lover boy. He didn't look up from his magazine. The Pakistani ordered another whisky and poured it into his beer. You must eat, she said. And she also said he had the nicest face she had ever seen. All he could eat, he replied, was chicken, but they didn't serve chicken here. They could send out for it and get it specially, she said. No, he said, he did not want it got specially. Then when her hand once more came to rest on his, he gripped it, and looked at the round stockings over her thighs.

Then you must have some dry beef, she said. What is that? he asked. It is very, very nice, she said. Her brother put down his magazine and nodded. She asked Angelo to bring a portion of Viande des Grisons.

When it arrived the young man stood up. Please, he said and stepped to the bar. She told her man from Karachi that her brother wanted to prepare the meat for him. The young man picked up the slice of lemon on the edge of the plate and squeezed drops of lemon juice on the paper-thin slices of reddish-brown meat. Then he took the pepper mill – a tall wooden one as large as a thermos flask – and bending over it, as though using all the power of his slender shoulders and thin arms, as though summoning every ounce of energy for the task, he ground the pepper over the slices of meat for the older man.

4

An hour's drive from the centre is a mountain. It is 1,800 metres high. In the hollows are small patches of frozen snow, over which children slide and toboggan on rubber mats – this even in June.

None of the ascents is steep or dangerous. If they take their time, quite elderly couples can walk to the summit.

Today is Sunday and there must be 3,000 people on this mountain.

The road stops a few hundred metres from the top. On the grass – springy as only grass that is several months of the year under snow can be – the cars and a bus are parked. In the evening when they are all gone, the hill looks like any other. There are no kiosks or litter bins. Only the grass that owes its special nature to the snow.

At the summit there are a few rocks. Otherwise the sides are all grass, and among the grass are mountain flowers: gentian, arnica, mountain anemones – and thousands of jonquils.

It is possible to scramble up the mountain from any direction, but there is a path which takes the easiest route. Along this path there is a constant traffic of couples, fathers carrying babies, grandparents, schoolchildren. Many of them are barefoot. From below, the procession, ascending and descending, looks a little like a medieval vision of some exchange with heaven. The more so because most of those coming down are carrying armfuls of jonquils, white-gold in colour.

From the summit one can see the ranges extending to the horizon. The rock joins with the sky and their common blue discounts every difference.

Towards the south one can also see the plain, intensely cultivated, the colour of greengages. Such a view is archetypal. It is the antithesis of a view of the grave.

Across the plain moves the shadow of one white cloud. Where the shadow is, the green is the green of laurel leaves.

The crowd, which is made up of hundreds of dispersed groups, is easy and at home. It is as if the mountain were their common ancestor.

5

Today there was a woman being bundled into a taxi: but she refused to bend her back, so she wouldn't fit inside the door. There were two men struggling with her. Quite respectable middle-aged men steel-ing themselves in righteousness against the doubting eyes of the crowd that had gathered. Then the woman began to shout. I couldn't understand a word. But she shouted in such a way that it was obvious she believed that across the street, somewhere near where I was standing, there was somebody who understood what she was suffer-ing and the reasonableness of her simple wish not to be bundled into the car and taken somewhere else. After several minutes' struggling the two men gave up: she wouldn't fit through the door. So they took her back, still shouting, and her knees bent as they dragged her along – she was only a woman of about forty-five – to the chemist's shop where they had originally been. Inside the shop she still fought, and one of the men had to stand with his back against the glass door to prevent her running out and away. It appeared that the chemist was trying to help them calm her. The taxi driver waited, the door of his taxi still open. Because one of the men was leaning with his back against the door, no customer could enter the shop. I watched through the window. There were the drugs and the medicines on the shelves. There was the woman with her will, that would have done what she wanted done and would prevent what she did not want. And between the shelves and the woman there were the men, hesitating.

1972

26

The eaters and the eaten

     ———

'The consumer society', so often and widely discussed as if it were a relatively new phenomenon, is the logical outcome of economic and technological processes which began at least a hundred years ago. Consumerism is intrinsic to nineteenth-century bourgeois culture. Consumption fulfils a cultural as well as an economic need. The nature of this need becomes clearer if we look at the most direct and simple form of consumption: eating.

How does the bourgeois approach his food? If we isolate and define this specific approach we will be able to recognize it when it is far more widely diffused.

The question could become complex because of national and historical differences. The French bourgeois attitude to food is not the same as the English. A German mayor sits down to his dinner with a somewhat different attitude from a Greek mayor. A fashionable banquet in Rome is not quite the same as one in Copenhagen. Many of the eating habits and attitudes described in Trollope and Balzac are no longer to be found anywhere.

Nevertheless an overall view, an outline, emerges if one compares the bourgeois manner of eating with the one, within the same geographical areas, from which it is most distinct: the peasant manner of eating. Working-class eating habits have less tradition than those of the other two classes because they are far more vulnerable to fluctuations of the economy.

On a world scale, the distinction between bourgeois and peasant is closely related to the brute contrast between plenty and scarcity. This contrast amounts to a war. But, for our limited purpose now, the distinction is not between the hungry and the overfed, but between two traditional views of the value of food, the significance of the meal and the act of eating.

At the outset it is worth noting a conflict in the bourgeois view. On the one hand, meals have a regular and symbolic importance in the life of the bourgeois. On the other hand, he considers that to discuss eating is frivolous. This article, for example, cannot by its nature be serious; and if it takes itself seriously, it is pretentious. Cookbooks are bestsellers and most newspapers have their food columns. But what they discuss is considered a mere embellishment and is (mostly) the domain of women. The bourgeois does not think of the act of eating as a fundamental one.

The principal regular meal. For the peasant this meal is usually at mid-day; for the bourgeois it is usually dinner in the evening. The practical reasons for this are so obvious that they need not be listed. What may be significant is that the peasant meal is in the middle of the day, surrounded by work. It is placed in the day's stomach. The bourgeois meal comes after the day's work and marks the transition between day and evening. It is closer to the day's head (if the day begins with getting to the feet) and to dreams.

At the peasant's table the relationship between implements, food and eaters is intimate, and a value is conferred on use and handling. Each person has his own knife which he may well take out of his pocket. The knife is worn, used for many purposes other than eating, and usefully sharp. Whenever possible the same plate is kept throughout the meal, and between dishes it is cleaned with bread which is eaten. Each eater takes his share of the food and drink which are placed before all. For example: he holds the bread to his body, cuts a piece of it towards himself, and puts the bread down for another. Likewise with cheese or sausage. Contiguity as between uses, users and foods is treated as natural. There is a minimum of division.

On the bourgeois table everything that can be is kept untouched and separate. Every dish has its own cutlery and plate. In general plates are not cleaned by eating – because eating and cleaning are distinct activities. Each eater (or a servant) holds the serving dish to allow another to serve himself. The meal is a series of discrete, untouched gifts.

To the peasant all food represents work accomplished. The work may or may not have been his own or that of his family, but if it isn't, the work represented is nevertheless directly exchangeable with his own work. Because food represents physical work, the eater's body already 'knows' the food it is going to eat. (The peasant's strong resistance to eating any 'foreign' food for the first time is partly because its origin in the work process is unknown.) He does not expect to be surprised by food – except, sometimes, by its quality. His food is familiar like his own body. Its action on his body is *continuous* with the previous action of the body (labour) on the food. He eats in the room in which the food is prepared and cooked.

To the bourgeois, food is not directly exchangeable with his own work or activities. (The quality attributable to home-grown veg- etables becomes exceptional.) Food is a commodity he buys. Meals, even when cooked at home, are purchased through a cash exchange. The purchase is delivered in a special room: the domestic dining- room, or restaurant. This room has no other purpose. It always has at least two doors or ways of entry. One door connects with his own daily life; through it he has entered in order to be served with food. The second door connects with the kitchen; through it the food is brought out and the waste is taken away. Thus, in the dining-room, food is abstracted from its own production and from the 'real' world of his daily activities. Behind the two doors lie secrets: secrets of recipes behind the kitchen door; professional or personal secrets, not to be discussed at table, behind the other.

Abstracted, framed, insulated, the eaters and what is eaten form an isolated moment. This moment has to create its own content out of the air. The content tends to be theatrical: the décor of the table with its silver, glass, linen, china, etc.; the lighting; the relative formality of dress; the careful seating arrangements whenever there are guests; the ritualistic etiquette of table manners; the formality of serving; the

29

transformation of the table between each act (course); and, finally, the leaving of the theatre together for a more dispersed and informal setting.

To the peasant, food represents work done and therefore repose. The fruit of labour is not only the 'fruit' but also the time, taken from work time, spent in eating the food. Feasts apart, he accepts at table the sedative effect of eating. The appetite, satisfied, is quietened.

To the bourgeois the drama of eating, far from being reposeful, is a stimulus. The theatrical invitation of the scene often provokes family dramas at meal times. The scene of the typical oedipal drama is not, as logically it might be, the bedroom, but the dinner table. The dining-room is the place of assembly where the bourgeois family appears to itself in public guise, and where its conflicting interests and power struggles are pursued in a highly formalized manner. The ideal bourgeois drama, however, is entertainment. The use of the word 'entertain' meaning to invite guests is significant here. Yet entertainment always proposes its opposite: boredom. Boredom haunts the insulated dining-room. Hence the conscious emphasis placed on dinner talk, wit and conversation. But the spectre of boredom also characterizes the way of eating.

The bourgeois overeats. Especially meat. A psychosomatic explanation may be that his highly developed sense of competition compels him to protect himself with a source of energy – proteins. (Just as his children protect themselves from the emotional cold with sweets.) The cultural explanation, however, is as important. If the scale of the meal is *spectacular*, all the eaters share in its achievement, and boredom is less likely. The shared achievement is not, fundamentally, culinary. The achievement is that of wealth. What wealth has obtained from nature is an affidavit that overproduction and infinite increase are natural. The variety, the quantity, the waste of food prove the *naturalness* of wealth.

In the nineteenth century with partridge, mutton and porridge for breakfast (in England), and three meats and two fish for dinner, the quantities were net, the proof extracted from nature arithmetical.

Today with modern means of transport and refrigeration, the accelerated pace of daily life and a different use of the 'servant' classes, the spectacular is achieved in another way. The most varied and exotic foods are acquired out of season, and the dishes come from all over the world. Canard à la Chinoise is placed beside Steak Tartare and Boeuf Bourguignon. The affidavit obtained is no longer just from nature concerning quantity. It is also from history to testify how wealth unites the world.

By using the vomitorium the Romans separated the palate from the stomach in the pursuit of 'pleasure'. The bourgeois separates the act of eating from the body so that it can become, first, a spectacular social claim. The significance of the act of eating asparagus is not: I am eating this with pleasure; but: we *can* eat this here and now. The typical bourgeois meal is for each eater a series of discrete gifts. Each gift should be a surprise. But the message in each gift is the same: *happy the world which feeds you.*

The distinction between the principal regular meal and the celebration or feast is very clear for the peasant, and often blurred for the bourgeois. (Which is why some of what I have written above borders, for the bourgeois, on the feast.) For the peasant what he eats and how he eats daily are continuous with the rest of his life. The rhythm of this life is cyclic. The repetition of meals is similar to, and connected with, the repetition of the seasons. His diet is local and seasonal. And so the foods available, the methods of cooking them, the variations in his diet, mark recurring moments throughout a lifetime. To become bored with eating is to be bored with life. This happens, but only to people whose unhappiness is very pronounced. The feast, small or large, is made to mark a special recurring moment or an unrepeatable occasion.

The bourgeois feast usually has more of a social than temporal significance. It is less a notch in time than the fulfilling of a social desideratum.

The feast for the peasant, when once the occasion has been given, begins with food and drink. It does so because food and drink have been reserved or put aside, on account of their rarity or special quality, for just such an occasion. Any feast, even if it is impromptu, has been partly prepared for for years. A feast is the consuming of the surplus saved and produced over and above daily needs. Expressing and using up some of this surplus, the feast is a double celebration – of the occasion which gives rise to it, and of the surplus itself. Hence its slow tempo, its generosity and the active high spirits which accompany it.

The feast for the bourgeois is an additional expense. What distinguishes its food from that of an ordinary meal is the amount of money spent. The true celebration of a surplus is beyond him, because he can never have a surplus of money.

The purpose of these comparisons is not to idealize the peasant. Peasant attitudes are mostly, in the strict sense of the word, *conservative*. At least until recently, the physical reality of the peasant's conservatism has hindered his understanding of the political realities of the modern world. These realities were originally a bourgeois creation. The bourgeois once had, and still to some degree retains, a mastery of the world of his own making.

I have tried to outline by using comparisons two modes of acquisition, of possessing, through the act of eating. If one examines each point of comparison, it becomes clear that the peasant way of eating is centred on the act of eating itself and on the food eaten: it is centripetal and physical. Whereas the bourgeois way of eating is centred on fantasy, ritual and spectacle: it is centrifugal and cultural. The first can complete itself in satisfaction; the second is never complete and gives rise to an appetite which, in essence, is insatiable.

1976

Dürer: a portrait of the artist

We are more than five hundred years away from Dürer's birth. (He was born on 21st May 1471, in Nuremberg.) Those five hundred years may seem long or short, according to one's viewpoint or mood. When they seem short, it appears to be possible to understand Dürer and an imaginary conversation with him becomes feasible. When they seem long, the world he lived in and his consciousness of it appear so remote that no dialogue is possible.

Dürer was the first painter to be obsessed by his own image. No other before him made so many self-portraits. Among his earliest works is a silverpoint drawing of himself aged thirteen. The drawing demonstrates that he was a prodigy – and that he found his own appearance startling and unforgettable. One of the things that made it startling was probably his awareness of his own genius. All his self-portraits reveal pride. It is as though one of the elements of the masterpiece which he intends each time to create is the look of genius that he is observing in his own eyes. In this, his self-portraits are the antithesis of Rembrandt's.

Why does a man paint himself? Among many motives, one is the same as that which prompts any man to have his portrait painted. It is to produce evidence, which will probably outlive him, that he once existed. His look will remain, and the double meaning of the word 'look' – signifying both his appearance and his gaze – suggests the mystery or enigma which is contained in that thought. His look interrogates us who stand before the portrait, trying to imagine the artist's life.

As I recall these two self-portraits of Dürer, one in Madrid and the other in Munich, I am aware of being – along with thousands of others – the imaginary spectator whose interest Dürer assumed about 485 years ago. Yet at the same time I ask myself how many of the words I am writing could have conveyed their present meaning to Dürer. We approach so close to his face and expression that it is hard to believe that a large part of his experience must escape us. Placing Dürer historically is not the same thing as recognizing his own experience. It seems to me important to point this out in the face of so many complacent assumptions of continuity between his time and ours. Complacent because the more this so-called continuity is emphasized, the more we tend, in a strange way, to congratulate ourselves on his genius.

Two years separate the two paintings which so obviously depict the same man in extremely different frames of mind. The second portrait, now in the Prado Museum, Madrid, shows the painter, aged twenty-seven, dressed like a Venetian courtier. He looks confident, proud, almost princely. There is perhaps a slight over-emphasis on his being dressed up, suggested by, for example, his gloved hands. The expression of his eyes is a little at odds with the debonair cap on his head. It may be that the portrait half-confesses that Dürer is dressing up for a part, that he aspires to a new role. He painted the picture four years after his first visit to Italy. During this visit he not only met Giovanni Bellini and discovered Venetian painting; he also came to realize for the first time how independent-minded and socially honoured painters could be. His Venetian costume and the landscape of the Alps seen through the window surely indicate that the painting refers back to his experience of Venice as a young man. Interpreted into absurdly crude terms, the painting looks as though it is saying: 'In Venice I took the measure of my own worth, and here in Germany I expect this worth to be recognized.' Since his return, he had begun to receive important commissions from Frederick the Wise, the Elector of Saxony. Later he would work for the Emperor Maximilian.

The portrait in Munich was painted in 1500. The painting shows the artist in a sombre coat against a dark background. The pose, his

34

hand which holds his coat together, the way his hair is arranged, the expression – or rather the holy lack of it – on his face all suggest, according to the pictorial conventions of the time, a portrait head of Christ. And although it cannot be proved, it seems likely that Dürer intended such a comparison, or at least that he wanted it to cross the spectator's mind.

His intention must have been far from being blasphemous. He was devoutly religious and although, in certain ways, he shared the Renaissance attitude towards science and reason, his religion was of a traditional kind. Later in his life he admired Luther morally and intellectually, but was himself incapable of breaking with the Catholic Church. The picture cannot be saying: 'I see myself as Christ.' It must be saying: 'I aspire through the suffering I know to the imitation of Christ.'

Yet, as with the other portrait, there is a theatrical element. In none of his self-portraits, apparently, could Dürer accept himself as he was. The ambition to be something other or more than himself always intervened. The only consistent record of himself he could accept was the monogram with which, unlike any previous artist, he signed almost everything he produced. When he looked at himself in the mirror he was always fascinated by the possible selves he saw there; sometimes the vision, as in the Madrid portrait, was extravagant, sometimes, as in the Munich portrait, it was full of foreboding.

What can explain the striking difference between the two paintings? In the year 1500 thousands of people in southern Germany believed that the world was just about to end. There was famine, plague and the new scourge of syphilis. The social conflicts, which were soon to lead to the Peasants' War, were intensifying. Crowds of labourers and peasants left their homes and became nomads searching for food, revenge – and salvation on the day on which the wrath of God would rain fire upon the earth, the sun would go out, and the heavens would be rolled up and put away like a manuscript.

Dürer, who throughout his whole life was preoccupied by the thought of approaching death, shared in the general terror. It was at

35

this time that he made for a relatively wide, popular audience his first important series of woodcuts, and the theme of this series was the Apocalypse.

The style of these engravings, not to mention the urgency of their message, is a further demonstration of how far away we now are from Dürer. According to our categories, their style looks incongruously and simultaneously Gothic, Renaissance, and Baroque. We see it historically bridging a century. For Dürer, as the *end* of history approached and as the Renaissance dream of Beauty, such as he had dreamt in Venice, receded, the style of these woodcuts must have been as instantaneous to that moment and as natural as the sound of his own voice.

I doubt, however, whether any specific event can explain the difference between the two self-portraits. They might have been painted in the same month of the same year; they are complementary to one another; together they form a kind of archway standing before Dürer's later works. They suggest the dilemma, the area of self-questioning, within which he worked as an artist.

Dürer's father was a Hungarian goldsmith who settled in the trading centre of Nuremberg. As the trade then demanded, he was a competent draughtsman and engraver. But in his attitudes and bearing he was a medieval craftsman. All he had to ask himself concerning his work was 'How?' No other questions posed themselves for him.

By the time he was twenty-three years old his son had become the painter in Europe who was furthest removed from the mentality of the medieval craftsman. He believed that the artist must discover the secrets of the universe in order to achieve Beauty. The first question in terms of art – and in terms of actually travelling (he travelled whenever he could) – was 'Whither?' Dürer could never have achieved this sense of independence and initiative without going to Italy. But, paradoxically, he then became more independent than any Italian painter, precisely because he was an outsider without a modern tradition – the German tradition, until he changed it, belonged to the past. He was the first, one-man, avant-garde.

It is this independence which is expressed in the Madrid portrait. The fact that he does not embrace this independence completely, that it is like a costume which he tries on, is perhaps explained by the fact that he was, after all, his father's son. His father's death in 1502 affected him greatly; he was deeply attached to him. Did he think of his difference from his father as something inevitable and ordained, or as a question of his own free choice, of which he could not be absolutely sure? At different times probably both. The Madrid portrait includes the slight element of doubt.

His independence, combined with the manner of his art, must have given Dürer an unusual sense of power. His art came closer to recreating nature than that of any artist before him. His ability to depict an object must have seemed – as it can still seem today (think of the watercolour drawings of flowers and animals) – miraculous. He used to speak of his portraits as *Konterfei*, a word which emphasizes the process of *making exactly like*.

Was his way of depicting, of creating again what he saw before him or in his dreams, in some way analogous to the process by which God was said to have created the world and all that was in it? Perhaps that question occurred to him. If so, it was not a sense of his own virtue which made him compare himself with the godhead, but his awareness of what appeared to be his own creativity. Yet despite this creativity, he was condemned to live as a man in a world full of suffering, a world against which his creative power was finally of no avail. His self-portrait as Christ is the portrait of a creator on the wrong side of creation, a creator who has played no part in creating himself.

Dürer's independence as an artist was sometimes incompatible with his half-medieval religious faith. These two self-portraits express the terms of this incompatibility. But to say this is to make a very abstract statement. We still do not enter Dürer's experience. He travelled six days once in a small boat to examine, like a scientist, the carcass of a whale. At the same time, he believed in the Horsemen of

Albrecht Dürer: *Self-portrait*

Albrecht Dürer: *Self-portrait*

the Apocalypse. He considered Luther to be 'God's instrument'. How did he concretely ask, how did he really answer, as he gazed at himself in the mirror, the question which his painted face hints at as we stare into it, the question which at its simplest is: 'Of what am I the instrument?'

1971

One night in Strasbourg

I had gone to the cinema. When I came out it was cold and wet. You could just make out the cathedral spire against the sky.

Between the cathedral and the station there are many cheap brasseries and cafés. I went into one where there was a crow in a cage, hung beside the bottles behind the counter. At that time I was thinking about a scenario for a film and this had led me to try to analyse the nature of passion. I had written some notes in a school exercise book which had squares instead of lines on its pages. I had bought the book in a village shop. Now with my back to the stove in the café in Strasbourg and a glass of tea and rum on the table in front of me, I began to read what I had written.

The beloved represents the self's potential. The self's potential for action is to be loved by the beloved again and again. Active and passive become reversible. Love creates the space for love. The love of the beloved 'completes' – as though one were talking of a single action instead of two – the love of the lover.

The waitress has sat down to eat her supper. She has long straw-coloured hair.

With all those with whom we are not in love we have too much in common to be in love. Passion is only for the opposite. There is no companionship in passion. But passion can confer the same freedom on both lovers. And their shared experience of this freedom – a freedom which in itself is astral and cold – may give rise between them to an incomparable tenderness. Each time, the reawakening of desire is the reconstituting of the opposite.

A man comes in who clearly comes in every night. About sixty. A state office employee. He goes up to talk to the crow in the cage. He speaks a bird language to it.

The modalities of the opposition cannot easily be seen by a third person. What is more, they are continually being transformed within the lovers' subjective relationship. Each new experience, each fresh aspect revealed of the other's character, makes it necessary to redefine the lines of opposition. This is a continual imaginative process. When it ceases, there is no more passion. To conceive of the loved one as *all that the self is not* means that together the lovers form a totality. Together they can be anything and everything. This is the promise which passion makes to the imagination. And because of this promise the imagination works tirelessly drawing and re-drawing the lines of opposition.

I pay the waitress with straw-coloured hair, nod to the habitué who talked to the crow and start to walk to the station. No stars. There is twenty minutes to wait for the train. I look around the large closed booking hall. Three men are sheltering in it. A man is standing up asleep against the ticket counter, his head resting against a poster of a Loire château. Another man, head on his knees, is sitting asleep on the footplate of a weighing machine. Its rubber covering is warmer than the floor. Because a weight has been registered but no money put in and the weight not printed on a card, two lights on the face of the machine flick on and off, ceaselessly demanding a fifty-centime coin. The most fortunate of the three is on the floor with his back pressed against the only radiator. On his head is a bright red knitted hat. The soles of his shoes have holes in them the size of eggcups. In his sleep he scratches his stomach.

Lovers incorporate the whole world into their totality. All the classic images of love poetry bear this out. The poet's love is 'demonstrated' by the river, the forest, the sky, the minerals in the earth, the silk worm, the stars, the frog, the owl, the moon.

The man on the floor pulls up his knees to his stomach.

The aspiration towards such 'correspondence' is expressed by poetry, but it is created by passion. Passion aspires to include the world in the act of love. To want to make love in the sea, flying through the sky, in this city, in that field, on sand, with leaves, with salt, with oil, with fruit, in the snow, etc., is not to need new stimuli but to express a truth which is inseparable from passion.

The man with the red cap has sat up and clambered to his feet. The man from the château takes his place by the radiator without a word. As he walks to the exit, the man with the red cap stops to adjust his trousers, which are halfway down his hips. He unclasps his belt and pulls up several shirts and a vest. His stomach and torso are tattooed. He beckons to me to come over. He is fat, his skin unexpectedly soft-looking. The tattoos show couples making love in many different ways: their outlines are in black, their sexual organs in red. Across his stomach and flanks the figures are as crowded as those in Michelangelo's 'Last Judgment'. The man shivers. 'What can you expect?' he says; he doesn't bother to put the coin in his pocket but holds it in his fist until he reaches the café opposite.

The lovers' *totality extends, in a different manner*, to include the social world. Every action, when it is voluntary, is undertaken in the name of the beloved. What the lover then changes in the world is an expression of his passion.

The man in the red cap is going into the café opposite.

Yet passion is a privilege. An economic and cultural one.

The train comes in. I get into a compartment where two men are sitting either side of the window. One is young with a round face and dark eyes; the second is about my age. We say good evening. Outside the rain is turning to snow. I find a pencil in my pocket: I want to write a few more lines.

Some attitudes are incompatible with passion. This is not a question of temperament. A cautious man, a mean man, a dishonest woman, a lethargic woman, a cantankerous couple may all be capable of passion. What makes a person refuse passion – or be incapable of pursuing a passion which has already been born, thus transforming it into a mere obsession – is his or her refusal of its totality. Within the lover's totality – as within any – there is the unknown: the unknown which is also conjured up by death, chaos, extremity. Those who are conditioned to treat the unknown as something exterior to themselves against which they must continually take measures and be on guard, may refuse passion. This is not a question of fearing the unknown. Everyone fears it. It is a question of where the unknown is located. Our culture encourages us to locate it outside ourselves. Always. Even disease is

43

thought of as coming from outside. To locate the unknown as being *out there* is incompatible with passion.

The young man, who is a Spaniard, suggests that I take his seat by the window where there is a small folding table on which it will be easier to write. They are going to Mulhouse where they work in the same factory. The older one had been there for seven years. His family are in Bilbao.

The totality of passion overlays (or undermines) the world. Lovers love one another *with* the world. (As one might say *with* their hearts or *with* caresses.) The world is the *form* of their passion and all the events which they experience or imagine are the imagery of their passion. This is why passion is ready to risk life. Life appears to be only its form.

The older Spaniard, who is my age, is working on a piece of paper torn from the stiff cover of a magazine. With his large thumbs and nicotine-stained fingers he is carefully tearing small pieces out of it. The younger man watches him with the pride of an impresario: he has seen him do this before. But there is no audience for this act. It is gratuitous, in the small hours of the morning. As the older man tears at the paper, he makes the silhouette of a figure . . . head, shoulders, bottom, feet. He folds the figure lengthways and sideways. Then very delicately he tears a piece out of its centre and folds the whole again. It has become a man, four inches high. When he pulls the folds open a penis stands up erect. When he closes them, the penis goes down. Because I am looking, he shows it to me. Otherwise he wouldn't have done so. The three of us smile. He says he can make it better than that. Almost gently he crumples the figure up in his hand. Under the folding table is an ashtray. He throws the figure into the ashtray, letting the lid close with a sharp *clack*. Then, with folded arms, he stares out of the window into the night.

1974

On the banks of the Sava

About twenty miles south west of Belgrade there is a small town called Obrenovac. The bus stops opposite the post office. There is a decorative flower bed with grass growing in it instead of flowers. Four men sit on the edge of it, leaning forward with their elbows on their knees, talking. Behind them is a small but well-stocked supermarket. Other shops in the main street are less like those of a consumer society. There is an ironmonger's with home-made stovepipes in the window. There are four or five tailor's shops with lengths of material for men's suits and hand-made *sajkace* – the Serbian dented cap for men – in their windows. A hairdresser. A baker with several different kinds of bread, including ring-shaped, seed-covered *djevreki*, and various sorts of strudels. Then a butcher with no meat in the window, but with carcasses hanging at the back of the shop.

In Russian cities the food displayed in shop windows often consists of painted wooden models, wooden chops, chickens, eggs. From a distance they sometimes look more convincing than real food because their colours are unusually vivid and distinct. The wooden meat is either lean (red) or fat (cream-coloured). There was a painter from Georgia towards the end of the last century called Pirosmanishvili who spent most of his life going from one tavern in Tiflis to another, painting inn signs. Many of them were of food. I have never seen paintings more expressive of hunger – or rather, of the dreams provoked by hunger. Tabletops like the earth and on them cheeses and joints of meat like huge buildings. Even the women he painted look edible, like Easter cakes. In Pirosmanishvili's work the Russian tradition of painting wooden models of food for shop windows found its only genius and master. Why is it that the real lamb

45

hanging at the back of the butcher's in Obrenovac unexpectedly, without premeditation, reminds me of his painting?

Further along the street is a bookshop in which most of the books have the appearance of school textbooks. I know already that when the children come out of school for lunch they will be wearing black overalls trimmed with white stitching.

But even if I ignored the shop windows and the children, and if I walked, as I often do, head down looking at my feet, I would still know which part of Europe I was in. The surface of the road is poor and where it is metalled the edges are rough and unfinished. This much, however, might be true of parts of France. Is it the strength with which the grass grows, pushing up lean and stalky wherever there is a gap or crack, that makes it so Slav? Is there something quintessential in the yellowy grass stalks and that dusty grey tar which may at any moment break into cobbles or fade away into earth? (It is necessary to insist that there is nothing exotic in such questions: their answers are literally part of the substratum of real, in no way romantic, events: for example, that dusty, tarry grey is the colour at the bottom of the tram-lines in Prague when it is dry and the sun catches in a muted acetylene blue on the uppermost surface of the rails.)

Or is the characteristic quality of the road more to do with the relative thinness of its surface? Is it that it has never been embedded in the earth but only laid on its surface? Is it that the road wears like a cloth rather than a solid structure?

Either side of the main street the houses are low. You can almost touch their roofs. They have double windows with a space the width of their walls between the panes. In this space in one window there is a pot of geraniums and, behind them, coarse lace curtains. The other window is slightly dusty. To look through the glass, with its transparent nap of dust, at the deep red flowers in the shade and then through the lace, the colour of string tied round parcels, into the brownish darkness of the room beyond is to rediscover something of one's childhood. Is this the result of stories read, or does its 'childishness' derive from the scale of the window and house?

Occasionally along the street pass buses, cars, open lorries and horses hauling four-wheeled wooden carts like open-ended, very elongated cradles. Their drivers, reins in hand, sit rounded and hunched up: as dogmatically immobile against the movement of the cart as stone piers against the movement of a river. There are also cyclists on tall black bicycles with their wheels far apart – so that the cyclist gives the impression of hurriedly following the front wheel instead of bearing down upon it.

At right angles to the main street are a number of rough roads which lead for half a mile or more towards the fields and woods and wasteland which surround the town. These are access roads to the houses on either side of them. Some of these houses are like suburban bungalows; others are old, very small cottages which contain no more than one room. A fair number have television aerials on their roofs – and, at the same time, wells in their gardens or courtyards, for water. It is these gardens and yards which fascinate me and which constitute the most striking visual element.

In some there are flowerbeds of roses and on the grass between them chickens and ducks. There are also cherry trees and pigs. On the outside of the fence, along the borders of the road, there is a goat chained to a stake and two white kids who butt each other, standing on their hind legs like beasts rampant in a heraldry that never existed here. In these gardens and yards (the distinction between the two terms is that a garden is private whereas a yard is the space on to which two or three houses give), there are also tables, jugs or pails of water, benches, chairs, creepers to give shade, tall grass, bare earth to be dampened in the summer so that it does not become too dusty, vegetables, acacia trees, and ritual space. These gardens and yards are like bodies accepted for what they are without pretence. They are neither neglected nor, in the strict sense, cultivated. Yet such a description imputes a moral awareness that is irrelevant. A strange undemonstrative equality has been established here between nature and tenant. They are neither impressive nor sordid. They suggest neither ambition nor despair. They are simply and consistently inhabited, like rooms built on the earth. You measure them according to a human time-scale. They are not immediate like herbaceous borders, nor are they timeless like forests. Everything in them is a little overgrown and everything is intentional. And this is evident without a person being in sight or a story being told – merely through the disposition of what is visible within them.

The town is not far from the banks of the Sava. The Sava rises in the Julian Alps and joins the Danube at Belgrade, where the confluence of the two large rivers, with its considerable expanse of shining water, affects the light above the city so that sometimes you have the impression, looking up a street, that over the brow of its hill there will be the sea. Here the river is strong, wide, muddy-grey coloured and opaque, though bright like the sky because it is fast-flowing. If one must use the misleading metaphor of a river to describe the nature of time, this is the kind of river one should visualize. It has weight, and this weight is a reminder of the scale of the land mass to which everything on its bank belongs. It is a river that ultimately celebrates not water, but land. At the end of the road which leads to it from the outskirts of Obrenovac there is a café where they grill the river fish and serve them with cabbage salad.

For some way the road back to Belgrade runs beside the Sava. The bus stops at each village, usually outside the café if there is one – if not, where a few men are sitting on cases and boxes talking, with a bottle of beer between their feet. The bus radio is on loud. Songs not unlike certain Greek ones. As the bus bowls along, the seats squeak and the windows rattle (if there is a pothole they clatter) and all these sounds are somehow accommodated by the music. People quite far away from the road look up at the approach of the bus because they hear the notes and the voice it is bringing nearer and then carrying away into the distance.

Why am I so conscious of the progress of these sounds through the landscape, along the road, down the river? It isn't that everything else is quiet. It isn't because everyone looks up as we pass. It is, I think, because everything I can see out of the window suggests an expanse, a continuity which forces me to be aware of, to trace, the length of our short noisy ride over it. But what is it that suggests this almost endless continuity? The light in the sky? The air? The specific changes of colour caused by distance here? Perhaps these play a part. But principally, I think, it is because no event in the landscape (no hill, no tree, no building) is so striking that it creates a natural focal centre to which everything else becomes subservient. Each event passes your eye on to another and then that one to another and another and another, so that there is no reason to suppose that the sequence need ever stop.

In Western European terms, the opposite of romantic is classic. This landscape, however, is the true antithesis of the romantic landscape. The romantic is always at the edge, at the end, of the possible. It proposes the ultimate – either sublimely or terribly. It is based on hierarchy, whereas here between the events of the landscape there is a restrained egalitarianism similar to that which was evident in the gardens between the human and the natural. It is the normalcy of this landscape which makes it seem boundless.

In the National Gallery at Belgrade there is not a single painting which bears witness to any of these quintessential qualities. Nor can I think of many paintings elsewhere that do so. It is not a landscape which lends itself to representational painting – but, rather, to film because it moves, or to embroidery and decoration because they ignore the difference between near and far. It is the landscape, however, evident behind the experience expressed in a great deal of Slav poetry. But one must be clear about what one is looking for. There is nothing arcadian or innocent or eternal or reassuring about its qualities. Such landscape encourages a passionate (not quietist) recognition of transcience.

1972

Four postcard poems

—

Teslic

There is the dust
of the dawn bus
on the unmade road
across the pass

In every village
girls who are woman
and boys with moustaches
wait to ride to school

The bus of knowledge is leaving
leaving the old behind
soon the dust will settle
on the unmade road

Bakar

The village which told stories
during the night of centuries
above the bay of the tuna
has fallen silent
astounded
by the news of the refinery
and its refrain
flaming continually
against the hills
even on the days of funerals

Soave

On her bicycle she rides
beside a dead canal
reciting the lines by Carducci
she learnt last week at school
on this canal when I was young
barges crossed so close
it was like a kiss . . .

Kalemegdan: Beograd

Beside the battlements
where the living defenders
joined the dead
still fighting
to defend their walls
lovers today
fondle and embrace
as the Sava takes
the arm of the Danube
to go together
into the bliss of some black sea
here the city was built
here children will be born

1979

On the Bosphorus

For ten days I kept notes (after ten days we fast become ignorant habitués), with the idea of later being able to reconstruct my first impressions of Istanbul.

The reconstruction was not so simple as it might have been. Political violence, including a massacre at Maras, had forced Prime Minister Bülent Ecevit to declare a state of siege in thirteen of the provinces.

Why describe the tiles of Rustan Pasa mosque – their deep red and green lost in an even deeper blue – in a city where martial law has just been declared?

In Turkish, the Bosphorus is called the straits of the throat, the place of the stranglehold. It has featured for millennia in every global strategy. In 1947 Truman claimed an essential strategic interest in Turkey, just as, after the First World War, Britain and France had done. But whereas the Turks fought and won their war of independence (1918–23) against the first claim, they were powerless against the second.

American intervention in Turkish politics has been constant ever since. Nobody in Turkey doubts that the destabilizing programme of the right is backed by the CIA. The United States probably fears two things: the repercussions in Turkey of the fall of the Shah in Iran, unless there is a 'strong' government in Ankara; and Ecevit's reform programme which, though moderate, is not compliant with western interests, and revives some of the promise of Atatürk's independence movement. Among many other consequences, if Ecevit is ousted, the American-trained torturers will return to their prison posts.

When the ferry leaves Kadikoy on the Asian side of the Bosphorus, on your right you see the massive block of the Selemiye barracks, with its four towers, sentinels at each corner. In 1971 – the last time there was martial law in Istanbul – many political prisoners (nearly all of the left) were interrogated there. If you look the other way, you see the railway station of Hayderpasa and the buffers, only a few yards from the water, stopping the lines which come from Baghdad, Calcutta and Goa. Nazim Hikmet, who spent thirteen years in Turkish prisons, wrote many lines about this railway station:

> A smell of fish in the sea
> bugs on every seat
>   spring has come to the station
> Baskets and bags
>   descend the station steps
>   go up the station steps
>   stop on the steps
> Beside a policeman a boy
> – of five, perhaps less –
>   goes down the steps.
> He has never had any papers
> but he is called Kemal.
> A bag
> a carpet bag climbs the steps.
> Kemal descending the steps
>   barefoot and shirtless
>   is quite alone
>   in this beautiful world.
> He has no memories except of hunger
>   and then vaguely
>   of a woman in a dark room.

Across the water, in the early morning sunlight, the mosques are the colour of ripe honeydew melons. The Blue Mosque with its six piercing minarets. Santa Sophia, taking advantage of its hill, immense, dominating its minarets so that they look no more than guardians of a breast. The so-called New Mosque, finished in 1660. On overcast days the same buildings across the straits look dull and

53

grey, like the skin of cooked carp. I glance back now at the bleak towers of the Selemiye barracks.

Thousands of jellyfish of all sizes, as large as dishes, as small as eggcups, contract and distend in the current. They are milky and half-transparent. The local pollution has killed off the mackerel who used to eat the jellyfish. Hence their profusion in hundreds of thousands. Popularly they are called water cunts.

Hundreds of people crowd the boat. Most of them commute every day. A few, who stand out because of their clothes and the amazement to be read on their faces, are crossing into Europe for the first time, and have come from distant parts of Anatolia. A woman of thirty-five, wearing a scarf over her hair and baggy cotton trousers, sits on the uppermost deck in the sunshine which dazzles off the surface of the water.

The plain of central Anatolia, surrounded by mountains, with deep snow in the winter and the dust of rocks in the summer, was one of the first sites of neolithic agriculture, and the communities were peace-loving and matriarchal. Today, eroded, it risks becoming a desert. The villages are dominated by the *aghas*, thieving officials who are also landowners. There has been no effective land reform, and the average annual income in 1977 was £10–£20.

Deliberately the woman holds her husband's hand. He is all that remains of the familiar. Together they look across at the famous skyline which is the breathtaking, incandescent, perfumed half-truth of the city. The hand which she holds is like many of the hands resting on laps on the deck. The idiom of the popular male Turkish hand: broad, heavy, plumper than you would guess (even when the body is emaciated), calloused, strong. Hands which do not look as if they have grown out of the earth like vines – the hands of old Spanish peasants, for example – but nomad hands which travel across the earth.

Speaking of his narrative poems, Hikmet once said he wanted to make poetry like a material for shirts, very fine, half silk, half cotton: silks which are also democratic because they absorb the sweat.

A beggar woman stands by the door to the saloon on the lower deck. In contrast to the heaviness of the male hands, the woman's hands are light. Hands which make cakes of dried cow dung for burning in central Anatolia, hands which plait the daughter's hair into strands. On her arm, the beggar woman carries a basket of sick cats: an emblem of pity, off which she scrapes a living. Most of those who pass place a coin in her outstretched hand.

Sometimes first impressions gather up some of the residue of centuries. The nomadic hand is not just an image; it has a history. Meanwhile, the torturers are capable, within a few days, of breaking entire nervous systems. The hell of politics – which is why politics compulsively seeks utopias – is that it has to straddle both times: millennia and a few days. I picture the face of a friend perhaps to be imprisoned again, his wife, his children. Since the foundation of the republic, this is the ninth time that martial law has been declared to deal with internal dissent. I see his clothes still hanging neatly in the wardrobe.

When the ferry passes the headland, eleven minarets become visible, and you can see clearly the camel chimneys of the kitchens of the Sultan's palace. This palace of Topkapi housed luxury and indulgence on such a scale that they percolated into the very dreams of the West; but in reality, as you can see today, it was no more than a labyrinthine monument to a dynastic paranoia.

Turning now against the current, black diesel smoke belches from the ship's funnel, obliterating Topkapi. Forty per cent of the population of Istanbul live in shanty towns which are invisible from the centre of the city. These shanty towns – each one with a population of at least 25,000 – are insanitary, overcrowded and desperate. They are also sites of super-exploitation (a shack may be sold for as much as £5,000).

Yet the decision to migrate to the city is not a stupid one. About a quarter of the men who live in the shanty towns are unemployed. The other three-quarters work for a future which may be illusory, but which was totally inconceivable in the village. The average wage in the city is between £20 and £30 a week.

The massacre at Maras was planned by fascists backed by the CIA. Yet to know this is to know little. Eric Hobsbawm wrote[1] recently that it has taken left-wing intellectuals a long time to condemn terrorism. Today left-wing terrorism in Turkey plays into the hands of those who want to re-establish a right-wing police state such as existed between 1950 and 1960 – to the enormous benefit of the *aghas*.

Yet however much one condemns terrorism, one must recognize that its popular (minority) appeal derives from experience which is bound to remain totally untouched by such tactical, or ethical, considerations. Popular violence is as arbitrary as the labour market, not more so. The violent outbreak, whether encouraged by the right or the left, is fed by the suppressed violence of countless initiatives *not* taken. Such outbreaks are the ferment of stagnation, kept at the right temperature by broken promises. For more than fifty years, since Atatürk's republic succeeded the sultanate, the peasants of central Anatolia, who fought for their independence, have been promised land and the means to cultivate it. But such changes as there have been have led to more suffering.

In the lower-deck saloon a salesman, who has bribed the stewards to let him sell, is holding up, high for all to see, a paper folder of needles. His patter is leisurely and soft-voiced. Those who sit or stand around him are mostly men. On the folder, which holds fifteen needles of different sizes, is printed in English HAPPY HOME NEEDLE BOOK, and around this title an illustration of three young white women wearing hats and ribbons in their hair. Both needles and folder were made in Japan.

The salesman is asking 20p. Slowly, one after another, the men buy. It is a bargain, a present and an injunction. Carefully they slip the folder into one of the pockets of their thin jackets. Tonight they will give them to their wives, as if the needles were seeds for a garden.

In Istanbul the domestic interior, in both the shanty towns and elsewhere, is a place of repose, in profound opposition to what lies outside the door. Cramped, badly roofed, crooked, cherished, these interiors are spaces like prayers, both because they oppose the traffic of the world as it is, and because they are a metaphor for the Garden of Eden or Paradise.

Interiors symbolically offer the same things as Paradise: repose, flowers, fruit, quiet, soft materials, sweetmeats, cleanliness, femininity. The offer can be as imposing (and vulgar) as one of the Sultan's rooms in the harem, or it can be as modest as the printed pattern on a square of cheap cotton, draped over a cushion on the floor of a shack.

It is clear that Ecevit will try to maintain control over the initiatives of the generals who are now responsible for the rule of each province. The politico-military tradition of imprisonment, assassination and execution is still a strong one in Turkey. When considering the power and decadence of the Ottoman empire, the west conveniently overlooks the fact that this empire is what protected Turkey from the first inroads of capitalism, western colonization and the supremacy of money over every other form of power. Capital assumes within itself all earlier forms of ruthlessness, and makes the old forms obsolete. This obsolescence permits the West a basis for its global hypocrisies, of which the latest is the 'human rights' issue.

A man stands by the ship's rail, staring down at the flashing water and the ghostly water cunts. The ship, seventeen years old, was built by the Fairfield Shipbuilding and Engineering Company, Govan, Glasgow. Until five years ago, he was a shoemaker in a village not far from Bolu. It took him two days to make a pair of shoes. Then factory-made shoes began to arrive in the village, and were sold cheaper than his. The cheaper, factory-made shoes meant that some children in some villages no longer went barefoot. No longer able to sell his shoes, he went to the state factory to ask for work. They told him he could hire a stamping machine for cutting out pieces of leather.

A pair of shoes consists of twenty-eight pieces. If he wanted to hire the machine, he must cut the necessary pieces of leather for 50,000 pairs a year. The machine was delivered to his shop. By working twelve hours every day, he fulfilled his quota. At the end of every week, the pieces, stacked in piles like dogs' tongues, filled the entire shop. There was only room for him to sit on his stool by the machine.

The next year he was told that, if he wanted to keep the machine, he must now cut enough pieces for 100,000 pairs of shoes. It was impossible, he said. Yet it proved possible. He worked twelve hours during the day, and his brother-in-law worked twelve hours during the night. In the room above, which was a metaphor for Paradise, the sound of the stamping machine never stopped day or night. In a year, the two men cut nearly three million pieces.

One evening he smashed his left hand, and the noise of the machine stopped. There was quiet beneath the carpet of the room above. The machine was loaded on to a lorry, and taken back to the factory. It was after that that he came to Istanbul to look for work. The expression in his eyes, as he tells his story, is familiar. You see it in the eyes of countless men in Istanbul. These men are no longer young; yet their look is not one of resignation, it is too intense for that. Each one is looking at his own life with the same knowingness, protective-ness and indulgence as he would look on a son. A calm Islamic irony.

The subjective opposites of Istanbul are not reason and unreason, nor virtue and sin, nor believer and infidel, nor wealth and poverty — colossal as the objective contrasts are. They are, or so it seemed to me, purity and foulness.

This polarity covers that of interior/exterior, but is not confined to it. For example, as well as separating carpet from earth, it separates milk and cow, perfume and stench, pleasure and ache. The popular luxuries — honey-sweet to the tooth, shiny to the eye, silken to the touch, fresh to the nose — offer amends for the natural foulness of the world. Many Turkish popular expressions and insults play across this polarity. 'He thinks,' they say about someone who is conceited, 'that he's the parsley in everyone's shit.'

Applied to class distinction, this same polarity of purity/foulness becomes vicious. The faces of the rich bourgeois women of Istanbul, sick with idleness, fat with sweetmeats, are among the most pitiless I have seen.

When friends of mine were prisoners in the Seleminye barracks, their wives took them attar of roses and essence of lemons.

The ferry also carries lorries. On the tailboard of a lorry from Konya is written: 'The money I make I earn with my own hands, so may Allah bless me.' The driver, with grey hair, is leaning against the bonnet, drinking tea out of a small, gilt-rimmed glass. On every deck there are vendors of tea with such glasses and bowls of sugar on brilliant copper trays. The tea drinkers sip, relax, and look at the shining water of the Bosphorus. Despite the thousands of passengers carried daily, the ferry boats are almost as clean as interiors. There are no streets to compare with their decks.

On each side of the lorry from Konya, the driver has had a small landscape painted. Both show a lake surrounded by hills. Above is the all-seeing eye, almond-shaped with long lashes, like a bridegroom's. The painted water of the lakes suggests peace and stillness. As he sips his tea, the driver talks to three small, dark-skinned men with passionate eyes. The passion may be personal, but it is also the passion you can see all over the world in the eyes of proud and oppressed minorities. The three men are Kurds.

Both in the main streets of Istanbul, and in the back streets where there are chickens and sheep, you see porters carrying bales of cloth, sheets of metal, carpets, machine parts, sacks of grain, furniture, packing cases. Most of these porters are Kurds from eastern Anatolia, on the borders of Iraq and Iran. They carry everything where the lorries cannot. And because the industrial part of the city is full of small workshops in streets too narrow for lorries, there is a great deal to carry from workplace to workplace.

Fixed to their backs is a kind of saddle, on which the load is piled and corded high above their heads. This way of carrying, and the weight of the loads, obliges them to stoop. They walk, when loaded, like jack knives half-shut. The three now listening to the lorry driver are sitting on their own saddles, sipping tea, gazing at the water and the approach to the Golden Horn. The cords with which they fasten their loads lie loose between their feet on the deck.

Altogether, the crossing takes twenty minutes (about the time needed to read this article). Beside the landing stage rowing boats rock in the choppy water. In some of them fires burn, the flames dancing to the rhythm of the slapping water. Over the fires, men are frying fish to sell to those on their way to work.

Beyond these pans – almost as wide as the boat – of frying fish, lie all the energies and torpor of the city: the workshops, the markets, the mafia, the Galata Bridge on which the crowd walking across is invariably twenty abreast (the bridge is a floating one and incessantly, almost imperceptibly, quivers like a horse's flank), the schools, the newspaper offices, the shanty towns, the abattoir, the headquarters of the political parties, the gunsmiths, the merchants, soldiers, beggars.

These are the last moments of peace before the driver starts up the engine of his lorry, and the porters hurry to the stern of the ship to be among the first to jump ashore. The tea vendors are collecting the empty glasses. It is as if, during the crossing, the Bosphorus induces the same mood as the painted lakes: as if the ferry boat, built in Glasgow in 1961, becomes an immense floating carpet, suspended in time above the shining water, between home and work, between effort and effort, between two continents. And this suspension, which I remember so vividly, corresponds now to the destiny of the country.

1979

Notes

1 'The new dissent: Intellectuals, society and the left,' *New Society*, 23 November, 1978.

Manhattan

As a moral idea, an abstraction, Manhattan has a place in everybody's thinking throughout the world. Manhattan represents: opportunity, the power of capital, white imperialism, glamour, poverty – depending upon the world view of the one who is thinking. Manhattan is a concept. It also exists. In its streets a visitor is at first astounded by both the power and the weakness of his previous imagination. From this astonishment comes a paradox. They are, at one and the same time, streets in a dream and the most real streets (offering nothing behind what *is*) that he has ever seen.

I can seize on details: wheel-less cars abandoned under hundreds of living-room windows as though on a deserted beach: a diamond brooch in the form of the word LOVE in a window at Tiffany's: figures on street corners in Harlem, guarding with defiance the space and repose within their black bodies, because it is the only space and repose which is inalienably theirs. There are no symbolic details here. What you see is what you see; nothing more. Meaning is where you are. There is no hidden significance, no inner meaning. I remember Lorca's poems about Manhattan:

> Life is no dream! Beware and beware and beware!
> We tumble downstairs to eat of the damp of the
>   earth
> or we climb to the snowy divide with the choir of
>   dead dahlias.
> But neither dream nor forgetfulness, is:
> brute flesh is.

The streets are worn and stained like interiors. The steps, railings, hydrants, kerbs, have not aged with constant use over a long period of

time. Rather they have been broken and damaged by violent succes-
sions, like a basin in a public lavatory, a cell door, a bed in a lodging
house. Each sidewalk has a terrible intimacy. At street level in
Manhattan there is no distinction whatsoever between intimate and
public events. (The distinction disappears in the same way on a
battlefield.)

Nor are there any barriers in space. No border which can be
reached is respected. Only the traffic lights work; otherwise there are
no civic conventions. What keeps people out (or in) are locks and, in
the case of the defeated, despair. Between the Bowery and Wall
Street or the Bowery and Madison Avenue, the traveller walks
through invisible rope after invisible rope, strung across the open
spaces at waist level. These ropes keep the derelict in; they are made
out of their own despair. Their despair is no secret: it is there in the
bricks injected and polished with dirt, the smashed windows, the
boarded-up shop fronts, the broken angles of the doorways, their
scavenger clothes, ageless and sexless.

There are many places in the world, cities and villages, where the
destitute are more numerous than in Manhattan. But here the
derelict possess nothing with which to make even a mute appeal.
They have become nothing more than what they appear to be. They
are nothing but their dereliction.

The skyscrapers establish their norm. One's eye wearies of making
the distinction between vertical and horizontal; the right angle no
longer reads as such; what might recede flatly into the distance
recedes instead, upwards, at an indeterminate angle into the sky. The
principle of the horizon is broken. If you picture the experienced
space of other cities as being sheets of paper laid out more or less flat
on their sides; here the sheet of paper has been twisted into a
paper-funnel bag. The loss of the essential right angle within
perception is compensated for by the proliferation of nearby rec-
tangles – doors, windows, walls, steps, grids. The paper funnel-bag is
made of graph paper with squares printed on it. It is filled with faces,
languages, cars, bottles, trees, fabrics, machines, plans, stairs, hands,

threats, promises, reports from all over the
world. The density of the working population of central Manhattan is a quarter
of a million per square mile. With such
density there is little space to look *through*.
To find space one must look *up*. There are
more jewellers than I have ever seen in a
city. As many rings on show as inhabitants.

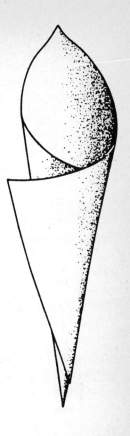

People are eating at all times, everywhere. The recipes come from all over the
world. But here food is what you put in
your mouth, here and now, and eat. It is
nothing else. It must have taken the im-
migrants a long time to learn this. Eating
here is private intake.

Everywhere there is talk. To talk. To
put outside. Talk to anyone who momentarily steps out of the crowd. In the crowd,
talk to whoever is available for a moment:
when alone, out loud to oneself. The talk
directly corresponds to what is going on in
one's head at that moment. What is going
on inside is immediately built outside in
words. And this acts as a kind of protection.

How does talk act as protection? Not in the obvious way. It isn't an
appeal for sympathy or special consideration. Better to ask: against
what does it protect? Against the space between the first person and
the next. This space is created by hopes. The other's and one's own.
It is a vertical space, a sheer drop.

Like lifts, hopes need shafts to travel up. To fall down one of these
shafts is easy. This is the fall into oblivion. Talk is a counter-agent to
oblivion. Nobody falls while talking to somebody else; the words
catch against the shaft and hold the speaker up. The falls occur in
silence.

What one might expect to happen on the inside, happens here on the outside. There is no interiority. There may be introspection, guilt, happiness, personal loss; but all of it surfaces and comes out in words, actions, habits, tics, which become events taking place on every floor in every block. It isn't that everything becomes public, for this would suggest that there is no solitariness. Rather, each soul is turned inside out and remains alone.

Walk again in the streets. Seventy per cent of the housing is more than fifty years old. The water tanks insulated with wood are *outside* on the roofs. The fire escapes, a foot above head level on the sidewalks, are clamped like grappling irons to the *outside* of each building, so that the streets become narrow passages between open-work iron. On the platforms of these vertical fire escapes, women stand and children sleep, as if inside a living-room. There is a specific history to each instance (the city water supplies and water pressure, nineteenth-century city fire regulations, summer city temperatures without air conditioning); but in each case the history is one of reducing economic margins to their absolute minimum for the sake of greater profit and expansion; and in each case the consequence is the putting outside of what, elsewhere, is normally within. The great glass skyscrapers, lit up at night, demonstrate the same principle and elevate it into mythology: their *interior* lighting becomes the dominant feature of the whole island's *exterior* nocturnal environment.

The principle is spiritual as well as physical – or, to put it more exactly, the principle, by denying interiority, makes the spiritual a category within the physical. And this is to be seen in the faces.

Elsewhere the traces left by experience on a person's face are the traces of meetings (or struggles) between the person's inner needs or intentions and the demands or offers of the outside world. Put differently: marks of experience on a face are the lines of conjuncture between two moulds; both moulds are social products, but one contains a self and the other history.

Here, by contrast, experience marks most faces only as direct impact. The marks are not the result of a struggle between two forces.

64

Neither self nor history is the key to them. The marks have been pressed out or imposed entirely by exterior events – as with the bodies of cars, pressed in manufacture or dented and bent after collision.

This does not mean that those who live in Manhattan are passive or inert. It means that *will* here invariably finds its object and then deposits its own power within that object. Aims cease to be guides and become magnets. The aim – which is seldom another human being – becomes beloved; promises the fulfilment of a passion. Yet to create the beloved aim, its lover has emptied himself. All obstacles met on the way are then received as blows. These blows are what I see on the faces.

To say that Manhattan is the purest locus of modern capitalism would be incorrect. Less than a fifth of the working population is engaged in manufacture. Yet it is the purest locus of the reflexes, thought patterns, compulsions and psychological inversions of capitalism. All the modes of its tireless energy, ruthlessness and despair are to be found here. For a short period, Amsterdam held a historically equivalent position in the seventeenth century. New York was then called New Amsterdam.

Cities on the West Coast can claim today to be more modern than New York. But they lack the historical element which is an essential spur to the energy created and demanded by capitalism. Manhattan is haunted by the dead. At street level, except in front of the downtown shop windows (where one can dream of a personal future), one walks through the silt and ashes of the past. The capitalist need for ceaseless economic expansion requires the subjective fear that the past, if one does not progress fast enough, may claim its own and avenge itself; it requires that its workers look back with fear on their own past.

The newly arrived immigrant looked out to sea, beyond the lagoon, and imagined that the line of clouds just above the horizon was an outline of land. I have seen that formation of clouds; it forms regularly. Again and again, he reminded himself that it could not be land, and that the eastern horizon held no promise. The impression persisted despite his logic. When finally he saw the clouds as clouds, and nothing but clouds – and if he never achieved this, his son would – he became an American and sent for his cousins.

Every hope leaves the self or seizes it, to take it with it in its vertical ascent. The vast majority never see their hopes realized. But they discover that they can no more recall the power of their own will back into themselves, than their ancestors could return to where they emigrated from. Manhattan is peopled by people resigned to being betrayed daily by their own hopes. From this comes their incomparable wit, their cynicism and what is taken to be their realism.

Yet realism is not confirmed by the place itself. The neutrality or 'objectivity' of the physical surroundings has disappeared. Too much has been projected on to them. Every surface on the island, however geometric or however worn down, has been prejudiced by hopes or their disappointment. The island is like a dream or nightmare being dreamt simultaneously by each of its inhabitants. I have said that nothing is symbolic here. But the symbolism of dreams is only a subject for speculation after waking. Within a dream there is no symbolism, everything is itself. Only itself. Yet in a dream everything *faces* the dreamer – in the sense that it addresses him as directly as if it were an inner feeling. In Manhattan there is no exterior without a *face* in this sense; no exterior therefore which can reassure. Millionaires sought a substitute reassurance in the surfaces of works of art, objects, buildings brought from Europe: surfaces which made self and history distinct again. For those who are not millionaires, there is nothing outside to reside in.

This is the pitiless contradiction of Manhattan. Substance has been robbed of its impartiality. The self has emigrated outward. When Dante described the circles of Hell, he had the code of Christian morality on which to base the architecture of damnation in which the lost souls found themselves. Manhattan is not Hell and the code of morality of Dante's time has been overthrown.

From the Empire State Building, at about 1,000 feet, the shape of the entire island is visible. Every American schoolchild, who can be, is taken there. 'Look at the people in the streets, look, they're small as ants.' All around, regular as formes of type at a printer's, other skyscrapers reach approximately the same height. Fifty feet below, men are laying concrete on a new tower. The 1,000 feet have been achieved and built foot by foot. To the south the recent Trade Towers are higher still . . .

Within the history of capitalism, Manhattan is the island reserved for those who are damned because they have hoped excessively.

1975

The theatre of indifference

A story I want to write soon concerns a man from a remote village who settles in a city. A very old story. But the late-twentieth-century city has changed the old story's meaning. Such a city, in its extreme form, I see as white and northern. Climate helps a little to regulate the frontier between public and private. A Mediterranean city, or a city in the south in the United States, is of a slightly different character.

How does such a city, in its extreme form, first strike the villager? To do justice to his impression, one must understand *what* is impressing him. One cannot accept the city's version of itself. The city has at least as many illusions about itself as he, at first, has about it.

Most things look or sound unfamiliar to him: buildings, traffic, crowds, lights, goods, words, perspectives. This newness is both shocking and exciting. It underlines the incredibility of the sentence: *I am here.*

Quickly, however, he has to find his way among people. At first he assumes that they are a traditional element in the city: that they are more or less like men and women he and his father knew. What distinguishes them are their possessions – including their ideas: but relations with them will be more or less similar. Soon he sees this is not the case. Between their expressions, under their words, through accompanying gestures of hand and body, in their glances, a mysterious and constant exchange is taking place. He asks: what is happening?

If the storyteller places himself equidistant from city and village, he may be able to offer a descriptive answer. But it will not be immediately accessible to the questioner. Economic need has forced the villager to the city. Once there, his ideological transformation begins with his questions *not* being answered.

A young woman crosses the street, or the bar, using every part of her body, her mouth, her eyes to proclaim her nubility. (He calls her *shameless* to himself, but explains it in terms of what he assumes to be her insatiable sexuality.) Two young men pretend to fight to attract the girl's attention. Circling one another like tom-cats, they never strike a blow. (He calls them *rivals*, armed with knives.) The girl watches them with a bored look. (He calls her *too frightened* to show emotion.) Police enter. The two immediately stop fighting. The faces of the police are without a trace of expression. Their eyes scan the public and they walk off. (He calls their impassiveness *impartiality*.) The mythic quality and appeal of the early Chaplin lay in his spontaneous ability to act out so convincingly such 'innocent' misinterpretations of the city.

For the first time the villager is seeing caricatures, not drawn on paper, but alive.

Graphic caricature began in eighteenth-century England and then had a second lease of life in nineteenth-century France. Today it is dead because life has outstripped it. Or, more accurately, because satire is only possible when a moral reserve still exists, and those reserves have been used up. We are too used to being appalled by ourselves to be able to react to the idea of caricature. Originally the tradition of graphic caricature constituted a rural critique of the towns, and it flourished when large areas of the countryside were first being absorbed by the new cities but before the norms of the city were accepted as natural. Drawn caricature exaggerated to the point of absurdity when compared with the supposed 'even tenor' of life. Living caricatures imply a life of unprecedented fervour, danger and hope; and to the outsider it is his exclusion from this exaggerated 'super-life' which now appears absurd.

Graphic caricatures were of social types. Their typology took account of social class, temperament, character and physique. Their content invoked class interests and social justice. The living caricatures are simply creatures of immediate circumstance. They involve no continuity. They are behaviourist. They are not caricatures of character but of performance. The roles performed may be influenced by social class. (The girl crossing the street or bar in that particular way is likely to belong to the petit rather than grand bourgeoisie; the police are mostly working class; and so on.) But the contingencies of the immediate situation hide the essential class conditions. Likewise the judgment the living caricature demands has nothing to do with social justice, but with the success or failure of the individual performance. The sum total of these performances make a collectivity. But it is the collectivity of theatre. Not a theatre of the absurd as some dramatic critics once believed, but a theatre of indifference.

Most public life in the city belongs to this theatre. Two activities, however, are excluded. The first is productive labour. And the second is the exercise of real power. These have become hidden, non-public activities. The assembly line is as private – in this sense – as the President's telephone. Public life concerns inessentials upon which the public have been persuaded to fix their hopes. Yet truth is not so easily ousted. It returns to transform public life into theatre. If a lie is accepted as truth, the real truth turns the false one into a merely theatrical truth.

The very cohesion of public life is now charged with this theatricality. Often it extends into domestic life – but here it is less evident to the newly arrived villager. In public nobody can escape it; every one is forced to be either spectator or performer. Some performers perform their refusal to perform. They play insignificant 'little men', or, if they are many, they may play a cohort of 'the silent majority'. The change-over from performer to spectator is almost instantaneous. It is also possible to be both at the same time: to be a performer towards one's immediate entourage and the spectator of a larger more distant performance. For example: at a railway station or in a restaurant.

The indifference is between spectator and performer. Between audience and players. The experience of every performer – that's to say everyone – has led him to believe that, as soon as he begins, the audience will leave, the theatre will empty. Equally, the experience of every spectator has led him to expect that the performance of another will be irrelevant and indifferent to his own personal situation.

The aim of the performer is to prevent at least a few members of the audience from leaving. His fear is to find himself performing in an empty theatre. (This can happen even when he is physically surrounded by hundreds of people.) There is an inverse ratio of numbers. If a performer chooses an audience of a hundred, he is, in one sense, further from his fear of an empty theatre. But a hundred can leave in seconds. If he chooses an audience of three, he will be able to hold at least one of them back for a longer period – until this third person is forced to *perform* boredom or indifference.

Performing in the theatre of indifference inevitably leads to assuming and cultivating exaggerated expressions. Including expressions of uninterest, independence, nonchalance. It leads to the hamming of everyday life. The most usual final appeal to the departing audience is violence. This may be in words (swearing, threats, shouts), in grimaces, or in action. Some crimes which take place are the theatre's purest expression.

Exaggeration and violence become habitual. The violence is in the *address* of the exaggeration. In this sense the girl's performed nubility was as violent as a pointed gun. Gradually the habit of exaggeration informs the physical being of the performer. He becomes the living caricature of the expression towards which he is most generally forced, either by temperament or situation, in his performances.

The existence of the theatre makes itself felt when there is not even a second person present, when the minimum requirement for any performance (two people) is lacking. Solitude is confused with the triumph of indifference and made entirely negative. The emptied theatre becomes the image of silence itself. To be alone in silence is to have failed to retain a single member of the audience. Hence the compulsive need to walk on again: to the corner shop to buy an evening paper; to the pub for half a pint. This helps to define the particular pathos of the old in the city.

Only one thing can defeat indifference: a star performance. The star is credited with all that has been suppressed in each spectator. The star is the only form of idol in the modern city. He fills the theatre. He promises that no indifference is final.

Following the example of the great stars, who occur in every spectacular activity from sport through crime to politics, everyone can aspire to be a small star of an occasion. If there are six customers in a shop, any one of them can be made a star, by the consensus of those present, elevated, for a brief instant, to that status by a remark, a reaction or a knack of physical presence. In a crowd on an escalator, in a line of traffic at the traffic lights, in a queue at the guichet, there is a chance, like that of winning a sweepstake, for anyone to briefly fill the theatre. During that instant a purely urban pleasure passes over the temporary star's face. An unexpectedly coy pleasure, comprising modesty and conceit. Like the pleasure of a child praised for something he has done by accident.

The theatre of indifference should not be subsumed under *the artificiality of city life*. It is a new phenomenon. The social life of a village is artificial in the sense that it is highly formalized. A village funeral, for example, is more, not less, formalized than any contemporary public event in a city. The antithesis of the theatre of indifference is not spontaneous simplicity, but drama in which both the principle protagonists and the audience have a common interest.

The historical precondition for the theatre of indifference is that everyone is consciously and helplessly dependent in most areas of their life on the opinions and decisions of others. To put it symbolically: the theatre is built on the ruins of the forum. Its precondition is the failure of democracy. The indifference is the result of the inevitable divergence of personal fantasies when isolated from any effective social action. The indifference is born of the equation between excessive mobility of private fantasy and social political stasis.

In the theatre of indifference, appearances hide failure, words hide facts, and symbols hide what they refer to.

A villager cannot conceive of the theatre of indifference. He has never seen people producing such a surplus of expression over and above what is necessary to express themselves. And so he assumes that their hidden lives are as rich and mysterious as their expressions are extreme. He demeans himself because he cannot yet see the invisible – that which, according to his imagination, must lie behind their expressions and behaviour. He believes that what is happening in the city exceeds his imagination and his previous dreams. Tragically he is right.

1975

3
TWO DREAMS

———

The city of Sodom

———

This image, which is a detail from a painting by Lucas van Leyden of 'Lot and His Daughters', shows the destruction of the city of Sodom. At first glance, its realism is striking. Many of us in our lifetime have seen cities burning like this one, the buildings reduced to bare cages for the savage fires within them. The electric colour of the water lit by flares seems strangely modern to have been painted by a sixteenth-century artist. Nevertheless Lucas van Leyden's vision of the wrath of God is fundamentally a medieval one. It is conceived according to two principles which are naturally opposed to one another: the order, the rationality of God, as opposed to the disorder, the chaos of the world of man. The city of men not only burns; it tilts into the sea; men run up its streets as up the slanting deck of a sinking ship. The masts of the ships smashed in the harbour are contrasted with the fore-ground tree which belongs to nature, created by God and relatively uncorrupted by the interference of man. In the whole picture the scale of the city is like that of a toy, the toy of a disobedient child who has provoked his father. The power of this father lies not only in his ability to rain fire down upon the city, but in the very form of the fire in the sky. It is symmetrical, ordered, lucid – like a perfectly developed part of a chrysanthemum. It is part of the order of justice which man fails to understand but cannot escape. Perhaps the reason why such an image can still work on one powerfully – if one allows it time – is to be found in the fact that in one's dreams and unconscious the notion of a higher order may still remain. The word 'father' can be very potent in this respect, while scenes of destruction by fire often possess, if we are not in immediate danger, something of the quality of a dream.

1972

Lucas van Leyden: *Lot and his Daughters* (detail)

The deluge

The notion of the destruction of the world existed long before men had the means to destroy it themselves. If one did not know the date of this watercolour, one might assume that it was a vision of atomic destruction. It was painted in 1525. The story of how it came to be painted is best told in Dürer's own words.

In the night between Wednesday and Thursday, after Whitsunday, I saw this appearance in my sleep – how many great waters fell from heaven. The first struck the earth about four miles away from me with terrific force and tremendous noise, and it broke up and drowned the whole land. I was so sore afraid that I awoke from it. Then the other waters fell, and as they fell they were very powerful and there were many of them, some further away, some nearer. And they came down from so great a height that they all seemed to fall with an equal slowness. But when the first water that touched the earth had very nearly reached it, it fell with such swiftness, with wind and roaring, and I was so sore afraid that when I awoke my whole body trembled and for a long while I could not recover myself. So when I arose in the morning I painted it above here as I saw it. God turn all things to the best.

Dürer was fifty-four when he painted this work.

Years previously, as a young man, he had made a series of woodcuts illustrating the end of the world as foreseen in the Apocalypse; these were full of conventional medieval symbols and figures. This dream is different. Its horror is not part of a doctrine or recipe. It is the spontaneous creation of Dürer's unconscious dreaming self. As in many nightmares, its ingredients include vast space, limitless water and a massive and oppressive sense of weight. Whether these elements relate to a dim recollection of the trauma of birth or to a premonition of death is not very important; what matters is that they augur a terrible finality. Yet the vision in itself is almost innocuous.

Albrecht Dürer: *The Deluge*

Our deepest fears reside just behind the everyday and the banal. The trickles of water are like those that run down a windowpane through which we are looking at the landscape. Suddenly there is a fearful change of scale. The trickle in the middle is seen to be four miles away and is thus immense, a vast deluge, the colour of blood seen through pale skin, the colour of a bruise which is the result of its own world-destroying blow.

1972

4

LOVE'S ABC

———

Kerchief

In the morning
folded with its wild flowers
washed and ironed
it takes up little space in the drawer.

Shaking it open
she ties it round her head.

In the evening she pulls it off
and lets it fall
still knotted to the floor.

On a cotton scarf
among printed flowers
a working day
has written its dream.

1985

Goya: the Maja, dressed and undressed

First, she lies on the couch in her fancy-dress costume: the costume which is the reason for her being called a Maja. Later, in the same pose, and on the same couch, she is naked.

Ever since the paintings were first hung in the Prado at the beginning of this century, people have asked: who is she? Is she the Duchess of Alba? A few years ago the body of the Duchess of Alba was exhumed and her skeleton measured in the hope that this would prove that it was not she who had posed! But then, if not she, who?

One tends to dismiss the question as part of the trivia of court gossip. But then when one looks at the two paintings there is indeed a mystery implied by them which fascinates. But the question has been wrongly put. It is not a question of *who*? We shall never know, and if we did we would not be much the wiser. It is a question of *why*? If we could answer that we might learn a little more about Goya.

My own explanation is that *nobody* posed for the nude version. Goya constructed the second painting from the first. With the dressed version in front of him, he undressed her in his imagination and put down on the canvas what he imagined. Look at the evidence.

There is the uncanny identity (except for the far leg) of the two poses. This can only have been the result of an *idea*: 'Now I will imagine her clothes are not there.' In actual poses, taken up on different occasions, there would be bound to be greater variation.

More important, there is the drawing of the nude, the way the forms of her body have been visualized. Consider her breasts – so rounded, high and each pointing outwards. No breasts, when a figure is lying, are shaped quite like that. In the dressed version we find the explanation. Bound and corseted, they assume exactly that shape and, supported, they will retain it even when the figure is lying. Goya has taken off the silk to reveal the skin, but has forgotten to reckon with the form changing.

The same is true of her upper arms, especially the near one. In the nude it is grotesquely, if not impossibly, fat – as thick as the thigh just above the knee. Again, in the dressed version we see why. To find the outline of a naked arm Goya has had to guess within the full, pleated shoulders and sleeves of her jacket, and has miscalculated by merely simplifying instead of reassessing the form.

Compared to the dressed version, the far leg in the nude has been slightly turned and brought towards us. If this had not been done, there would have been a space visible between her legs and the whole boat-like form of her body would have been lost. Then, paradoxically, the nude would have looked *less* like the dressed figure. Yet if the leg were really moved in this way, the position of both hips would change too. And what makes the hips, stomach and thighs of the nude seem to float in space – so that we cannot be certain at what angle they are to the bed – is that, although the far leg has been shifted, the form of the near hip and thigh has been taken absolutely directly from the clothed body, as though the silk there was a mist that had suddenly lifted.

Indeed the whole near line of her body as it touches the pillows and sheet, from armpit to toe, is as unconvincing in the nude as it is convincing in the first painting. In the first, the pillows and the couch sometimes yield to the form of the body, sometimes press against it: the line where they meet is like a stitched line – the thread disappearing and reappearing. Yet the line in the nude version is like the frayed edge of a cut-out, with none of this 'give-and-take' which a figure and its surroundings always establish in reality.

The face of the nude jumps forward from the body, not because it has been changed or painted afterwards (as some writers have suggested), but because it has been *seen* instead of conjured up. The more one looks at it, the more one realizes how extraordinarily vague and insubstantial the naked body is. At first its radiance deceives one into thinking that this is the glow of flesh. But is it not really closer to the light of an apparition? Her face is tangible. Her body is not.

Goya was a supremely gifted draughtsman with great powers of invention. He drew figures and animals in action so swift that clearly he must have drawn them without reference to any model. Like Hokusai, he knew what things looked like almost instinctively. His knowledge of appearances was contained in the very movement of his fingers and wrist as he drew. How then is it possible that the lack of a model for this nude should have made his painting unconvincing and artificial?

The answer, I think, has to be found in his motive for painting the two pictures. It is possible that both paintings were commissioned as a new kind of scandalous *trompe-l'oeil* – in which in the twinkling of an eye a woman's clothes disappeared. Yet at that stage of his life Goya was not the man to accept commissions on other men's trivial terms. So if these pictures were commissioned, he must have had his own subjective reasons for complying.

What then was his motive? Was it, as seemed obvious at first, to confess or celebrate a love affair? This would be more credible if we could believe that the nude had really been painted from life. Was it to brag of an affair that had not in fact taken place? This contradicts Goya's character; his art is unusually free from any form of bravado. I suggest that Goya painted the first version as an informal portrait of a friend (or possibly mistress), but that as he did so he became obsessed by the idea that suddenly, as she lay there in her fancy dress looking at him, she might have no clothes on.

Why 'obsessed' by this? Men are always undressing women with their eyes as a quite casual form of make-believe. Could it be that Goya was obsessed because he was afraid of his own sexuality?

There is a constant undercurrent in Goya which connects sex with violence. The witches are born of this. And so, partly, are his protests against the horrors of war. It is generally assumed that he protested because of what he witnessed in the hell of the Peninsular War. This is true. In all conscience he identified himself with the victims. But with despair and horror he also recognized a potential self in the torturers.

The same undercurrent blazes as ruthless pride in the eyes of the women he finds attractive. Across the full, loose mouths of dozens of faces, including his own, it flickers as a taunting provocation. It is there in the charged disgust with which he paints men naked, always equating their nakedness with bestiality – as with the madmen in the madhouse, the Indians practising cannibalism, the priests awhoring. It is present in the so-called 'Black' paintings which record orgies of violence. But most persistently it is evident in the way he painted all flesh.

It is difficult to describe this in words, yet it is what makes nearly every Goya portrait unmistakably his. The flesh has an expression of its own – as features do in portraits by other painters. The expression varies according to the sitter, but it is always a variation on the same demand: the demand for flesh as food for an appetite. Nor is that a rhetorical metaphor. It is almost literally true. Sometimes the flesh has a bloom on it like fruit. Sometimes it is flushed and hungry-looking, ready to devour. Usually – and this is the fulcrum of his intense psychological insight – it suggests both simultaneously: the devourer and the to-be-devoured. All Goya's monstrous fears are summed up in this. His most horrific vision is of Satan eating the bodies of men.

One can even recognize the same agony in the apparently mundane painting of the butcher's table. I know of no other still life in the world which so emphasizes that a piece of meat was recently living, sentient flesh, which so combines the emotive with the literal meaning of the word 'butchery'. The terror of this picture, painted by a man who has enjoyed meat all his life, is that it is *not* a still life.

If I am right in this, if Goya painted the nude Maja because he was haunted by the fact that he imagined her naked – that is to say imagined her flesh with all its provocation – we can begin to explain why the painting is so artificial. He painted it to exorcise a ghost. Like the bats, dogs and witches, she is another of the monsters released by 'the sleep of reason', but, unlike them, she is beautiful because desirable. Yet to exorcise her as a ghost, to call her by her proper name, he had to identify her as closely as possible with the painting of her dressed. He was not painting a nude. He was painting the apparition of a nude within a dressed woman. This is why he was tied so faithfully to the dressed version and why his usual powers of invention were so unusually inhibited.

I am not suggesting that Goya intended us to interpret the two paintings in this way. He expected them to be taken at their face value: the woman dressed and the woman undressed. What I am suggesting is that the second, nude version was probably an *invention* and that perhaps Goya became imaginatively and emotionally involved in its 'pretence' because he was trying to exorcise his own desires.

Why do these two paintings seem surprisingly modern? We assumed that the painter and model were lovers when we took it for granted that she agreed to pose for the two pictures. But their power, as we now see it, depends upon there being so *little* development between them. The difference is only that she is undressed. This should change everything, but in fact it only changes our way of looking at her. She herself has the same expression, the same pose, the same distance. All the great nudes of the past offer invitations to share their golden age; they are naked in order to seduce and transform us. The Maja is naked but indifferent. It is as though she is not aware of being seen – as though we were peeping at her secretly through a keyhole. Or rather, more accurately, as though she did not know that her clothes had become 'invisible'.

In this, as in much else, Goya was prophetic. He was the first artist to paint the nude as a stranger; to separate sex from intimacy; to substitute an aesthetic of sex for an energy of sex. It is in the nature of energy to break bounds: and it is the function of aesthetics to construct them. Goya, as I have suggested, may have had his own reason for fearing energy. In the second half of the twentieth century the aestheticism of sex helps to keep a consumer society stimulated, competitive and dissatisfied.

1969

Bonnard

Since his death in 1947 at the age of eighty, Pierre Bonnard's reputation has grown fairly steadily, and in the last five years or so quite dramatically. Some now claim that he is *the* greatest painter of the century. Twenty years ago he was considered a minor master.

This change in his reputation coincides with a general retreat among certain intellectuals from political realities and confidence. There is very little of the post-1914 world in Bonnard's work. There is very little to disturb – except perhaps the unnatural peacefulness of it all. His art is intimate, contemplative, privileged, secluded. It is an art about cultivating one's own garden.

It is necessary to say this so that the more extreme recent claims for Bonnard can be placed in an historical context. Bonnard was essentially a conservative artist – although an original one. The fact that he is praised as 'a pure painter' underlines this. The purity consisted in his being able to accept the world as he found it. Was Bonnard a greater artist than Brancusi – not to mention Picasso, or Giacometti? Each period assesses all surviving artists according to its own needs. What is more interesting is why Bonnard will undoubtedly survive. The conventional answer, which begs the question, is that he was a great colourist. What was his colour for?

Bonnard painted landscapes, still lifes, occasional portraits, very occasional mythological pieces, interiors, meals and nudes. The nudes seem to me to be far and away the best pictures.

In all his works after about 1911 Bonnard used colours in a roughly similar way. Before then – with the help of the examples of Renoir, Degas, Gauguin – he was still discovering himself as a colourist; after 1911 he by no means stopped developing, but it was a development along an already established line. The typical mature Bonnard bias of colour – towards marble whites, magenta, pale cadmium yellow, ceramic blues, terracotta reds, silver greys, stained purple, all unified like reflections on the inside of an oyster – this bias tends in the landscapes to make them look mythical, even faery; in the still lifes it tends to give the fruit or the glasses or the napkins a silken glamour, as though they were part of a legendary tapestry woven from threads whose colours are too intense, too glossy; but in the nudes the same bias seems only to add conviction. It is the means of seeing the women through Bonnard's eyes. The colours confirm the woman.

Then what does it mean to see a woman through Bonnard's eyes? In a canvas painted in 1899, long before he was painting with typical Bonnard colours, a young woman sprawls across a low bed. One of her legs trails off the bed on to the floor: otherwise, she is lying very flat on her back. It is called 'L'Indolente: Femme assoupie sur un lit'.

The title, the pose and the art-nouveau shapes of the folds and shadows all suggest a cultivated *fin de siècle* form of eroticism very different from the frankness of Bonnard's later works; yet this picture – perhaps just because it doesn't engage us – offers us a clear clue.

Continue to look at the picture and the woman begins to disappear – or at least her presence becomes ambiguous. The shadow down her near side and flank becomes almost indistinguishable from the cast shadow on the bed. The light falling on her stomach and far leg marries them to the golden-lit bed. The shadows which reveal the form of a calf pressed against a thigh, of her sex as it curves down and round to become the separation between her buttocks, of an arm thrown across her breasts – these eddy and flow in exactly the same rhythm as the folds of the sheet and counterpane.

The picture, remaining a fairly conventional one, does not actually belie its title: the woman continues to exist. But it is easy to see how the painting is pulling towards a very different image: the image of the imprint of a woman on an *empty* bed. Yeats:

> . . . the mountain grass
> Cannot but keep the form
> Where the mountain hare has lain.[1]

Alternatively one might describe the same state of affairs in terms of the opposite process: the image of a woman losing her physical limits, overflowing, overlapping every surface until she is no less and no more than the *genius loci* of the whole room.

Before I saw the Bonnard exhibition at the Royal Academy in London in 1966, I was vaguely aware of this ambiguity in Bonnard's work between presence and absence, and I explained it to myself in terms of his being a predominantly nostalgic artist: as though the picture was all he could ever save of the subject from the sweep of time passing. Now this seems far too crude an explanation. Nor is there anything nostalgic about 'Femme assoupie sur un lit', painted at the age of thirty-two. We must go further.

The risk of loss in Bonnard's work does not appear to be a factor of distance. The far-away always looks benign. One has only to compare his seascapes with those of Courbet to appreciate the difference. It is proximity which leads to dissolution with Bonnard. Features are lost, not in distance, but, as it were, in the near. Nor is this an optical question of something being too close for the eye to focus. The closeness also has to be measured in emotional terms of tenderness and intimacy. Thus 'loss' becomes the wrong word, and nostalgia the wrong category. What happens is that the body which is very near – in every sense of the word – becomes the axis of everything that is seen; everything that is visible relates to it; it acquires a domain to inhabit; but by the same token it has to lose the precision of its own fixed position in time and space.

The process may sound complex, but in fact it is related to the common experience of falling in love. Bonnard's important nudes are the visual expressions of something very close to Stendhal's famous definition of the process of 'crystallization' in love:

A man takes pleasure in adorning with a thousand perfections the woman of whose love he is certain; he recites to himself, with infinite complacency, every item that makes up his happiness. It is like exaggerating the attractions of a superb property that has just fallen into our hands, which is still unknown, but of the possession of which we are assured . . . In the salt mines of Salzburg they throw into the abandoned depths of a mine a branch of a tree stripped of its leaves by winter; two or three months later they draw it out, covered with sparkling crystallizations: the smallest twigs, those which are no larger than the foot of a titmouse, are covered with an infinity of diamonds, shifting and dazzling; it is impossible any longer to recognize the original branch.[2]

Many other painters have of course idealized women whom they have painted. But straightforward idealization becomes in effect indistinguishable from flattery or pure fantasy. It in no way does justice to the energy involved in the psychological state of being in love. What makes Bonnard's contribution unique is the way that he shows in pictorial terms how the image of the beloved emanates *outwards from her* with such dominance that finally her actual physical presence becomes curiously incidental and in itself indefinable. (If it could be defined, it would become banal.)

Bonnard said something similar himself:

By the seduction of the first idea the painter attains to the universal. It is the seduction which determines the choice of the motif and which corresponds exactly to the painting. If this seduction, if the first idea vanishes all that remains . . . is the object which invades and dominates the painter.[3]

Everything about the nudes Bonnard painted between the two world wars confirms this interpretation of their meaning, confirms it visually, not sentimentally. In the bath nudes, in which the woman lying in her bath is seen from above as through a skylight, the surface of the water serves two pictorial functions simultaneously. First it diffuses the image of her whole body, which, whilst remaining recognizable, sexual, female, becomes as varied and changeable and large as a sunset or an aurora borealis; secondly, it seals off the body from us. Only the light from it comes through the water to reflect off the bathroom walls. Thus she is potentially everywhere, except specifically here. She is lost in the near. Meanwhile what structurally pins down these paintings to prevent their presence becoming as ambiguous as hers is the geometric patterning of the surrounding tiles or linoleum or towelling.

In other paintings of standing nudes, the actual surface of the picture serves a similar function to the surface of the water. Now it is as though a large part or almost all of her body had been left unpainted and was simply the brown cardboardy colour of the original canvas. (In fact this is not the case: but it is the deliberate effect achieved by very careful colour and tonal planning.) All the objects around her – curtains, discarded clothes, a basin, a lamp, chairs, her dog – frame her in light and colour as the sea frames an island. In doing so, they break forward towards us, and draw back into depth. But she remains fixed to the surface of the canvas, simultaneously an absence and a presence. Every mark of colour is related to her, and yet she is no more than a shadow against the colours.

In a beautiful painting of 1916–19 she stands upright on tiptoe. It is a very tall painting. A rectangular bar of light falls down the length of her body. Parallel to this bar, just beside it and similar in colour, is a rectangular strip of wallpapered wall. On the wallpaper are pinkish flowers. On the bar of light is her nipple, the shadow of a rib, the slight shade like a petal under her knee. Once again the surface of that bar of light holds her back, makes her less than present; but also once again, she is ubiquitous: the designs on the wallpaper are the flowers of her body.

In the 'Grand Nu Bleu' of 1924, she almost fills the canvas as she bends to dry a foot. This time no surface or bar of light imposes on her. But the extremism of the painting of her body itself dissolves her. The painting is, as always, tender: its extremism lies in its rendering of what is near and what is far. The distance between her near raised thigh and the inside of the far thigh of the leg on which she is standing – the distance of the caress of one hand underneath her – is made by the force of colour to be felt as a landscape distance: just as the degree to which the calf of that standing leg swells towards us is made to seem like the emerging of a near white hill from the blue recession of a plain running to the horizon. Her body is her habitation – the whole world in which she and the painter live; and at the same time it is immeasurable.

It would be easy to quote other examples: paintings with mirrors, paintings with landscapes into which her face flows away like a sound, paintings in which her body is seen like a sleeve turned inside out. All of them establish with all of Bonnard's artfulness and skill as a draughtsman and colourist how her image emanates outwards from her until she is to be found everywhere except within the limits of her physical presence.

And now we come to the harsh paradox which I believe is the pivot of Bonnard's art. Most of his nudes are directly or indirectly of a girl whom he met when she was sixteen and with whom he spent the rest of his life until she died at the age of sixty-two. The girl became a tragically neurasthenic woman: a frightened recluse, beside herself, and with an obsession about constantly washing and bathing. Bonnard remained loyal to her.

Thus the starting point for these nudes was an unhappy woman, obsessed with her toilet, excessively demanding and half 'absent' as a personality. Accepting this as a fact, Bonnard, by the strength of his devotion to her or by his cunning as an artist or perhaps by both, was able to transform the literal into a far deeper and more general truth: the woman who was only half present into the image of the ardently beloved.

It is a classic example of how art is born of conflict. In art, Bonnard said, *il faut mentir*. The trouble with the landscapes and still lifes and meals – the weakness expressed through their colour – is that in them the surrounding world conflicts are still ignored and the personal tragedy is temporarily put aside. It may sound callous, but it seems probable that his tragedy, by forcing Bonnard to express and marvellously celebrate a common experience, ensured his survival as an artist.

1969

Notes

1   *Collected Poems of W. B. Yeats*, London, Macmillan, 1951, p. 168; New York, Macmillan, 1951.

2   Stendhal, *De L'Amour*, Paris, Editions de Cluny, 1938, p. 43 (trans. by the author). Cf. Stendhal, *Love*, trans. G. and S. Sale, Harmondsworth, Penguin Classics, 1975, p. 45; Viking Penguin Inc.

3   Quoted in *Pierre Bonnard*, London, Royal Academy Catalogue, 1966.

Modigliani's alphabet of love

The photographs show a man who fits his own laconic description of himself: born in Livorno, Jew, painter. Sad, vital, furious and tender, a man never quite filling his own appearance, a man searching behind appearances. A man who painted unseeing eyes – often closed, and even when open without iris or pupils, and yet eyes which in their very absence speak. A man whose intimacy had always to traverse great distances. A man maybe like music, present and yet detached from the visible. And nevertheless a painter.

With van Gogh, Modigliani is probably one of the most regarded of modern artists. I mean that literally: the most looked-at by the most people. How many postcards of Modigliani at this moment on how many walls? He appeals particularly but not exclusively to the young. The young of succeeding generations.

This popular reputation has not been much encouraged by museums and art experts. In the art world during the last forty years Amadeo Modigliani, who died sixty years ago, has been acknowledged and, mostly, left aside. He may even be the only twentieth-century painter to have won, in this sense, an independent acknowledgment. Without cultural retailers. Beyond the reach of critics. Why should this be so?

In themselves his paintings demand little explanation. Indeed they impose a kind of silence, a listening. The whirrings of analysis become more than usually pretentious. Yet the answer to the question has to be found within the paintings. A sociology of popular taste will not help much. Nor can much weight be given to the 'Modigliani legend'. His life story, lending itself easily to film and sensational biographies, his apotheosis as the *peintre maudit* of Montparnasse in

99

its heyday, the many women in his life, his poverty, his addictions, his early death, provoking the suicide of Jeanne Hebuterne, last companion, now buried near him in the cemetery of Père Lachaise: all this has become well known, but it has little to do with why his paintings speak to so many people.

And in this, Modigliani's case is very different from van Gogh's. The legend of van Gogh's life enters the paintings, the two tumults mix. Whereas Modigliani's paintings, instantly recognizable as they are, remain at a profound level anonymous. In face of them, it is not the trace or the struggle of a painter that we confront, but a completed image, its very completeness imposing a kind of listening, during which the painter slips away, and gradually through the image, the subject comes closer.

In the history of art there are portraits which *announce* the men and women portrayed – Holbein, Velasquez, Manet . . . there are others which call them back – Fra Angelico, Goya, Modigliani, among others. The special appeal of Modigliani is surely related to his method as a painter. Not his technical procedure as such, but the method by which his vision transformed the visible. All painting, even hyper-realism, transforms.

Only by considering a painting's method, the practice of its transformation, can we be confident about the direction of its image, the direction of the image's passage towards us and past us. Every painting comes from far away (many fail to reach us), yet we only receive a painting fully if we are looking in the direction from which it has come. This is why seeing a painting is so different from seeing an object.

A single drawn curve on a flat surface – not a straight line – is already playing with the special power of drawn imagery. The curve stays on the surface like that of the letter *C* when written, and, at the same time, it can leave the surface and be filled out by an approaching volume which may be a pebble, an orange, a shoulder.

Modigliani began each painting with curves. The curve of an eyebrow, the shoulders, a head, a hip, a knee, the knuckles. And after hours of work, correction, refinement, searching, he hoped to re-find, preserve, the double function of the curve. He hoped to find curves that simultaneously would be both letter and flesh, would constitute something like a person's name to those who know the person. The name which is both word and physical presence. ANTONIA.

At the time of Cubism and its collages, it was not unusual for painters to introduce written words or even single letters into their paintings. And therefore one should not attach too much importance to Modigliani doing the same. And yet when he did do so, the letters always spelt out the name of the sitter: they did in their way what the paint was doing in its way – both recalling the person.

More profound and important, however, is that where there are no words, the curves in Modigliani's paintings, the curves with which he began, are still both two-dimensional like print, and three-dimensional like the line of a cheek or breast. It is this which gives to almost every figure painted by Modigliani something of the quality of a silhouette – although in fact these figures glow, and are, in other ways, the opposite of silhouettes. But a silhouette is both substance and two-dimensional sign. A silhouette is both writing and existence.

Let us now consider the long, often violent process by which he proceeded from the initial curves to the finished vibrant static image. What did he intuitively seek through this process? He sought an invented letter, a monogram, a shape, which would *print as permanent* the transient living form he was looking at.

The achieving of such a shape was the result of numerous corrections and redrawn simplifications. Unlike many artists, Modigliani began with a simplification and drawing was the process of letting the living form complicate it. In his masterpieces like 'Nu Assis à la Chemise' (1917), 'Elvira Assise' (1918), 'La Belle Romaine' (1917) or 'Chaim Soutine' (1916), the dialectic between simplification and complexity becomes hypnotic: what our eyes see swings like a pendulum, ceaselessly, between the two.

And it is here that we find Modigliani's remarkable visual originality. He discovered new simplifications. Or, to put it, I think, more accurately, he allowed the model, in that life and in that pose, to offer him new simplifications. When this happened, a shape, that part of the simplified invented letter, which meant an arm resting on the table, an elbow resting on a hip, a pair of legs crossed, this shape, cut for the first and unique time during the drawing of those sessions, turned like a key in its lock, and a door swung open on the very life of the limbs in question.

An invented letter, a monogram, a name, the profile of a key – each of these comparisons stresses the stamped emblematic quality of the drawing in Modigliani's paintings. But what of their colour? His colours are as instantly recognizable as his use of lines and curves. And as amazing. Nobody for at least two centuries painted flesh as radiantly as he did. And then, if in one's mind one compares him with Titian or Rubens, what is specific to his use of colour becomes clearer. It is complementary to what we have already seen about his drawing.

His colour is sensuously, mysteriously (how did he achieve that glow and bloom?) articulated to the present, to the tangible and to what extends in space, *and* it is also emblematic. The radiance of the body becomes an emblematic field of intimacy. It is at one and the same time body, and the aura of that body as lovingly perceived by another. I put it like that because the other is not necessarily or exclusively a lover in the sexual sense. The bodies painted by Modigliani are more transcendent than those painted by Titian or Rubens. They have perhaps a certain affinity with some figures by Botticelli, but Botticelli's art was social, its symbolism and myths were public, whereas Modigliani's are solitary and private.

When critics discuss the influences behind Modigliani's art (he was thirty and had seven more years to live when he achieved his true independence), they speak of the Italian primitives, Byzantine art, Ingres, Toulouse-Lautrec, Cézanne, Brancusi, African sculpture. The latter had a very direct influence on his carving which, in my opinion, is unremarkable when compared to his painting. His sculpture remains a casing: the spirit of the subject is never freed. None of the visual dialectic we have examined can easily apply to sculpture.

Yet it has always seemed to me that if Modigliani's art has a close affinity with another, it is with the art of the Russian icon – although here there was probably no direct influence. The profound affinity is not stylistic. There may sometimes be a superficial resemblance in the 'silhouettes' of the figures, but in general the icon figures are more fluid, less taut; their grace was a given, and did not have to be rescued anew each time. The resemblance lies in the quality of the presence of the figures.

They are attendant. They have been called back, and they wait. They wait with such patience, such calm, that one can almost say that they wait with abandon, and what they have abandoned is time. They are still like a coastline is still before the endless movement of the sea. They are there for when all has been said and done. And this distance – which is not a question of superiority but of span, in the sense of a roof spanning what happens in a house – means that in their presence there is a quality of absence. All this is at the first degree. At the second, as soon as they enter the mind of the spectator – and it is this which they are awaiting – they become more present than the immediate.

Obviously this affinity cannot be pushed too far. On one hand, there are religous images of a traditional faith; on the other, secular images wrenched from a lonely and tempestuous modern life. Yet Modigliani's admiration for the mystical poetry of Max Jacob, much of his reading, and the titles he gave to some of his paintings, are a reminder that he at least might not have found the comparison surprising.

Let me now resume what we have so far noticed, before attempting an answer to the question with which I began. Modigliani wanted his paintings to *name* his subjects. He wanted them to have the constancy of a sign – like a monogram or an initial – and, equally, he wanted them to possess the variability, the temperamentality, the sentience of the flesh. He wanted his paintings to summon up the presence of the sitter and to diffuse it, but diffuse it as an aura within his and the spectator's imagination or memory.

He wanted his paintings to address both the flesh and the soul. And in his best works – through his method as a painter, not through simple nostalgia or yearning – this is what he achieved.

His paintings are so widely acknowledged because they speak of love. Often explicitly sexual, sometimes not. Many painters have painted images of lovers, others – like Picasso – have painted images polarized by their own desire, but Modigliani painted images such as love invents to picture a loved one. (When no tenderness existed between him and his model, he failed and produced mere exercises.)

That he was usually able to achieve this without sentimentality was the consequence of his extraordinary rigour. He knew that the problem was to find and reveal the structural laws, the gestalt, of some of the ways by which love visualizes a loved one. He was concerned with romantic love, seduction; his images are about being in love. They are distinct from, for example, Rembrandt's images of love as familiarity and communion.

Nevertheless, despite his romanticism, Modigliani refused the obvious romantic short cuts of symbols, gestures, smiles or expressions. This is probably the reason why he often suppressed the look of the eyes. He was, at his strongest, not interested in the obvious signs of reciprocal love. But only in how love holds and transports its own image of a loved one. How the image concentrates, diffuses, distinguishes, and is both emblem and existence, like a name.
ANTONIA.

Everything begins with the skin, the flesh, the surface of that body, the envelope of that soul. Whether the body is naked or clothed, whether the extent of that skin is finally bordered by a fringe of hair, by a neckline of a dress, or by a contour of a torso or a flank, makes little difference. Whether the body is male or female makes no difference. All that makes a difference is whether the painter had, or had not, crossed that frontier of imaginary intimacy on the far side of which a vertiginous tenderness begins. Everything begins with the skin and what outlines it. And everything is completed there too. Along that outline are assembled the stakes of Modigliani's art.

And what is at stake? The ancient – and how ancient! – meeting between the finite and the infinite. That meeting, that recurring rendezvous, only takes place, so far as we know, within the human mind and heart. And it is both very complex and very simple. A loved one is finite. The feelings provoked are felt as infinite. Against the law of entropy, there is only the faith of love. But if this were all, there would be no outline, only a blending, a merging of the two.

A loved one is also singular, distinct, separate. The more closely one defines, regardless of any given values, the more intimately one loves. The finite outline is a proof of its opposite, the infinity of emotion provoked by what the outline contains. This is the deepest reason for the frequent elongation of Modigliani's figures and faces. The elongation is the result of the closest possible definition, of wanting to be closer.

And the infinite? The infinite in Modigliani's painting, as in the icons, abandons space and enters the realm of time in order to try to overcome it. The infinite seeks a sign, an emblem: it attaches itself to a name which belongs to a language that, unlike the body, endures. ANTONIA.

I would not suggest that the entire secret of Modigliani's art or of what his paintings say is identical to the secret of being in love. But the two do have something in common. And it may be this which has escaped the art theorists, but not those who pin up in their rooms postcards of Amadeo Modigliani's paintings.

1981

The Hals mystery

———

Stories arrive in the head in order to be told. Sometimes paintings do the same. I will describe it as closely as I can. First, however, I will place it art-historically as the experts always do. The painting is by Franz Hals. My guess would be that it was painted sometime between 1645 and 1650.

The year 1645 was a turning point in Hals's career as a portrait painter. He was in his sixties. Until then he had been much sought after and commissioned. From then onwards, until his death as a pauper twenty years later, his reputation steadily declined. This change of fortune corresponded with the emergence of a different kind of vanity.

Now I will try to describe the painting. The large canvas is a horizontal one – 1.85 by 1.30 metres. The reclining figure is a little less than life size. For a Hals – whose careless working methods often led to the pigment cracking – the painting is in good condition; should it ever find its way to a saleroom, it would fetch – given that its subject matter is unique in Hals's *oeuvre* – anything between two and six million dollars. One should bear in mind that, as from now, forgeries may be possible.

So far the identity of the model is understandably a mystery. She lies there naked on the bed, looking at the painter. Obviously there was some complicity between them. Fast as Hals worked, she is bound to have posed during several hours for him. Yet her look is appraising and sceptical.

Was she Hals's mistress? Was she the wife of a Haarlem burgher who comissioned the painting; and if so, where did such a patron intend to hang it? Was she a prostitute who begged Hals to do this painting of herself – perhaps to hang in her own room? Was she one of the painter's own daughters? (There is an opening here to a promising career for one of the more detective of our European art historians.)

What is happening in this room? The painting gave me the impression that neither painter nor model saw beyond their present acts, and therefore it is these, undertaken for their own sake, which remain so mysterious. Her act of lying there on the dishevelled bed in front of the painter, and his act of scrutinizing and painting her in such a way that her appearances were likely to outlive them both.

Apart from the model, the bottom two-thirds of the canvas are filled with the bed, or rather with the tousled, creased white sheet. The top third is filled with a wall behind the bed. There is nothing to be seen on the wall, which is a pale brown, the colour of flax or cardboard, such as Hals often used as a background. The woman, with her head to the left, lies along and slightly across the bed. There is no pillow. Her head, turned so as to watch the painter, is pillowed on her own two hands.

Her torso is twisted, for whereas her bust is a little turned towards the artist, her hips face the ceiling and her legs trail away to the far side of the bed near the wall. Her skin is fair, in places pink. Her left elbow and foot break the line of the bed and are profiled against the brown wall. Her hair is black, crow black. And so strong are the art-historical conventions by which we are conditioned that, in this seventeenth-century painting, one is as surprised by the fact that she has pubic hair as one would be surprised in life by its absence.

How easily can you imagine a naked body painted by Hals? One has to discard all those black clothes which frame the experiencing faces and nervous hands, and then picture a whole body painted with the same degree of intense laconic observation. Not strictly an observation of forms as such – Hals was the most anti-Platonic of painters – but of all the traces of experience left on those forms.

He painted her breasts as if they were entire faces, the far one in profile, the near one in a three-quarter view, her flanks as if they were hands with the tips of their fingers disappearing into the black hair of her stomach. One of her knees is painted as if it revealed as much about her reactions as her chin. The result is disconcerting because we are unused to seeing the experience of a body painted in this way; most nudes are as innocent of experience as aims unachieved. And disconcerting, for another reason yet to be defined, because of the painter's total concentration on painting her – her, nobody else and no fantasy of her.

It is perhaps the sheet which most immediately proposes that the painter was Hals. Nobody but he could have painted linen with such violence and panache – as though the innocence suggested by perfectly ironed white linen was intolerable to his view of experience. Every cuff he painted in his portraits informs on the habitual movements of the wrist it hides. And here nothing is hidden. The gathered, crumpled, slewed sheet, its folds like grey twigs woven together to make a nest, and its highlights like falling water, is unambiguously eloquent about what has happened on the bed.

What is more nuanced is the relation between the sheet, the bed and the figure now lying so still upon it. There is a pathos in this relationship which has nothing to do with the egotism of the painter. (Indeed perhaps he never touched her and the eloquence of the sheet is that of a sexagenarian's memory.) The tonal relationship between the two is subtle, in places her body is scarcely darker than the sheet. I was reminded a little of Manet's 'Olympia' – Manet who so much admired Hals. But there, at this purely optical level, the resemblance ends, for whereas 'Olympia', so evidently a woman of leisure and pleasure, reclines on her bed attended by a black servant, one is persuaded that the woman now lying on the bed painted by Hals will later remake it and wash and iron the sheets. And the pathos lies precisely in the repetition of this cycle: woman as agent of total abandon, woman in her role as cleaner, folder, tidier. If her face mocks, it mocks, among other things, the surprise men feel at this contrast – men who vainly pride themselves on their homogeneity.

Her face is unexpected. As the body is undressed, the look,

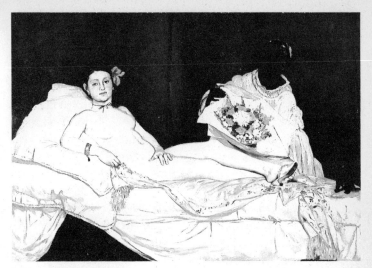

Edouard Manet: *Olympia*

according to the convention of the nude, must simply invite or become masked. On no account should the look be as honest as the stripped body. And in this painting it is even worse, for the body too has been painted like a face open to its own experience.

Yet Hals was unaware of, or indifferent to, the achievement of honesty. The painting has a desperation within it which at first I did not understand. The energy of the brush strokes is sexual and, at the same time, the paroxysm of a terrible impatience. Impatience with what?

In my mind's eye I compared the painting with Rembrandt's 'Bathsheba' which (if I'm right about the dates) was painted at almost the same time, in 1654. The two paintings have one thing in common. Neither painter wished to idealize his model, and this meant that neither painter wished to make a distinction, in terms of looking, between the painted face and body. Otherwise the two paintings are not only different but opposed. By this opposition the Rembrandt helped me to understand the Hals.

Rembrandt's image of Bathsheba is that of a woman loved by the image maker. Her nakedness is, as it were, original. She is as she is, before putting her clothes on and meeting the world, before being judged by others. Her nakedness is a function of her being and it glows with the light of her being.

The model for Bathsheba was Hendrickye, Rembrandt's mistress. Yet the painter's refusal to idealize her cannot simply be explained by his passion. At least two other factors have to be taken into account.

First there is the realist tradition of seventeenth-century Dutch painting. This was inseparable from another 'realism' which was an essential ideological weapon in the rise to an independent, purely secular power by the Dutch trading and merchant bourgeoisie. And second, *contradicting this*, Rembrandt's religious view of the world. It was this dialectical combination which allowed or prompted the older Rembrandt to apply a realist practice more radically than any other Dutch painter to the subject of individual experience. It is not his choice of biblical subjects which matters here, but the fact that his

Rembrandt: *Bathsheba*

religious view offered him the principle of *redemption*, and this enabled him to look unflinchingly at the ravages of experience with a minimal, tenuous hope.

All the tragic figures painted by Rembrandt in the second half of his life – Hannan, Saul, Jacob, Homer, Julius Civilis, the self-portraits – are attendant. None of their tragedies is baulked and yet *being painted* allows them to wait; what they await is meaning, a final meaning to be conferred upon their entire experience.

The nakedness of the woman on the bed painted by Hals is very different from Bathsheba's. She is not in a natural state, prior to putting her clothes on. She has only recently taken them off, and it is her raw experience, just brought back from the world outside the room with the flax-coloured wall, that lies on the bed. She does not, like Bathsheba, glow from the light of her being. It is simply her flushed perspiring skin that glows. Hals did not believe in the principle of redemption. There was nothing to counteract the realist practice, there was only his rashness and courage in pursuing it. It is irrelevant to ask whether or not she was his mistress, loved or unloved. He painted her in the only way he could. Perhaps the famous speed with which he painted was partly the result of summoning the necessary courage for this, of wanting to be finished with such looking as quickly as possible.

Of course there is pleasure in the painting. The pleasure is not embedded in the act of painting – as with Veronese or Monet – but the painting refers to pleasure. Not only because of the history which the sheet tells (or pretends to tell like a storyteller) but also because of the pleasure to be found in the body lying on it.

The hair-thin cracks of the pigment, far from destroying, seem to enhance the luminosity and warmth of the woman's skin. In places it is only this warmth which distinguishes the body from the sheet: the sheet by contrast looks almost greenish like ice. Hals's genius was to render the full physical quality of such superficiality. It's as if in painting he gradually approached his subjects until he and they were cheek to cheek. And this time in this skin-to-skin proximity, there was already pleasure. Add to this that nakedness can reduce us all to two common denominators and that from this simplification comes a kind of assuagement.

I am aware of failing to describe properly the desperation of the painting. I will try again, beginning more abstractly. The era of fully fledged capitalism, which opened in seventeenth-century Holland, opened with both confidence and despair. The former – confidence in individuality, navigation, free enterprise, trade, the *bourse* – is part of accepted history. The despair has tended to be overlooked or, like Pascal's, explained in other terms. Yet part of the striking evidence for this despair is portrait after portrait painted by Hals from the 1630s onwards. We see in these portraits of men (not of the women) a whole new typology of social types and, depending upon the individual case, a new kind of anxiety or despair. If we are to believe Hals – and he is nothing else if not credible – then today's world did not arrive with great rejoicing.

In face of the painting of the woman on the bed I understood for the first time to what degree, and how, Hals may have shared the despair he so often found in his sitters. A potential despair was intrinsic to his practice of painting. He painted appearances. Because the visible *appears* one can wrongly assume that all painting is about appearances. Until the seventeenth century most painting was about inventing a visible world; this invented world borrowed a great deal from the actual world but excluded contingency. It drew – in all senses of the word – conclusions. After the seventeenth century a lot of painting was concerned with disguising appearances; the task of the new academies was to teach the disguises. Hals began and ended with appearances. He was the only painter whose work was profoundly prophetic of the photograph, though none of his paintings is 'photographic'.

What did it mean for Hals as a painter to begin and end with appearances? His practice as a painter was not to reduce a bouquet of flowers to their appearance, nor a dead partridge, nor distant figures in the street; it was to reduce closely observed *experience* to appear-

Franz Hals: *The Gipsy Girl*

ance. The pitilessness of this exercise paralleled the pitilessness of every value being systematically reduced to the value of money.

Today, three centuries later, and after decades of publicity and consumerism, we can note how the thrust of capital finally emptied everything of its content and left only the shard of appearances. We see this now because a political alternative exists. For Hals there was no such alternative, any more than there was redemption.

When he was painting those portraits of men whose names we no longer know, the *equivalence* between his practice and their experiences of contemporary society may well have afforded him and them – if they were prescient enough – a certain satisfaction. Artists cannot change or make history. The most they can do is to strip it of pretences. And there are different ways of doing this, including that of demonstrating an existent heartlessness.

Yet when Hals came to paint the woman on the bed it was different. Part of the power of nakedness is that it seems to be unhistorical. Much of the century and much of the decade are taken off with the clothes. Nakedness seems to return us to nature. *Seems* because such a notion ignores social relations, the forms of emotion and the bias of consciousness. Yet it is not entirely illusory, for the power of human sexuality – its capacity to become a passion – depends upon the promise of a new beginning. And this *new* is felt as not only referring to the individual destiny, but equally to the cosmic which, in some strange way, during such a moment, both fills and transcends history. The evidence for the fact that it happens like this is the repetition in love poetry everywhere, even during revolutions, of cosmic metaphors.

In this painting there could be no equivalence between Hals's practice as a painter and his subject, for his subject was charged, however prematurely, however nostalgically, with the potential promise of a new beginning. Hals painted the body on the bed with the consummate skill that he had acquired. He painted its experience as appearance. Yet his act of painting the woman with the crow black hair could not respond to the sight of her. He could invent nothing

Nude by Franz Hals

new and he stood there, desperate, at the very edge of appearances.

And then? I imagine Hals putting down his brushes and palette and sitting down on a chair. By now the woman had already gone out and the bed was stripped. Seated, Hals closed his eyes. He did not close them in order to doze. With his eyes shut, he might envisage, as a blind man envisages, other pictures painted at another time.

1979

5
THE LAST PICTURES

———

In a Moscow cemetery

———

The snow had thawed a week before, and the earth, just uncovered, was dishevelled like somebody woken up too early. In patches, new grass was growing, but mostly the grass was last year's: lank, lifeless and almost white. The earth, awoken too early, was stumbling towards a window. The immense sky was white, full of light and tactful. It told no stories, made no jokes. Earth and sky are always a couple.

Between them a wind blew. North-east veering to east. A routine unexceptional wind. It made people button their coats, the women adjust the kerchiefs on their heads, but across the plain it scarcely ruffled the surface of the million puddles. The earth had thrown a mud-coloured shawl over her shoulders.

Flying low over the waterlogged soil, jackdaws and crows let themselves be carried sideways by the wind. Now that the snow had gone, worms would become visible. Across the mud, lorries were transporting gravel. On one of the two building sites a crane was lifting concrete joists to an open fourth storey, which was as yet no more than a skeletal platform. Nothing there, between earth and sky, would ever be entirely finished.

Many people were arriving and leaving, a few in cars, most in lorries or old buses. There was no town to be seen. And yet you could sense the presence of a city not so far away: a question of sounds, the silence was still shallow, not yet deep like the ocean.

Twenty people got down from one of the buses, the last four carrying a coffin. Their faces – like those of other groups – were closed but not locked. Each face had pulled the door to – and, within, each one was conversing with an old certainty.

They carried the coffin over the pallid grass towards a wooden structure, rather like the stand on which generals take up their positions, so as to be better seen when reviewing their troops. A woman, who had been sheltering from the wind in a hut, stepped out, a camera slung round her neck. She was the temporary specialist of last pictures. The coffin, its lid now removed, was placed on one of the lower steps of the wooden stand in such a way that it was inclined towards the photographer so that the woman inside the coffin should be visible. She must have been about seventy years old. The group of family and friends took up their position on the other steps of the stand.

Photography, because it stops the flow of life, is always flirting with death, but the temporary specialist of last pictures was only concerned that nobody in the group should be excluded by the frame. The photos were in black and white. The yellow daffodils surrounding the coffin would print out as pale grey, only the sky would be almost its real colour. She beckoned to the figures on the right to close in.

The image she saw through the viewfinder was not grief-stricken. Everyone knew that grief is private and long and has never spared anyone, and that the photograph they had ordered was a public record in which grief had no place. They looked hard at the camera, as if the old woman in the coffin was a newborn child, or a wild boar shot by hunters, or a trophy won by their team. This is how it appeared through the viewfinder.

The cemetery was very large but almost invisible because so low on the ground. For once, the equality of the dead was a perceptible fact. There were no outstanding monuments, no hopeless mausoleums. When the new grass came, it would grow between all. Around some of the graves there were low railings, no higher than hay, and inside the railings, small wooden tables and seats, which all winter long were buried under the snow, just as in ancient Egypt mirrors and jewels were buried in the sand with the royal dead, with the difference that, here, after the thaw the tables and seats could also serve the living.

The burial ground was divided up into plots of about an acre, each one numbered. The numbers were stencilled on wooden boards, nailed to posts, stuck into the earth. These numbers, too, were buried under the snow in the winter.

On some of the headstones there were sepia oval photos behind glass. It is strange how we distinguish one person from another. The visible outward differences are relatively so slight – as between two sparrows – yet by these differences we distinguish a being whose uniqueness seems to us to be as large as the sky.

The gravediggers, whose jokes are the same on every continent, had dug up many mounds of earth. The soil there was acid.

The cemetery was begun in the 1960s, the plots with the lowest numbers being the earliest. In each plot there were those who died young, and those who lived to an old age. But in the first plots those who had died in their forties or early fifties were far more numerous. These men and women had lived through the war and the purges. They had survived to die early. All illnesses are clinical, and some are also historical.

Silver birches grow quickly and they were already growing between the graves. Soon their leaves would be in bud and then the blood-red catkins, now hanging from their branches like swabs of lint, would fall on to the acid earth. Of all trees, birches are perhaps the most like grass. They are small, pliant, slender; and if they promise a kind of permanence, it has nothing to do with solidity or longevity – as with an oak or a linden – but only with the fact that they seed and spread quickly. They are ephemeral and recurring – like words, like a form of conversation between earth and sky.

Between the trees you could glimpse figures, figures of the living. The family who had just been photographed were carrying wreaths of daffodils, whose yellow was strident as a keening.

> And perhaps, Jesus, holding your feet on
> my knees

I am leaning to embrace
The square shaft of the cross,
Losing consciousness as I strain your
    body to me
Preparing you for burial

Pasternak

The lid was placed on the coffin for the last time and nailed down.

Nearby, a middle-aged woman on her knees was cleaning an old grave as though it were her kitchen floor. The ground was water-logged, and when she stood up, her wide knees were black with rain water.

Far away the tractors were pulling their trailers of heaped gravel; the crane was delivering concrete slabs to the fifth storey; and the jackdaws, in that place where nothing would ever be entirely finished, were letting themselves be carried sideways by the wind.

A couple sat at one of the wooden tables. The woman brought out her string bag, wrapped in newspaper, a bottle and three glasses. Her husband filled the three glasses. They drank with the man beneath the earth, pouring his glass of vodka into the grass.

The specialist of last pictures had by now taken another dozen. A colleague had just phoned her, in her hut, to tell her that some raincoats had been delivered to the shop near the bridge over the canal. She would stop there on her way home tonight to see whether they had her son's size. The coffin she could see through the viewfinder was small, the child inside no more than ten years old.

Among the first plots a solitary man in a raincoat, leaning against a birch tree, was sobbing, his fists thrust deep into his pockets. In some puddles, cloud was reflected; into others soil had crumbled, muddying them, so that there were no reflections. The man glanced up at the sky with a look of recognition. Had they, one evening when they were both drunk, reminisced together?

With questions and partial answers, mourners and visitors to the cemetery were trying to make sense of the deaths and their own lives, just as previously the dead had done. This work of the imagination, to which everybody and everything contributes, can never be entirely finished, either in the Khovanskoie cemetery, twenty miles south of Moscow, or anywhere else in the world.

1983

Ernst Fischer: a philosopher and death

———

It was the last day of his life. Of course we did not know it then – not until almost ten o'clock in the evening. Three of us spent the day with him: Lou (his wife), Anya and myself. I can write now only of my own experience of that day. If I tried to write about theirs – much as I was conscious of it at the time and later – I would nevertheless run the risk of writing fiction.

Ernst Fischer was in the habit of spending the summer in a small village in Styria. He and Lou stayed in the house of three sisters who were old friends and who had been Austrian Communists with Ernst and his two brothers in the 1930s. The youngest of the three sisters, who now runs the house, was imprisoned by the Nazis for hiding and aiding political refugees. The man with whom she was then in love was beheaded for a similar political offence.

It is necessary to describe this in order not to give a false impression of the garden which surrounds their house. The garden is full of flowers, large trees, grass banks and a lawn. A stream flows through it, conducted through a wooden pipe the diameter of an immense barrel. It runs the length of the garden, then across fields to a small dynamo which belongs to a neighbour. Everywhere in the garden there is the sound of water, gentle but persistent. There are two small fountains: tiny pin-like jets of water force their way hissing through holes in the wooden barrel-line; water flows into and empties continually from a nineteenth-century swimming pool (built by the grandfather of the three sisters): in this pool, now surrounded by tall grass, and itself green, trout swim and occasionally jump splashing to the surface.

It often rains in Styria, and if you are in this house you sometimes have the impression that it is still raining after it has stopped on account of the sound of water in the garden. Yet the garden is not damp and many colours of many flowers break up its greenness. The garden is a kind of sanctuary. But to grasp its full meaning one must, as I said, remember that in its outhouses men and women were hiding for their lives thirty years ago and were protected by the three sisters who now arrange vases of flowers and let rooms to a few old friends in the summer in order to make ends meet.

When I arrived in the morning Ernst was walking in the garden. He was thin and upright. And he trod very lightly, as though his weight, such as it was, was never fully planted on the ground. He wore a wide-brimmed white and grey hat which Lou had recently bought for him. He wore the hat like he wore all his clothes, lightly, elegantly, but without concern. He was fastidious – not about details of dress, but about the nature of appearances.

The gate to the garden was difficult to open and shut, but he had mastered it and so, as usual, he fastened it behind me. The previous day Lou had felt somewhat unwell. I enquired how she was. 'She is better,' he said, 'you have only to look at her!' He said this with youthful, unrestricted pleasure. He was seventy-three years old and when he was dying the doctor, who did not know him, said he looked older, but he had none of the muted expressions of the old. He took present pleasures at their full face-value and his capacity to do this was in no way diminished by political disappointment or by the bad news which since 1968 had persistently arrived from so many places. He was a man without a trace, without a line on his face, of bitterness. Some, I suppose, might therefore call him an innocent. They would be wrong. He was a man who refused to jettison or diminish his very high quotient of belief. Instead he readjusted its objects and their relative order. Recently he *believed* in scepticism. He even believed in the necessity of apocalyptic visions in the hope that they would act as warnings.

It is the surety and strength of his convictions which now make it seem that he died so suddenly. His health had been frail since childhood. He was often ill. Recently his eyesight had begun to fail and he could read only with a powerful magnifying glass – more often Lou read to him. Yet despite this it was quite impossible for anyone who knew him to suppose that he was dying slowly, that every year he belonged a little less vehemently to life. He was fully alive because he was fully convinced.

What was he convinced of? His books, his political interventions, his speeches are there on record to answer the question. Or do they not answer it fully enough? He was convinced that capitalism would eventually destroy man – or be overthrown. He had no illusions about the ruthlessness of the ruling class everywhere. He recognized that we lacked a model for Socialism. He was impressed by and highly interested in what is happening in China, but he did not believe in a Chinese model. What is so hard, he said, is that we are forced back to offering visions.

We walked towards the end of the garden, where there is a small lawn surrounded by bushes and a willow tree. He used to lie there talking with animated gestures, fingers plucking, hands turning out and drawing in – as though literally winding the wool from off his listeners' eyes. As he talked, his shoulders bent forward to follow his hands; as he listened, his head inclined forward to follow the speaker's words. (He knew the exact angle at which to adjust the back of his deckchair.)

Now the same lawn, the deckchairs piled in the outhouse, appears oppressively, flagrantly empty. It is far harder to walk across it without a shiver than it was to turn down the sheet and look again and again at his face. The Russian believers say that the spirits of the departed stay in their familiar surroundings for forty days. Perhaps this is based on a fairly accurate observation of the stages of mourning. At any rate it is hard for me to believe that if a total stranger wandered into the garden now, he would not notice that the end under the willow tree surrounded by bushes was flagrantly empty, like a deserted house on the point of becoming a ruin. Its emptiness is palpable. And yet it is not.

It had already begun to rain and so we went to sit in his room for a while before going out to lunch. We used to sit, the four of us, round a small round table, talking. Sometimes I faced the window and looked out at the trees and the forests on the hills. That morning I pointed out that when the frame with the mosquito net was fitted over the window, everything looked more or less two-dimensional and so composed itself. We give too much weight to space, I went on – there's perhaps more of nature in a Persian carpet than in most landscape paintings. 'We'll take the hills down, push the trees aside and hang up carpets for you,' said Ernst. 'Your other trousers,' remarked Lou, 'why don't you put them on as we're going out?' Whilst he changed we went on talking. 'There,' he said, smiling ironically at the task he had just performed, 'is that better now?' 'They are very elegant, but they are the same pair!' I said. He laughed, delighted at this remark. Delighted because it emphasized that he had changed his trousers only to satisfy Lou's whim, and that that was reason enough for him; delighted because an insignificant difference was treated as though it didn't exist; delighted because, encapsulated in a tiny joke, there was a tiny conspiracy against the existent.

The Etruscans buried their dead in chambers under the ground and on the walls they painted scenes of pleasure and everyday life such as the dead had known. To have the light to see what they were painting they made a small hole in the ground above and then used mirrors to reflect the sunlight onto the particular image on which they were working. With words I try to decorate, as though it were a tomb, the last day of his life.

We were going to have lunch in a *pension* high up in the forests and hills. The idea was to look and see whether it would be suitable for Ernst to work there during September or October. Earlier in the year Lou had written to dozens of small hotels and boarding houses and this was the only one which was cheap and sounded promising. They wanted to take advantage of my having a car to go and have a look.

There are no scandals to make. But there is a contrast to draw.

Two days after his death there was a long article about him in *Le Monde*. 'Little by little,' it wrote, 'Ernst Fischer has established himself as one of the most original and rewarding thinkers of "heretical" Marxism.' He had influenced an entire generation of the left in Austria. During the last four years he was continually denounced in Eastern Europe for the significant influence he had had on the thinking of the Czechs who had created the Prague Spring. His books were translated into most languages. But the conditions of his life during the last five years were cramped and harsh. The Fischers had little money, were always subject to financial worries, and lived in a small, noisy workers' flat in Vienna. Why not? I hear his opponents ask. Was he better than the workers? No, but he needed professional working conditions. In any case he himself did not complain. But with the unceasing noise of families and radios in the flats above and on each side he found it impossible to work as concentratedly in Vienna as he wished to do and was capable of doing. Hence the annual search for quiet, cheap places in the country – where three months might represent so many chapters completed. The three sisters' house was not available after August.

We drove up a steep dust road through the forest. Once I asked a child the way in my terrible German and the child did not understand and simply stuffed her fist into her mouth in amazement. The others laughed at me. It was raining lightly: the trees were absolutely still. And I remember thinking as I drove round the hairpin bends that if I could define or realize the nature of the submission of the trees, I would learn something about the human body too – at least about the human body when loved. The rain ran down the trees. A leaf is so easily moved. A breath of wind is sufficient. And yet not a leaf moved.

We found the *pension*. The young woman and her husband were expecting us and they showed us to a long table where some other guests were already eating. The room was large with a bare wooden floor and big windows from which you looked over the shoulders of some nearby steep fields across the forest to the plain below. It was not unlike a canteen in a youth hostel, except that there were cushions on the benches and flowers on the tables. The food was simple but good. After the meal we were to be shown the rooms. The husband came over with an architect's plan in his hands. 'By next year everything will be different,' he explained; 'the owners want to make more money and so they're going to convert the rooms and put bathrooms in and put up their prices. But this autumn you can still have the two rooms on the top floor as they are, and there'll be nobody else up there, you'll be quiet.'

We climbed to the rooms. They were identical, side by side, with the lavatory on the same landing opposite them. Each room was narrow, with a bed against the wall, a wash-basin and an austere cupboard, and at the end of it a window with a view of miles and miles of landscape. 'You can put a table in front of the window and work here.' 'Yes, yes,' he said. 'You'll finish the book.' 'Perhaps not all of it, but I could get much done.' 'You must take it,' I said. I visualized him sitting at the table in front of the window, looking down at the still trees. The book was the second volume of his autobiography. It covered the period 1945–55 – when he had been very active in Austrian and international politics – and it was to deal principally with the development and consequences of the Cold War which he saw, I think, as the counter-revolutionary reaction, on both sides of what was to become the Iron Curtain, to the popular victories of 1945. I visualized his magnifying glass on the small table, his note-pad, the pile of current reference books, the chair pushed away when, stiffly but light on his feet, he had gone downstairs to take his regular walk before lunch. 'You must take it,' I said again.

We went for a walk together, the walk into the forest he would take each morning. I asked him why in the first volume of his memoirs he wrote in several distinctly different styles.

'Each style belongs to a different person.'

'To a different aspect of yourself?'

'No, rather it belongs to a different self.'

'Do these different selves coexist, or, when one is predominant, are the others absent?'

131

'They are present together at the same time. None can disappear. The two strongest are my violent, hot, extremist, romantic self and the other my distant, sceptical self.'

'Do they discourse together in your head?'

'No.' (He had a special way of saying No. As if he had long ago considered the question at length and after much patient investigation had arrived at the answer.)

'They watch each other,' he continued. 'The sculptor Hrdlicka has done a head of me in marble. It makes me look much younger than I am. But you can see these two predominant selves in me – each corresponding to a side of my face. One is perhaps a little like Danton, the other a little like Voltaire.'

As we walked along the forest path, I changed sides so as to examine his face, first from the right and then from the left. Each eye was different and was confirmed in its difference by the corner of the mouth on each side of his face. The right side was tender and wild. He had mentioned Danton. I thought rather of an animal: perhaps a kind of goat, light on its feet, a chamois maybe. The left side was sceptical but harsher: it made judgments but kept them to itself, it appealed to reason with an unswerving certainty. The left side would have been inflexible had it not been compelled to live with the right. I changed sides again to check my observations.

'And have their relative strengths always been the same?' I asked.

'The sceptical self has become stronger,' he said. 'But there are other selves too.' He smiled at me and took my arm and added, as though to reassure me: 'Its hegemony is not complete!'

He said this a little breathlessly and in a slightly deeper voice than usual – in the voice in which he spoke when moved, for example when embracing a person he loved.

His walk was very characteristic. His hips moved stiffly, but otherwise he walked like a young man, quickly, lightly, to the rhythm of his own reflections. 'The present book,' he said, 'is written in a consistent style – detached, reasoning, cool.'

'Because it comes later?'

'No, because it is not really about myself. It is about an historical period. The first volume is also about myself and I could not have told the truth if I had written it all in the same voice. There was no self which was above the struggle of the others and could have told the story evenly. The categories we make between different aspects of experience – so that, for instance, some people say I should not have spoken about love *and* about the Comintern in the same book – these categories are mostly there for the convenience of liars.'

'Does one self hide its decisions from the others?'

Maybe he didn't hear the question. Maybe he wanted to say what he said whatever the question.

'My first decision,' he said, 'was not to die. I decided when I was a child, in a sick-bed, with death at hand, that I wanted to live.'

From the *pension* we drove down to Graz. Lou and Anya needed to do some shopping; Ernst and I installed ourselves in the lounge of an old hotel by the river. It was in this hotel that I had come to see Ernst on my way to Prague in the summer of '68. He had given me addresses, advice, information, and summarized for me the historical back-ground to the new events taking place. Our interpretation of these events was not exactly the same, but it seems pointless now to try to define our small differences. Not because Ernst is dead, but because those events were buried alive and we see only their large contours heaped beneath the earth. Our specific points of difference no longer exist because the choices to which they applied no longer exist. Nor will they ever exist again in quite the same way. Opportunities can be irretrievably lost and then their loss is like a death. When the Russian tanks entered Prague in August 1968 Ernst was absolutely lucid about that death.

In the lounge of the hotel I remembered the occasion of four years before. He had already been worried. Unlike many Czechs, he considered it quite likely that Brezhnev would order the Red Army to move in. But he still hoped. And this hope still carried within it all the other hopes which had been born in Prague that spring.

After 1968 Ernst began to concentrate his thoughts on the past. But he remained incorrigibly orientated towards the future. His view of the past was for the benefit of the future – for the benefit of the great or terrible transformations it held in store. But after '68 he recognized that the path towards any revolutionary transformation was bound to be long and tortuous and that Socialism in Europe would be deferred beyond his life-span. Hence the best use of his remaining time was to bear witness to the past.

We did not talk about this in the hotel, for there was nothing new to decide. The important thing was to finish the second volume of his memoirs and that very morning we had found a way of making this happen more quickly. Instead, we talked of love: or, more exactly, about the state of being in love. Our talk followed roughly these lines.

The capacity to fall in love is now thought of as natural and universal – and as a passive capacity. (Love strikes. Love-struck.) Yet there have been whole periods when the possibility of falling in love did not exist. Being in love in fact depends upon the possibility of free active choice – or anyway an apparent possibility. What does the lover choose? He chooses to stake the world (the whole of his life) against the beloved. The beloved concentrates all the possibilities of the world within her and thus offers the realization of all his own potentialities. The beloved for the lover empties the world of hope (the world that does not include her). Strictly speaking, being in love is a mood in so far as it is infinitely extensive – it reaches beyond the stars; but it cannot develop without changing its nature, and so it cannot endure.

The equivalence between the beloved and the world is confirmed by sex. To make love with the beloved is, subjectively, to possess and be possessed by the world. Ideally, what remains outside the experience is – nothing. Death of course is within it.

This provokes the imagination to its very depths. One wants to use the world in the act of love. One wants to make love with fish, with fruit, with hills, with forests, in the sea.

And those, said Ernst, 'are the metamorphoses! It is nearly always that way round in Ovid. The beloved becomes a tree, a stream, a hill. Ovid's *Metamorphoses* are not poetic conceits, they are really about the relation between the world and the poet in love.'

I looked into his eyes. They were pale. (Invariably they were moist with the strain of seeing.) They were pale like some blue flower bleached to a whitish grey by the sun. Yet despite their moisture and their paleness, the light which had bleached them was still reflected in them.

'The passion of my life,' he said, 'was Lou. I had many love affairs. Some of them, when I was a student here in Graz, in this hotel. I was married. With all the other women I loved there was a debate, a discourse about our different interests. With Lou there is no discourse because our interests are the same. I don't mean we never argue. She argued for Trotsky when I was still a Stalinist. But our interest – below all our interests – is singular. When I first met her, I said No. I remember the evening very well. I knew immediately I saw her, and I said No to myself. I knew that if I had a love affair with her, everything would stop. I would never love another woman. I would live monogamously. I thought I would not be able to work. We would do nothing except make love over and over again. The world would never be the same. She knew too. Before going home to Berlin she asked me very calmly: "Do you want me to stay?" "No," I said.'

Lou came back from the shops with some cheeses and yoghurts she had bought.

'Today we have talked for hours about me,' said Ernst, 'you don't talk about yourself. Tomorrow we shall talk about you.'

On the way out of Graz I stopped at a bookshop to find Ernst a copy of some poems by the Serbian poet Miodrag Pavlovic. Ernst had said sometime during the afternoon that he no longer wrote poems and no longer saw the purpose of poetry. 'It may be,' he added, 'that my idea of poetry is outdated.' I wanted him to read Pavlovic's poems. I gave him the book in the car. 'I already have it,' he said. But he put his hand on my shoulders. For the last time without suffering.

We were going to have supper in the café in the village. On the stairs outside his room, Ernst, who was behind me, suddenly but softly cried out. I turned round immediately. He had both his hands pressed to the small of his back. 'Sit down,' I said, 'lie down.' He took no notice. He was looking past me into the distance. His attention was there, not here. At the time I thought this was because the pain was bad. But it seemed to pass quite quickly. He descended the stairs – no more slowly than usual. The three sisters were waiting at the front door to wish us good night. We stopped a moment to talk. Ernst explained that his rheumatism had jabbed him in the back.

There was a curious distance about him. Either he consciously suspected what had happened, or else the chamois in him, the animal that was so strong in him, had already left to look for a secluded place in which to die. I question whether I am now using hindsight. I am not. He was already distant.

We walked, chatting, through the garden past the sounds of water. Ernst opened the gate and fastened it because it was difficult, for the last time.

We sat at our usual table in the public bar of the café. Some people were having their evening drink. They went out. The landlord, a man only interested in stalking and shooting deer, switched off two of the lights and went out to fetch our soup. Lou was furious and shouted after him. He didn't hear. She got up, went behind the bar and switched on the two lights again. 'I would have done the same,' I said. Ernst smiled at Lou and then at Anya and me. 'If you and Lou lived together,' he said, 'it would be explosive.'

When the next course came Ernst was unable to eat it. The landlord came up to enquire whether it was not good. 'It is excellently prepared,' said Ernst, holding up the untouched plate of food in front of him, 'and excellently cooked, but I am afraid that I cannot eat it.'

He looked pale and he said he had pains in the lower part of his stomach.

'Let us go back,' I said. Again he appeared – in response to the suggestion – to look into the distance. 'Not yet,' he said, 'in a little while.'

We finished eating. He was unsteady on his feet but he insisted on standing alone. On the way to the door he placed his hand on my shoulder – as he had in the car. But it expressed something very different. And the touch of his hand was now even lighter.

After we had driven a few hundred metres he said: 'I think I may be going to faint.' I stopped and put my arm round him. His head fell on my shoulder. He was breathing in short gasps. With his left, sceptical eye he looked hard up into my face. A sceptical, questioning, unswerving look. Then his look became unseeing. The light which had bleached his eyes was no longer in them. He was breathing heavily.

Anya flagged down a passing car and went back to the village to fetch help. She came back in another car. When she opened the door of our car, Ernst tried to move his feet out. It was his last instinctive movement – to be ordered, willed, neat.

When we reached the house, the news had preceded us and the gates, which were difficult, were already open so that we could drive up to the front door. The young man who had brought Anya from the village carried Ernst indoors and upstairs over his shoulders. I walked behind to stop his head banging against the door-jambs. We laid him down on his bed. We did helpless things to occupy ourselves whilst waiting for the doctor. But even waiting for the doctor was a pretext. There was nothing to do. We massaged his feet, we fetched a hot-water bottle, we felt his pulse. I stroked his cold head. His brown hands on the white sheet, curled up but not grasping, looked quite separate from the rest of the body. They appeared cut off by his cuffs. Like the forefeet cut off from an animal found dead in the forest.

The doctor arrived. A man of fifty. Tired, pale-faced, sweating. He wore a peasant's suit without a tie. He was like a veterinary surgeon. 'Hold his arm,' he said, 'whilst I give this injection.' He inserted the needle finely in the vein so that the liquid should flow along it like the water along the barrel-pipe in the garden. At this moment we were alone in the room together. The doctor shook his head. 'How old is he?' 'Seventy-three.' 'He looks older,' he said.

'He looked younger when he was alive,' I said.

'Has he had an infarctus before?'

'Yes.'

'He has no chance this time,' he said.

Lou, Anya, the three sisters and I stood around his bed. He had gone.

Besides painting scenes from everyday life on the walls of their tombs, the Etruscans carved on the lids of their sarcophagi full-length figures representing the dead. Usually these figures are half-reclining, raised on one elbow, feet and legs relaxed as though on a couch, but head and neck alert as they gaze into the distance. Many thousands of such carvings were executed quickly and more or less according to a formula. But however stereotyped the rest of these figures, their alertness as they look into the distance is striking. Given the context, the distance is surely a temporal rather than a spatial one: the distance is the future the dead projected when alive. They look into that distance as though they could stretch out a hand and touch it.

I can make no sarcophagus carving. But there are pages written by Ernst Fischer where it seems to me that the writer wrote adopting an equivalent stance, achieving a similar quality of expectation.

1974

François, Georges and Amélie: a requiem in three parts

———

François

François was killed on a Saturday night. Just as it was getting dark. A car coming from behind knocked him over. The young driver of the car, who didn't stop, was fortunate because the autopsy showed that François was drunk. Even before the result of the autopsy, nobody in the village imagined anything different. If it was Saturday night and François wasn't at the farm, he was on one of his weekend walks and drunk. But usually, when very drunk, he was still attentive and careful about traffic.

He was seventy-six. He owned what he was wearing, a few clothes he had left in the stable, a mouth-organ and the money which the police found tied into a plastic bag that he carried on a cord round his neck.

Owning so little, what gave him pleasure? The mountains, women, music and red wine. This makes him sound like a bohemian – he who, even in his extravagant boasts and jokes, never left the valley of two adjacent rivers.

Why have I put off for so long trying to describe and remember your funeral? Because after it, you were not for once in the café telling a story about the late departed? Because I'm waiting for next summer when your absence will become more acute?

A knock on the door with your stick, and you walk in without waiting for an answer. Your creased face folded yet again into a smile. You give a long kiss to B. A smile of relish. Then through the door into the next room – as though it were beyond human ingenuity to invent a right that you wouldn't have in this mountain chalet where you once came to be congratulated on still being alive.

'There's a man with the same name as me who has just died over there!' You pointed across the valley to the second river far below. 'There were those who thought it was me, me who was dead! Me!'

You opened your mouth and spread out your arms like a jack-in-box and roared with laughter.

'To those who are alive!' And we clinked our glasses together. Do you remember?

There were only a few people at the funeral, because nobody thought of putting a notice in the local paper and François was buried, not in the village, but in the small town where he was killed.

Nobody knows what happened to the money he carried round his neck. It amounted to several hundred pounds. When he was at the farm, he hid it. You can leave your money around, he said to his boss, I won't touch it, I have my own. He worked in exchange for his keep, not for wages, and in this way he kept his independence. He worked when he liked, he left when he liked.

If there were any remaining members of his family left, none of them appeared. Small towns now have an exclusive deal with some undertaking firm. It's arranged by the mayor. In exchange for this exclusivity, the firm agrees to supply one free funeral a year. In the case of a pauper, this saves the community money. The firm in question gave a free funeral to François, which didn't include flowers.

He had looked after animals all his life, either in the valley or on the mountain. He was used to their company. Of the company of men – not women – he was more suspicious. They didn't all necessarily accept the authority he took upon himself.

'I've had enough of his cows eating *my* grass!' Every summer François re-started a wrangle about grazing.

'It's not even your grass!' said a young man standing at the counter.

'If I see *him*, I'll punch his face in!'

'You're too old to punch anything in!'

'And at your age, you know nothing. Nothing. I've been a shepherd for fifty years!'

The little group followed the coffin down the street towards the cemetery. As they passed the steamed-up windows of a café, six men came out to join the procession. They left their glasses half-full on the counter for they would soon be back.

When he was young he enjoyed dancing; later he liked to make people dance. And so whenever he heard of a celebration taking place and he was able to go, he took his mouth-organ. One Saturday night at a friend's birthday party he lost it.

I was there when his boss's wife gave him another to replace the one he had lost. The three of us were sitting outside the chalet. The water was flowing into the wooden trough. There were some geese by our feet. Some parachutists had just jumped off the mountain and were drifting down to the valley. He took the mouth-organ out of its box. He examined it on every side to ensure that it included no secret which he didn't already know. He tried holding it in his hands, as he would when playing, but without raising it to his lips. Then he put it back into its box and slipped the box into his pocket. It was no longer a present, it was his.

The small group of us filed past the coffin. His, just as his completed life had now become his.

Georges

Georges was killed on a Monday when working by the bridge over the Foron. It was in the afternoon. Young Bernard came into the stable with the news at milking time the same evening. The vet was there looking at the calf who had had something wrong with its stomach since birth.

'He's dead!' cried out Claire in protest. Then she addressed each person in the stable as if hoping that one of them might contradict her. 'Jeanne, he's dead! Theophile, he's dead! Monsieur, he's dead!'

Jeanne said nothing but she clenched her jaw, and her eyes were filled with tears. The three men stood in silence without moving, the vet holding the syringe in his hand against his own arm.

He was carried down the river before anybody could reach him and drowned.

Bernard, who had never before been the bearer of such bad news, walked solemnly out of the stable. Then, a little later, after the vet had left, the words came.

'Where is the justice?'

'His arm was sticking out from the rocks, that's how they found him.'

'It takes away even your will to work.'

'There were three of them unblocking a drain, and then the water broke through without any warning.'

'Without any warning.'

Georges was twenty-eight. He had been married three years before. The couple didn't yet have any children. His body was wounded all over by the rocks against which the river had flung him. All over he was grazed and cut. But the bruises, which would have appeared, didn't come, because he was dead.

His body was taken home to his wife with a bandage round his head to hide the worst wounds. He was laid out on his large bed, and friends and relatives came to pay him their last respects. Each night Martine, his wife, lay beside him.

'He must have been outside the blankets,' she announced the first morning, 'for I could feel that he was a little cold.'

On the third day when it was time to place him in his coffin, she said: 'Now it is time to close it, his poor corpse is beginning to smell.'

During those three days, his death haunted the village too. It was an unnatural death which had come as brutally and unexpectedly as the mass of water which engulfed him. All the rivers and streams around the village were swollen and white with froth. Everywhere there was the sound of the water which killed him. He was too young, he carried too many hopes away with him. A thousand people came to the funeral on Thursday.

When the coffin came out of the church, Martine was supported on either side by two of his brothers. They carried her, for her legs trailed behind her, and following the coffin, she wailed: 'Jo-Jo, no! Jo-Jo, no!' Georges, whom everyone knew as Jo-Jo, could not reply.

A thousand men and women stood in silence and witnessed the chief mourner's fight, her heaving fight, not for breath but to be able to stop breathing.

Above the cemetery the orchards were littered with broken branches torn from the apple trees by the snow which, melting now, swelled the rivers.

During the next two weeks Martine hoped against hope that she might have conceived just before Georges's death. And then again the blood came.

Amélie

Amélie never saw a doctor in her life until four days before. And unhappily it turned out to be too late. She was eighty-two; she had congestion on both lungs and her heart gave up.

She lived with her son who was already a widower. This son had been born when his mother was seventeen. She had not been able to marry the boy's father, because he, the father, was only thirteen.

Everyone knew the story of Amélie's life. She was a woman of great endurance. She worked every day on the farm with her son until she was taken ill for the first and last time. She was, it was often said, a force of nature.

Fifteen years after the birth of her son, she became pregnant again. Still unmarried, she was living with her mother. This was at the time of the Popular Front, Franco's victory in Spain, the approaching holocaust. Her mother was old and her eyes were failing. And so, on this second occasion, Amélie decided to spare her mother's feelings –

or was it, too, in order to spare herself from her mother's nagging and execration? In any case, she kept her pregnancy a secret. She was already a large woman, and she bound her belly tightly so that its rising was not very pronounced.

On the evening when her labour began, she climbed up into the barn and there, during the night, delivered her own baby, alone. The baby was a girl, and this daughter, now a middle-aged woman, was standing against the cemetery wall whilst neighbours and friends came and offered their condolences for her mother's death.

On Amélie's coffin, in the middle of the cemetery, there was a wreath, the size of a counterpane, of red and pink carnations. The colours of blood and youth.

Before dawn, fifty years ago, Amélie took the train to the nearest town and there left her newborn daughter at the house of a woman with whom she had already come to an arrangement. The same evening she was back home, working in the stable, as if nothing had happened to either her body or heart.

Amélie's mother never knew that she had a grand-daughter, but there were neighbours who had been aware of Amélie's condition and who now whispered that she had murdered her child.

The police from the town made an official investigation. They came to cross-question Amélie, who laughed in the inspector's face. What I've done is no crime, she said. You can accuse me of nothing, except – here she shut her eyes – of being too good-natured!

As soon as her mother died, Amélie brought her daughter back home. And when her village schooling was over, she sent her daughter to a secondary school, so that she would not be condemned to being a peasant, if, by chance, she had the opportunity of choosing.

This daughter did not take up the choice; she married locally and had two children. One of these children, now a young woman of seventeen, was at the funeral. Six months earlier she had given birth to a baby. The father had gone back to his own country – he was a pastrycook – and she had not pursued him to insist that he should marry her. She stood there now, her long hair loose on her shoulders, looking boldly and solemnly at those who had come to bury her grandmother.

At most funerals in the village there are at least 200 mourners. And Amélie's was no exception. They came because they respected her, because the last service they could offer her was to pray for her, because their absence might be noticed, because when, for each of them, their turn came to join the population of the village dead beneath the ground, a population which, counted over the centuries, was now that of a small city, each hoped to benefit from the same gesture of solidarity.

Yet this afternoon the funeral was ending differently. The priest was as usual blessing the family grave into which later the coffin would be lowered. But in the cypress tree a bird was singing. Nobody knew what kind of bird it was. Its song was so loud and shrill that the priest's prayers and the amens of the two choirboys were quite inaudible. The entire cemetery was filled with the thrills and warbling of this song.

And there was scarcely a woman or man standing in the February sunlight, their arms folded, or their large hands clasped behind the back, who did not think: throughout the years, across the generations, a force drives on, like the sap now rising, and it is implacable and destructive and reproductive; it makes mouths open, eyes burn, hands join. (They were gazing as much at the grand-daughter as at the coffin with its red and pink flowers.) And this force condemns to work and to sacrifice, also it kills, and it sings, even at this moment is singing, and will never stop.

1980

145

Drawn to that moment

When my father died recently, I did several drawings of him in his coffin. Drawings of his face and head.

There is a story about Kokoschka teaching a life class. The students were uninspired. So he spoke to the model and instructed him to pretend to collapse. When he had fallen over, Kokoschka rushed over to him, listened to his heart and announced to the shocked students that he was dead. A little afterwards the model got to his feet and resumed the pose. 'Now draw him,' said Kokoschka, 'as though you were aware that he was alive and not dead!'

One can imagine that the students, after this theatrical experience, drew with more verve. Yet to draw the truly dead involves an ever greater sense of urgency. What you are drawing will never be seen again, by you or by anybody else. In the whole course of time past and time to come, this moment is unique: the last opportunity to draw what will never again be visible, which has occurred once and which will never reoccur.

Because the faculty of sight is continuous, because visual categories (red, yellow, dark, thick, thin) remain constant, and because so many things appear to remain in place, one tends to forget that the visual is always the result of an unrepeatable, momentary encounter. Appearances, at any given moment, are a construction emerging from the debris of everything which has previously appeared. It is something like this that I understand in those words of Cézanne which so often come back to me: 'One minute in the life of the world is going by. Paint it as it is.'

Beside my father's coffin I summoned such skill as I have as a draughtsman, to apply it *directly* to the task in hand. I say *directly* because often skill in drawing expresses itself as a manner, and then its application to what is being drawn is indirect. Mannerism – in the general rather than art-historical sense – comes from the need to invent urgency, to produce an 'urgent' drawing, instead of submitting to the urgency of what is. Here I was using my small skill to save a likeness, as a lifesaver uses his much greater skill as a swimmer to save a life. People talk of freshness of vision, of the intensity of seeing for the first time, but the intensity of seeing for the last time is, I believe, greater. Of all that I could see only the drawing would remain. I was the last ever to look on the face I was drawing. I wept whilst I strove to draw with complete objectivity.

As I drew his mouth, his brows, his eyelids, as their specific forms emerged with lines from the whiteness of the paper, I felt the history and the experience which had made them as they were. His life was now as finite as the rectangle of paper on which I was drawing, but within it, in a way infinitely more mysterious than any drawing, his character and destiny had emerged. I was making a record and his face was already only a record of his life. Each drawing then was nothing but the site of a departure.

They remained. I looked at them and found that they resembled my father. Or, more strictly, that they resembled him as he was when dead. Nobody could ever mistake these drawings as ones of an old man sleeping. Why not? I ask myself. And the answer, I think, is in the way they are drawn. Nobody would draw a sleeping man with such objectivity. About this quality there is finality. Objectivity is what is left when something is finished.

I chose one drawing to frame and hang on the wall in front of the table at which I work. Gradually and consistently the relationship of his drawing to my father changed – or changed for me.

There are several ways of describing the change. The content of the drawing increased. The drawing, instead of marking the site of a departure, began to mark the site of an arrival. The forms, drawn, filled out. The drawing became the immediate locus of my memories of my father. The drawing was no longer deserted but inhabited. For each form, between the pencil marks and the white paper they marked, there was now a door through which moments of a life could enter: the drawing, instead of being simply an object of perception, with one face, had moved forward to become double-faced, and worked like a filter: from behind, it drew out my memories of the past whilst, forwards, it projected an image which, unchanging, was becoming increasingly familiar. My father came back to give the image of his death mask a kind of life.

If I look at the drawing now I scarcely see the face of a dead man; instead I see aspects of my father's life. Yet if somebody from the village came in, he would see only a drawing of a death mask. It is still unmistakably that. The change which has taken place is subjective. Yet, in a more general sense, if such a subjective process did not exist, neither would drawings.

The advent of the cinema and television means that we now define drawings (or paintings) as *static* images. What we often overlook is that their virtue, their very function, depended upon this. The need to discover the camera, and the instantaneous or moving image, arose for many different reasons but it was not in order to *improve* on the static image, or, if it was presented in those terms, it was only because the meaning of the static image had been lost. In the nineteenth century when social time became unilinear, vectorial and regularly exchangeable, the instant became the maximum which could be grasped or preserved. The plate camera and the pocket watch, the reflex camera and the wrist-watch, are twin inventions. A drawing or painting presupposes another view of time.

Any image – like the image read from the retina – records an appearance which will disappear. The faculty of sight developed as an active response to continually changing contingencies. The more it developed, the more complex the set of appearances it could construct from events. (An event in itself has no appearances.) Recognition is an essential part of this construction. And recognition depends upon the phenomenon of reappearance sometimes occurring in the ceaseless flux of disappearance. Thus, if appearances, at any given moment, are a construction emerging from the debris of all that has previously appeared, it is understandable that this very construction may give birth to the idea that everything will one day be recognizable, and the flux of disappearance cease. Such an idea is more than a personal dream; it has supplied the energy for a large part of human culture. For example: the story triumphs over oblivion; music offers a centre; the drawing challenges disappearance.

What is the nature of this challenge? A fossil also 'challenges' disappearance but the challenge is meaningless. A photograph challenges disappearance but its challenge is different from that of the fossil or the drawing.

The fossil is the result of random chance. The photographed image has been selected for preservation. The drawn image contains the experience of looking. A photograph is evidence of an encounter between event and photographer. A drawing slowly questions an event's appearance and in doing so reminds us that appearances are always a construction with a history. (Our aspiration towards objectivity can only proceed from the admission of subjectivity.) We use photographs by taking them with us, in our lives, our arguments, our memories; it is we who *move* them. Whereas a drawing or painting forces us to *stop* and enter its time. A photograph is static because it has stopped time. A drawing or painting is static because it encompasses time.

I should perhaps explain here why I make a certain distinction between drawings and paintings. Drawings reveal the process of their own making, their own looking, more clearly. The imitative facility of a painting often acts as a disguise – i.e. what it refers to becomes more impressive than the reason for referring to it. Great paintings are not disguised in this way. But even a third-rate drawing reveals the process of its own creation.

How does a drawing or painting encompass time? What does it hold in its stillness? A drawing is more than a memento – a device for bringing back memories of time past. The 'space' that my drawing offers for my father's return into it is quite distinct from that offered by a letter from him, an object owned by him or, as I have tried to explain, a photograph of him. And here it is incidental that I am looking at a drawing which I drew myself. An equivalent drawing by anybody else would offer the same 'space'.

To draw is to look, examining the structure of appearances. A drawing of a tree shows, not a tree, but a tree-being-looked-at. Whereas the sight of a tree is registered almost instantaneously, the examination of the sight of a tree (a tree-being-looked-at) not only takes minutes or hours instead of a fraction of a second, it also involves, derives from, and refers back to, much previous experience of looking. Within the instant of the sight of a tree is established a life-experience. This is how the act of drawing refuses the process of disappearances and proposes the simultaneity of a multitude of moments.

From each glance a drawing assembles a little evidence, but it consists of the evidence of many glances which can be seen together. On one hand, there is no sight in nature as unchanging as that of a drawing or painting. On the other hand, what is unchanging in a drawing consists of so many assembled moments that they con-stitute a totality rather than a fragment. The static image of a draw-ing or painting is the result of the opposition of two dynamic processes. Disappearances opposed by assemblage. If, for diagram-matic convenience, one accepts the metaphor of time as a flow, a river, then the act of drawing, by driving upstream, achieves the stationary.

Vermeer's view of Delft across the canal displays this as no theoretical explanation ever can. The painted moment has remained (almost) unchanged for three centuries. The reflections in the water have not moved. Yet this painted moment, as we look at it, has a plenitude and actuality that we experience only rarely in life. We experience everything we see in the painting as *absolutely* momentary. At the same time the experience is repeatable the next day or in ten years. It would be naïve to suppose that this has to do with accuracy: Delft at any given moment never looked like this painting. It has to do with the density per square millimetre of Vermeer's looking, with the density per square millimetre of assembled moments.

As a drawing, the drawing above my table is unremarkable. But it works in accord with the same hopes and principles which have led me to draw for thousands of years. It works because from being a site of departure, it has become a site of arrival.

Every day more of my father's life returns to the drawing in front of me.

1976

The unsaid

—

On my table
a pile of letters
not yet replied to
the earliest dated
three years before.
One evening I decide
the time has come
to deal with them all.
Letters from poets
more lyrical than I
requesting advice,
letters from institutions
inviting me to speak
on communication
or the use of art . . .
from an insurance company
a reminder explaining
I had overlooked
the obligatory premium
against natural disasters,
a birthday card.

Among the post unanswered
two letters
from close friends.
The handwritings,
one fat and one thin,

not easy to decypher,
yet over the years
I had read them avidly
finding encouragement.

Now both are dead
their last letters
lost in a pile:
both killed themselves
one with a gun
one in a canal.

1985

6

THE *WORK* OF ART

━━

On a Degas bronze of a dancer

———

You say the leg supports the body
But have you never seen
The seed in the ankle
   Whence the body grows?

You say (if you are the builder of bridges
I think you are) each pose
Must have its natural equilibrium
But have you never seen
Recalcitrant muscles of dancers
   Hold their unnatural own?

You say (if as rational
As I hope you are) the biped's evolution
Was accomplished long ago
But have you never seen
The still miraculous sign
A little in from the hip
Predicting nine inches below
   Bodies fork in two?

Then let us look together
(We who both know
Light's the go-between
Of space and time)
Let us look at this figure
To verify
   I my goddess
   And you the stress.

Think in terms of bridges.
See, the road of leg and back
Hingeing at hip and shoulder
Holds firm from palm to heel
Single leg as pier
Thigh above the knee
Cantilevering member.

Think in terms of bridges
Over what men once called Lethe.
See, the ordinary body we cross through
Vulnerable, inhabited, warm
Stands the strain too.
Dead Load, Live Load
And Longitudinal Drag.

So let the bridge this dancer arches for us
Stand the strain of all old prejudice
So let's verify again,
　　You my goddess
　　And I the stress.

1960

The moment of Cubism

This essay is dedicated to Barbara Niven who prompted it in an ABC teashop off the Gray's Inn Road a long time ago.

> Certains hommes sont des collines
>   Qui s'élèvent entre les hommes
> Et voient au loin tout l'avenir
>   Mieux que s'il était présent
> Plus net que s'il était passé.   Apollinaire

> The things that Picasso and I
> said to one another during those years will never be said again,
> and even if they were,
> no one would understand them any more.
> It was like
> being roped together on a mountain.   Georges Braque

> There are happy moments,
> but no happy periods in history.   Arnold Hauser

> The work of art is therefore
> only a halt in the becoming
> and not a frozen aim on its own.   El Lissitzky

I find it hard to believe that the most extreme Cubist works were painted over fifty years ago. It is true that I would not expect them to have been painted today. They are both too optimistic and too revolutionary for that. Perhaps in a way I am surprised that they have been painted at all. It would seem more likely that they were yet to be painted.

Do I make things unnecessarily complicated? Would it not be more helpful to say simply: the few great Cubist works were painted between 1907 and 1914? And perhaps to qualify this by adding that a few more, by Juan Gris, were painted a little later?

And anyway is it not nonsense to think of Cubism having not yet taken place when we are surrounded in daily life by the apparent effects of Cubism? All modern design, architecture and town planning seems inconceivable without the initial example of Cubism.

Nevertheless I must insist on the sensation I have in front of the works themselves: the sensation that the works and I, as I look at them, are caught, pinned down, in an enclave of time, waiting to be released and to continue a journey that began in 1907.

Cubism was a style of painting which evolved very quickly, and whose various stages can be fairly specifically defined.[1] Yet there were also Cubist poets, Cubist sculptors, and later on so-called Cubist designers and architects. Certain original stylistic features of Cubism can be found in the pioneer works of other movements: Suprematism, Constructivism, Futurism, Vorticism, the de Stijl movement.

The question thus arises: can Cubism be adequately defined as a style? It seems unlikely. Nor can it be defined as a policy. There was never any Cubist manifesto. The opinions and outlook of Picasso, Braque, Léger or Juan Gris were clearly very different even during the few years when their paintings had many features in common. Is it not enough that the category of Cubism includes those works that are now generally agreed to be within it? This is enough for dealers, collectors, and cataloguers who go by the name of art historians. But it is not, I believe, enough for you or me.

Even those whom the stylistic category satisfies are wont to say that Cubism constituted a revolutionary change in the history of art. Later we shall analyse this change in detail. The concept of painting as it had existed since the Renaissance was overthrown. The idea of art holding up a mirror to nature became a nostalgic one: a means of diminishing instead of interpreting reality.

If the word 'revolution' is used seriously and not merely as an epithet for this season's novelties, it implies a process. No revolution is simply the result of personal originality. The maximum that such originality can achieve is madness: madness is revolutionary freedom confined to the self.

Cubism cannot be explained in terms of the genius of its exponents. And this is emphasized by the fact that most of them became less profound artists when they ceased to be Cubists. Even Braque and Picasso never surpassed the works of their Cubist period: and a great deal of their later work was inferior.

The story of how Cubism happened in terms of painting and of the leading protagonists has been told many times. The protagonists themselves found it extremely difficult – both at the time and afterwards – to explain the meaning of what they were doing.

To the Cubists, Cubism was spontaneous. To us it is part of history. But a curiously unfinished part. Cubism should be considered not as a stylistic category but as a moment (even if a moment lasting six or seven years) experienced by a certain number of people. A strangely placed moment.

It was a moment in which the promises of the future were more substantial than the present. With the important exception of the avant-garde artists during a few years after 1917 in Moscow, the confidence of the Cubists has never since been equalled among artists.

D. H. Kahnweiler, who was a friend of the Cubists and their dealer, has written:

I lived those seven crucial years from 1907 to 1914 with my painter friends . . . what occurred at that time in the plastic arts will be understood only if one bears in mind that a new epoch was being born, in which man (all mankind in fact) was undergoing a transformation more radical than any other known within historical times.[2]

What was the nature of this transformation? I have outlined elsewhere (in *The Success and Failure of Picasso*) the relation between Cubism and the economic, technological and scientific developments of the period. There seems little point in repeating this here: rather, I would like to try to push a little further our definition of the philosophic meaning of these developments and their coincidence.

An interlocking world system of imperialism; opposed to it, a socialist international; the founding of modern physics, physiology and sociology; the increasing use of electricity, the invention of radio and the cinema; the beginnings of mass production; the publishing of mass-circulation newspapers; the new structural possibilities offered by the availability of steel and aluminium; the rapid development of chemical industries and the production of synthetic materials; the appearance of the motor-car and the aeroplane: what did all this mean?

The question may seem so vast that it leads to despair. Yet there are rare historical moments to which such a question can perhaps be applied. These are moments of convergence, when numerous developments enter a period of similar qualitative change, before diverging into a multiplicity of new terms. Few of those who live through such a moment can grasp the full significance of the qualitative change taking place; but everybody is aware of the times changing: the future, instead of offering continuity, appears to advance towards them.

This was surely the case in Europe from about 1900 to 1914 – although one must remember, when studying the evidence, that the reaction of many people to their own awareness of change is to pretend to ignore it.

Apollinaire, who was the greatest and most representative poet of the Cubist movement, repeatedly refers to the future in his poetry.

> Where my youth fell
> You see the flame of the future
> You must know that I speak today
> To tell the whole world
> That the art of prophecy is born at last.

The developments which converged at the beginning of the twentieth century in Europe changed the meaning of both time and space. All, in different ways, some inhuman and others full of promise, offered a liberation from the immediate, from the rigid distinction between absence and presence. The concept of the field, first put forward by Faraday when wrestling with the problem – as defined in traditional terms – of 'action at a distance', entered now, unacknowledged, into all modes of planning and calculation and even into many modes of feeling. There was a startling extension through time and space of human power and knowledge. For the first time the world, as a totality, ceased to be an abstraction and became *realizable*.

If Apollinaire was the greatest Cubist poet, Blaise Cendrars was the first. His poem, 'Les Pâques à New York' (1912) had a profound influence on Apollinaire and demonstrated to him how radically one could break with tradition. The three major poems of Cendrars at this time were all concerned with travelling – but travelling in a new sense across a *realizable* globe. In 'Le Panama ou Les Aventures de Mes Sept Oncles' he writes:

> Poetry dates from today
>> The milky way round my neck
>> The two hemispheres on my eyes
>>> At full speed
>> There are no more breakdowns
> If I had the time to save a little money I'd
>> be flying in the air show
> I have reserved my seat in the first train through
>> the tunnel under the Channel
> I am the first pilot to cross the Atlantic solo
> 900 millions

The 900 millions probably refers to the then estimated population of the world.

It is important to see how philosophically far-reaching were the consequences of this change and why it can be termed qualitative. It was not merely a question of faster transport, quicker messages, a more complex scientific vocabulary, larger accumulations of capital, wider markets, international organizations, etc. The process of the secularization of the world was at last complete. Arguments against the existence of God had achieved little. But now man was able to extend *himself* indefinitely beyond the immediate: he took over the territory in space and time where God had been presumed to exist.

'Zone', the poem that Apollinaire wrote under the immediate influence of Cendrars, contains the following lines:

> Christ pupil of the eye
> Twentieth pupil of the centuries knows how
> This century changed into a bird ascends like Jesus
> Devils in pits raise their heads to watch it
> They say it's imitating Simon Magus of Judea
> If it can fly, we'll call it the fly one
> Angels swing past its trapeze
> Icarus Enoch Elias Apollonius of Tyana
> Hover round the first aeroplane
> Dispersing at times to let through the priests
> As they bear the Holy Eucharist
> Forever ascending and raising the Host . . .[3]

The second consequence concerned the relation of the self to the secularized world. There was no longer any essential discontinuity between the individual and the general. The invisible and the multiple no longer intervened between each individual and the world. It was becoming more and more difficult to think in terms of having been *placed* in the world. A man was part of the world and indivisible from it. In an entirely original sense, which remains at the basis of modern consciousness, a man *was* the world which he inherited.

Again, Apollinaire expresses this:

> I have known since then the bouquet of the world
> I am drunk from having drunk the universe whole.

All the previous spiritual problems of religion and morality would now be increasingly concentrated in a man's choice of attitude to the existing state of the world considered as his own existing state.

It is now only against the world, within his own consciousness, that he can measure his stature. He is enhanced or diminished according to how he acts towards the enhancement or diminishment of the world. His self apart from the world, his self wrenched from its global context – the sum of all existing social contexts – is a mere biological accident. The secularization of the world exacts its price as well as offering the privilege of a choice, clearer than any other in history.

Apollinaire:

> I am everywhere or rather I start to be everywhere
> It is I who am starting this thing of the centuries
> to come.

As soon as more than one man says this, or feels it, or aspires towards feeling it – and one must remember that the notion and the feeling are the consequence of numerous material developments impinging upon millions of lives – as soon as this happens, the unity of the world has been proposed.

The term 'unity of the world' can acquire a dangerously utopian aura. But only if it is thought to be politically applicable to the world as it is. A *sine qua non* for the unity of the world is the end of exploitation. The evasion of this fact is what renders the term utopian.

Meanwhile the term has other significations. In many respects (the Declaration of Human Rights, military strategy, communications, etc.) the world since 1900 has been treated as a single unit. The unity of the world has received *de facto* recognition.

Today we know that the world should be unified, just as we know that all men should have equal rights. Insofar as a man denies this or acquiesces in its denial, he denies the unity of his own self. Hence the profound psychological sickness of the imperialist countries, hence the corruption implicit in so much of their learning – when knowledge is used to deny knowledge.

At the moment of Cubism, no denials were necessary. It was a moment of prophecy, but prophecy as the basis of a transformation that had actually begun.

Apollinaire:

> Already I hear the shrill sound of the friend's voice to come
> Who walks with you in Europe
> Whilst never leaving America . . .

I do not wish to suggest a general period of ebullient optimism. It was a period of poverty, exploitation, fear and desperation. The majority could only be concerned with the means of their survival, and millions did not survive. But for those who asked questions, there were new positive answers whose authenticity seemed to be guaranteed by the existence of new forces.

The socialist movements in Europe (with the exception of that in Germany and sections of the trade-union movement in the United States) were convinced that they were on the eve of revolution and that the revolution would spread to become a world revolution. This belief was shared even by those who disagreed about the political means necessary – by syndicalists, parliamentarians, communists and anarchists.

A particular kind of suffering was coming to an end: the suffering of hopelessness and defeat. People now believed, if not for themselves then for the future, in victory. The belief was often strongest where the conditions were worst. Everyone who was exploited or downtrodden and who had the strength left to ask about the purpose of his miserable life was able to hear in answer the echo of declarations like that of Lucheni, the Italian anarchist who stabbed the Empress of Austria in 1898: 'The hour is not far distant when a new sun will shine upon all men alike'; or like that of Kalyaev in 1905 who, on being sentenced to death for the assassination of the Governor-General of Moscow, told the court 'to learn to look the advancing revolution straight in the eye'.

An end was in sight. The limitless, which until now had always reminded men of the unattainability of their hopes, became suddenly an encouragement. The world became a starting point.

The small circle of Cubist painters and writers were not directly involved in politics. They did not think in political terms. Yet they were concerned with a revolutionary transformation of the world. How was this possible? Again we find the answer in the historical timing of the Cubist movement. It was not then essential for a man's intellectual integrity to make a political choice. Many developments, as they converged to undergo an equivalent qualitative change, appeared to promise a transformed world. The promise was an overall one.

'All is possible,' wrote André Salmon, another Cubist poet, 'everything is realizable everywhere and with everything.'

Imperialism had begun the process of unifying the world. Mass production promised eventually a world of plenty. Mass-circulation newspapers promised informed democracy. The aeroplane promised to make the dream of Icarus real. The terrible contradictions born of the convergence were not yet clear. They became evident in 1914 and they were first politically polarized by the Russian Revolution of 1917. El Lissitzky, one of the great innovators of Russian revolutionary art until this art was suppressed, implies in a biographical note how the moment of political choice came from the conditions of the Cubist moment:

The Film of El's Life till 1926[4]
BIRTH: My generation was born
a few dozen years
before the Great October Revolution.
ANCESTORS: A few centuries ago our ancestors had the luck
to make the great voyages of discovery.
WE: We, the grandchildren of Columbus,
are creating the epoch of the most glorious inventions.
They have made our globe very small,
but have
expanded our space
and intensified our time.
SENSATIONS: My life is accompanied
by unprecedented sensations.
Barely five years old I had the rubber leads
of Edison's phonograph stuck in my ears.

Eight years,
and I was chasing after the first electric tram in Smolensk,
the diabolical force
which drove the peasant horses out of the town.
COMPRESSION OF MATTER: The steam engine rocked my
cradle.
In the meantime it has gone the way of all ichthyosauruses.
Machines are ceasing
to have fat bellies full of intestines.
Already we have the compressed skulls
of dynamos with their electric brains.
Matter and mind
are directly transmitted through crankshafts
and thus made to work.
Gravity and inertia are being overcome.
1918: In 1918 in Moscow before my eyes
the short-circuit sparked
which split the world in
half.
This stroke drove our present apart
like a wedge
between yesterday and tomorrow.
My work
too
forms part of driving the wedge
further
in.
One belongs here or there:
there is no middle.

The Cubist movement ended in France in 1914. With the war a new
kind of suffering was born. Men were forced to face for the first time
the full horror – not of hell, or damnation, or a lost battle, or famine,
or plague – but the full horror of what stood in the way of their own
progress. And they were forced to face this in terms of their own
responsibility, not in terms of a simple confrontation as between
clearly defined enemies.

The scale of the waste and the irrationality and the degree to which
men could be persuaded and forced to deny their own interests led to

the belief that there were incomprehensible and blind forces at work. But since these forces could no longer be accommodated by religion, and since there was no ritual by which they could be approached or appeased, each man had to live with them *within himself*, as best he could. Within him they destroyed his will and confidence.

On the last page of *All Quiet on the Western Front* the hero thinks:

I am very quiet. Let the months and years come, they can take nothing from me, they can take nothing more. I am so alone, and so without hope that I can confront them without fear. The life that has borne me through these years is still in my hands and my eyes. Whether I have subdued it, I know not. But so long as it is there it will seek its own way out, heedless of the will that is within me.[5]

The new kind of suffering which was born in 1914 and has persisted in Western Europe until the present day is an inverted suffering. Men fought within themselves about the meaning of events, identity, hope. This was the negative possibility implicit in the new relation of the self to the world. The life they experienced became a chaos within them. They became lost within themselves.

Instead of apprehending (in however simple and direct a way) the processes which were rendering their own destinies identical with the world's, they submitted to the new condition passively. That is to say the world, which was nevertheless indivisibly part of them, reverted *in their minds* to being the old world which was separate from them and opposed them: it was as though they had been forced to devour God, heaven and hell and live for ever with the fragments inside themselves. It was indeed a new and terrible form of suffering and it coincided with the widespread, deliberate use of false ideological propaganda as a weapon. Such propaganda preserves within people outdated structures of feeling and thinking whilst forcing new experiences upon them. It transforms them into puppets – whilst most of the strain brought about by the transformation remains politically harmless as inevitably *incoherent* frustration. The only purpose of such propaganda is to make people deny and then abandon the selves which otherwise their own experience would create.

In 'La Jolie Rousse', Apollinaire's last long poem (he died in 1918), his vision of the future, after his experience of the war, has become a source of suffering as much as of hope. How can he reconcile what he has seen with what he once foresaw? From now on there can be no unpolitical prophecies.

> We are not your enemies
> We want to take over vast strange territories
> Where the flowering mystery waits to be picked
> Where there are fires and colours never yet seen
> A thousand imponderable apparitions
> Which must be given reality
> We wish to explore the vast domain of goodness
>   where everything is silent
> And time can be pursued or brought back
> Pity us who fight continually on the frontiers
> Of the infinite and the future
> Pity for our mistakes pity for our sins.
>
> The violence of summer is here
> My youth like the spring is dead
> Now, O sun, is the time of scorching Reason
> Laugh then laugh at me
> Men from everywhere and more particularly here
> For there are so many things I dare not tell you
> So many things you will not let me say
> Have pity on me.

We can now begin to understand the central paradox of Cubism. The spirit of Cubism was objective. Hence its calm and its comparative anonymity as between artists. Hence also the accuracy of its technical prophecies. I live in a satellite city that has been built during the last five years. The character of the pattern of what I now see out of the window as I write can be traced directly back to the Cubist pictures of 1911 and 1912. Yet the Cubist spirit seems to us today to be curiously distant and disengaged.

This is because the Cubists took no account of politics *as we have since experienced them*. In common with even their experienced political contemporaries, they did not imagine and did not foresee the extent, depth and duration of the suffering which would be involved in the political struggle to realize what had so clearly become possible and what has since become imperative.

The Cubists imagined the world transformed, but not the process of transformation.

Cubism changed the nature of the relationship between the painted image and reality, and by so doing it expressed a new relationship between man and reality.

Many writers have pointed out that Cubism marked a break in the history of art comparable to that of the Renaissance in relation to medieval art. That is not to say that Cubism can be equated with the Renaissance. The confidence of the Renaissance lasted for about sixty years (approximately from 1420 to 1480): that of Cubism lasted for about six years. However, the Renaissance remains a point of departure for appreciating Cubism.

In the early Renaissance the aim of art was to imitate nature. Alberti formulated this view: 'The function of the painter is to render with lines and colours, on a given panel or wall, the visible surface of any body, so that at a certain distance and from a certain position it appears in relief and just like the body itself.'[6]

It was not, of course, as simple as that. There were the mathematical problems of linear perspective which Alberti himself solved. There was the question of choice – that is to say the question of the artist doing justice to nature by choosing to represent what was typical of nature at her best.

Yet the artist's relation to nature was comparable to that of the scientist. Like the scientist, the artist applied reason and method to the study of the world. He observed and ordered his findings. The parallelism of the two disciplines is later demonstrated by the example of Leonardo.

Although often employed far less accurately during the following centuries, the metaphorical model for the function of painting at this time was *the mirror*. Alberti cites Narcissus when he sees himself reflected in the water as the first painter. The mirror renders the appearances of nature and simultaneously delivers them into the hands of man.

It is extremely hard to reconstruct the attitudes of the past. In the light of more recent developments and the questions raised by them, we tend to iron out the ambiguities which may have existed before the questions were formed. In the early Renaissance, for example, the humanist view and a medieval Christian view could still be easily combined. Man became the equal of God, but both retained their traditional positions. Arnold Hauser writes of the early Renaissance: 'The seat of God was the centre round which the heavenly spheres revolved, the earth was the centre of the material universe, and man himself a self-contained microcosm round which, as it were, revolved the whole of nature, just as the celestial bodies revolved round that fixed star, the earth.'[7]

Thus man could observe nature around him on every side and be enhanced both by what he observed and by his own ability to observe. He had no need to consider that he was essentially part of that nature. *Man was the eye for which reality had been made visual*: the ideal eye, the eye of the viewing point of Renaissance perspective. The human greatness of his eye lay in its ability to reflect and contain, like a mirror, what was.

The Copernican revolution, Protestantism, the Counter-Reformation destroyed the Renaissance position. With this destruction modern subjectivity was born. The artist becomes primarily concerned with creation. His own genius takes the place of nature as the marvel. It is the gift of his genius, his 'spirit', his 'grace' which makes him god-like. At the same time the equality between man and god is totally destroyed. Mystery enters art to emphasize the inequality. A century after Alberti's claim that art and science are parallel activities, Michelangelo speaks – no longer of imitating nature – but of imitating Christ: 'In order to imitate in some degree the venerable image of Our Lord, it is not enough to be a painter, a great and skilful master; I believe that one must further be of blameless life, even if possible a saint, that the Holy Spirit may inspire one's understanding.'[8]

It would take us too far from our field even to attempt to trace the history of art from Michelangelo onwards – Mannerism, the Baroque, seventeenth- and eighteenth-century classicism. What is relevant to our purpose is that, from Michelangelo until the French Revolution, the metaphorical model for the function of painting becomes the *theatre stage*. It may seem unlikely that the same model works for a visionary like El Greco, a Stoic like Poussin (who actually worked from stage models he built himself) and a middle-class moralist like Chardin. Yet all the artists of these two centuries shared certain assumptions. For them all the power of art lay in its *artificiality*. That is to say they were concerned with constructing comprehensive examples of some truth such as could not be met with in such an ecstatic, pointed, sublime or meaningful way in life itself.

Painting became a schematic art. The painter's task was no longer to represent or imitate what existed: it was to summarize experience. Nature is now what man has to redeem himself from. The artist becomes responsible not simply for the means of conveying a truth, but also for the truth itself. Painting ceases to be a branch of natural science and becomes a branch of the moral sciences.

In the theatre the spectator faces events from whose consequences he is immune; he may be affected emotionally and morally but he is physically removed, protected, separate, from what is happening before his eyes. What is happening is artificial. It is *he* who now represents nature – not the work of art. And if, at the same time, it is from himself that he must redeem himself, this represents the contradiction of the Cartesian division which prophetically or actually so dominated these two centuries.

Rousseau, Kant and the French Revolution – or rather, all the developments which lay behind the thought of the philosophers and the actions of the Revolution – made it impossible to go on believing in constructed order as against natural chaos. The metaphorical model changed again, and once more it applies over a long period despite dramatic changes of style. The new model is that of the *personal account*. Nature no longer confirms or enhances the artist as he investigates it. Nor is he any longer concerned with creating 'artificial' examples, for these depend upon the common recognition of certain moral values. He is now alone, surrounded by nature, from which his own experience separates him.

Nature is what he sees *through* his experience. There is thus in all nineteenth-century art – from the 'pathetic fallacy' of the Romantics to the 'optics' of the Impressionists – considerable confusion about where the artist's experience stops and nature begins. The artist's personal account is his attempt to make his experience as real as nature, which he can never reach, by communicating it to others. The considerable suffering of most nineteenth-century artists arose out of this contradiction: because they were alienated from nature, they needed to present *themselves* as nature to others.

Speech, as the recounting of experience and the means of making it real, preoccupied the Romantics. Hence their constant comparisons between paintings and poetry. Géricault, whose 'Raft of the Medusa' was the first painting of a contemporary event consciously based on eyewitness accounts, wrote in 1821: 'How I should like to be able to show our cleverest painters several portraits, which are such close resemblances to nature, whose easy pose leaves nothing to be desired, and of which one can really say that all they lack is the power of speech.'[9]

In 1850 Delacroix wrote: 'I have told myself a hundred times that painting – that is to say, the material thing called painting – was no more than the pretext, the bridge between the mind of the painter and that of the spectator.'[10]

For Corot experience was a far less flamboyant and more modest affair than for the Romantics. But nevertheless he still emphasized how essential the personal and the relative are to art. In 1856 he wrote: 'Reality is one part of art: feeling completes it . . . before any site and any object, abandon yourself to your first impression. If you have really been touched, you will convey to others the sincerity of your emotion.'[11]

Zola, who was one of the first defenders of the Impressionists, defined a work of art as 'a corner of nature seen through a temperament'. The definition applies to the whole of the nineteenth century and is another way of describing the same metaphorical model.

Monet was the most theoretical of the Impressionists and the most anxious to break through the century's barrier of subjectivity. For him (at least theoretically) the role of his temperament was reduced to that of the process of perception. He speaks of a 'close fusion' with nature. But the result of this fusion, however harmonious, is a sense of powerlessness – which suggests that, bereft of his subjectivity, he has nothing to put in its place. Nature is no longer a field for study, it has become an overwhelming force. One way or another the confrontation between the artist and nature in the nineteenth century is an unequal one. Either the heart of man or the grandeur of nature dominates. Monet wrote:

I have painted for half a century, and will soon have passed my sixty-ninth year, but, far from decreasing, my sensitivity has sharpened with age. As long as constant contact with the outside world can sustain the ardour of my curiosity, and my hand remains the quick and faithful servant of my perception, I have nothing to fear from old age. I have no other wish than a close fusion with nature, and I desire no other fate than (according to Goethe) to have worked and lived in harmony with her rules. Beside her grandeur, her power and her immorality, the human creature seems but a miserable atom.

I am well aware of the schematic nature of this brief survey. Is not Delacroix in some senses a transitional figure between the eighteenth and nineteenth centuries? And was not Raphael another transitional figure who confounds such simple categories? The scheme, however, is true enough to help us appreciate the nature of the change which Cubism represented.

The metaphorical model of Cubism is the *diagram*: the diagram being a visible, symbolic representation of invisible processes, forces, structures. A diagram need not eschew certain aspects of appearances: but these too will be treated symbolically as *signs*, not as imitations or re-creations.

The model of the *diagram* differs from that of the *mirror* in that it suggests a concern with what is not self-evident. It differs from the model of the *theatre stage* in that it does not have to concentrate upon climaxes but can reveal the continuous. It differs from the model of the *personal account* in that it aims at a general truth.

The Renaissance artist imitated nature. The Mannerist and Classic artist reconstructed examples from nature in order to transcend nature. The nineteenth-century artist experienced nature. The Cubist realized that his awareness of nature was part of nature.

Heisenberg speaks as a modern physicist. 'Natural science does not simply describe and explain nature; it is part of the interplay between nature and ourselves: it describes nature as exposed to our method of questioning.'[12] Similarly, the frontal facing of nature became inadequate in art.

How did the Cubists express their imitation of the new relation existing between man and nature?

1   *By their use of space*

Cubism broke the illusionist three-dimensional space which had existed in painting since the Renaissance. It did not destroy it. Nor did it muffle it – as Gauguin and the Pont-Aven school had done. It broke its continuity. There is space in a Cubist painting in that one form can be inferred to be behind another. But the relation between any two forms does not, as it does in illusionist space, establish the rule for all the spatial relationships between all the forms portrayed in the picture. This is possible without a nightmarish deformation of space, because the two-dimensional surface of the picture is always there as arbiter and resolver of different claims. The picture surface acts in a Cubist painting as the constant which allows us to appreciate the variables. Before and after every sortie of our imagination into the problematic spaces and through the interconnections of a Cubist painting, we find our gaze resettled on the picture surface, aware once more of two-dimensional shapes on a two-dimensional board or canvas.

This makes it impossible to *confront* the objects or forms in a Cubist work. Not only because of the multiplicity of viewpoints – so that, say, a view of a table from below is combined with a view of the table from above and from the side – but also because the forms portrayed never present themselves as a totality. The totality is the surface of the picture, *which is now the origin and sum of all that one sees*. The viewing point of Renaissance perspective, fixed and outside the picture, but to which everything within the picture was drawn, has become a field of vision which is the picture itself.

It took Picasso and Braque three years to arrive at this extraordinary transformation. In most of their pictures from 1907 to 1910 there are still compromises with Renaissance space. The effect of this is to deform the subject. The figure or landscape becomes the construction, instead of the construction being the picture acting as an expression of the relation between viewer and subject.[13]

After 1910 all references to appearances are made as signs on the picture surface. A circle for a top of a bottle, a lozenge for an eye, letters for a newspaper, a volute for the head of a violin, etc. Collage was an extension of the same principle. Part of the actual or imitation surface of an object was stuck on to the surface of the picture as a sign referring to, but not imitating, its appearance. A little later painting borrowed from this experience of collage, so that, say, a pair of lips or a bunch of grapes might be referred to by a drawing which 'pretended' to be on a piece of white paper stuck on to the picture surface.

2   *By their treatment of form*

It was this which gave the Cubists their name. They were said to paint everything in *cubes*. Afterwards this was connected with Cézanne's remark: 'Treat nature by the cylinder, by the sphere, the cone, everything in proper perspective.' And from then on the misunderstanding has continued – encouraged, let it be said, by a lot of confused assertions by some of the lesser Cubists themselves.

The misunderstanding is that the Cubist wanted to simplify – for the sake of simplification. In some of the Picassos and Braques of 1908 it may look as though this is the case. Before finding their new vision, they had to jettison traditional complexities. But their aim was to arrive at a far more complex image of reality than had ever been attempted in painting before.

To appreciate this we must abandon a habit of centuries: the habit of looking at every object or body as though it were complete in itself, its completeness making it separate. The Cubists were concerned with the interaction between objects.

They reduced forms to a combination of cubes, cones, cylinders – or, later, to arrangements of flatly articulated facets or planes with sharp edges – so that the elements of any one form were interchangeable with another, whether a hill, a woman, a violin, a carafe, a table or a hand. Thus, as against the Cubist discontinuity of space, they created a continuity of structure. Yet when we talk of the Cubist discontinuity of space, it is only to distinguish it from the convention of linear Renaissance perspective.

Space is part of the continuity of the events within it. It is in itself an event, comparable with other events. It is not a mere container. And this is what the few Cubist masterpieces show us. The space between objects is part of the same structure as the objects themselves. The forms are simply reversed so that, say, the top of a head is a convex element and the adjacent space which it does not fill is a concave element.

The Cubists created the possibility of art revealing processes instead of static entities. The content of their art consists of various modes of interaction: the interaction between different aspects of the same event, between empty space and filled space, between structure and movement, between the seer and the thing seen.

Rather than ask of a Cubist picture: Is it true? or: Is it sincere? one should ask: Does it continue?

Today it is easy to see that, since Cubism, painting has become more and more diagrammatic, even when there has been no direct Cubist influence – as, say, in Surrealism. Eddie Wolfram in an article about Francis Bacon has written: 'Painting today functions directly as a conceptual activity in philosophical terms and the art object acts only as a cypher reference to tangible reality.'[14]

This was part of the Cubist prophecy. But only part. Byzantine art might equally well be accommodated within Wolfram's definition. To understand the full Cubist prophecy we must examine the content of their art.

A Cubist painting like Picasso's 'Bottle and Glasses' of 1911 is two-dimensional insofar as one's eye comes back again and again to the surface of the picture. We start from the surface, we follow a sequence of forms which leads into the picture, and then suddenly we arrive back at the surface again and deposit our newly acquired knowledge upon it, before making another foray. This is why I called the Cubist picture-surface the origin and sum of all that we can see in the picture. There is nothing decorative about such two-dimensionality, nor is it merely an area offering possibilities of juxtaposition for dissociated images – as in the case of much recent neo-Dadaist or pop art. We begin with the surface, but since everything in the picture refers back to the surface we begin with the conclusion. We then search – not for an explanation, as we do if presented with an image with a single, predominant meaning (a man laughing, a mountain, a reclining nude), but for some understanding of the configuration of events whose interaction is the conclusion from which we began. When we 'deposit our newly acquired know-ledge upon the picture surface', what we in fact do is find the sign for what we have just discovered: a sign which was always there but which previously we could not read.

To make the point clearer it is worth comparing a Cubist picture with any work in the Renaissance tradition. Let us say Pollaiuolo's 'Martyrdom of St Sebastian'. In front of the Pollaiuolo the spectator completes the picture. It is the spectator who draws the conclusions and infers all except the aesthetic relations between the pieces of evidence offered – the archers, the martyr, the plain laid out behind, etc. It is he who through his reading of what is portrayed seals its unity of meaning. The work is presented to him. One has the feeling almost that St Sebastian was martyred so that he should be able to explain this picture. The complexity of the forms and the scale of the space depicted enhance the sense of achievement, of grasp.

In a Cubist picture, the conclusion and the connections are given. They are what the picture is made of. They are its content. The spectator has to find his place *within* this content whilst the complexity of the forms and the 'discontinuity' of the space remind him that his view from that place is bound to be only partial.

Such content and its functioning was prophetic because it coincided with the new scientific view of nature which rejected simple causality and the single permanent all-seeing viewpoint.

Heisenberg writes:

One may say that the human ability to understand may be in a certain sense unlimited. But the existing scientific concepts cover always only a very limited part of reality, and the other part that has not yet been understood is infinite. Whenever we proceed from the known to the unknown we may hope to understand, but we may have to learn at the same time a new meaning of the word understanding.[15]

Such a notion implies a change in the methodology of research and invention. W. Grey Walter, the physiologist, writes:

Classical physiology, as we have seen, tolerated only one single unknown quantity in its equations – in any experiment there could be only one thing at a time under investigation . . . We cannot extract one independent variable in the classical manner; we have to deal with the interaction of many unknowns and variables, all the time . . . In practice, this implies that not one but many – as many as possible – observations must be made at once and compared with one another, and that whenever possible a simple known variable should be used to modify the several complex unknowns so that their tendencies and interdependence can be assessed.[16]

The best Cubist works of 1910, 1911 and 1912 were sustained and precise models for the method of searching and testing described above. That is to say, they force the senses and imagination of the spectator to calculate, omit, doubt and conclude according to a pattern which closely resembles the one involved in scientific observation. The difference is a question of appeal. Because the act of looking at a picture is far less concentrated, the picture can appeal to wider and more various areas of the spectator's previous experience. Art is concerned with memory: experiment is concerned with predictions.

Outside the modern laboratory, the need to adapt oneself constantly to presented totalities – rather than making inventories or supplying a transcendental meaning as in front of the Pollaiuolo – is a feature of modern experience which affects everybody through the mass media and modern communication systems.

Marshall McLuhan is a manic exaggerator, but he has seen certain truths clearly:

In the electric age, when our central nervous system is technologically extended to involve us in the whole of mankind and to incorporate the whole of mankind in us, we necessarily participate, in depth, in the consequences of our every action . . . The aspiration of our time for wholeness, empathy and depth of awareness is a natural adjunct of electric technology. The age of mechanical industry that preceded us found vehement assertion of private outlook the natural mode of expression . . . The mark of our time is its revolution against imposed patterns. We are suddenly eager to have things and people declare their beings totally.[17]

The Cubists were the first artists to attempt to paint totalities rather than agglomerations.

I must emphasize again that the Cubists were not aware of all that we are now reading into their art. Picasso and Braque and Léger kept silent because they knew that they might be doing more than they knew. The lesser Cubists tended to believe that their break with tradition had freed them from the bondage of appearances so that they might deal with some kind of spiritual essence. The idea that their art coincided with the implications of certain new scientific and technological developments was entertained but never fully worked out. There is no evidence at all that they recognized as such the qualitative change which had taken place in the world. It is for these reasons that I have constantly referred to their *intimation* of a transformed world: it amounted to no more than that.

One cannot explain the exact dates of the maximum Cubist achievement. Why 1910 to 1912 rather than 1905 to 1907? Nor is it possible to explain *exactly* why certain artists, at exactly the same time, arrived at a very different view of the world – artists ranging from Bonnard to Duchamp or de Chirico. To do so we would need to know an *impossible* amount about each separate individual development. (In that impossibility – which is an absolute one – lies our freedom from determinism.)

We have to work with partial explanations. With the advantage of sixty years' hindsight, the correlations I have tried to establish between Cubism and the rest of history seem to me to be undeniable. The precise route of the connections remains unknown. They do not inform us about the intentions of the artists: they do not explain exactly why Cubism took place in the manner it did; but they do help to disclose the widest possible continuing meaning of Cubism.

Two more reservations. Because Cubism represented so fundamental a revolution in the history of art, I have had to discuss it as though it were pure theory. Only in this way could I make its revolutionary content clear. But naturally it was not pure theory. It was nothing like so neat, consistent or reduced. There are Cubist paintings full of anomalies and marvellous gratuitous tenderness and confused excitement. We see the beginning in the light of the conclusions it suggested. But it was only a beginning, and a beginning cut short.

For all their insight into the inadequacy of appearances and of the frontal view of nature, the Cubists used such appearances as their means of reference to nature. In the maelstrom of their new constructions, their liaison with the events which provoked them is shown by way of a simple, almost naïve reference to a pipe stuck in the 'sitter's' mouth, a bunch of grapes, a fruit dish or the title of a daily newspaper. Even in some of the most 'hermetic' paintings – for example Braque's 'Le Portugais' – you can find naturalistic allusions to details of the subject's appearance, such as the buttons on the musician's jacket, buried intact within the construction. There are only a very few works – for instance Picasso's 'Le Modèle' of 1912 – where such allusions have been totally dispensed with.

The difficulties were probably both intellectual and sentimental. The naturalistic allusions seemed necessary in order to offer a measure for judging the transformation. Perhaps also the Cubists were reluctant to part with appearances because they suspected that in art they could never be the same again. The details are smuggled in and hidden as mementoes.

The second reservation concerns the social content of Cubism – or, rather, its lack of it. One cannot expect of a Cubist painting the same kind of social content as one finds in a Brueghel or a Courbet. The mass media and the arrival of new publics have profoundly changed the social role of the fine arts. It remains true, however, that the Cubists – during the moment of Cubism – were unconcerned about the personalized human and social implications of what they were doing. This, I think, is because they had to simplify. The problem before them was so complex that their manner of stating it and their trying to solve it absorbed all their attention. As innovators they wanted to make their experiments in the simplest possible conditions; consequently, they took as subjects whatever was at hand and made least demands. The content of these works is the relation between the seer and the seen. This relation is only possible given the fact that the seer inherits a precise historical, economic and social situation. Otherwise they become meaningless. They do not illustrate a human or social situation, they posit it.

I spoke of the continuing meaning of Cubism. To some degree this meaning has changed and will change again according to the needs of the present. The bearings we read with the aid of Cubism vary according to our position. What is the reading now?

It is being more and more urgently claimed that 'the modern tradition' begins with Jarry, Duchamp and the Dadaists. This confers legitimacy upon the recent developments of neo-Dadaism, auto-destructive art, happenings, etc. The claim implies that what separates the characteristic art of the twentieth century from the art of all previous centuries is its acceptance of unreason, its social desperation, its extreme subjectivity and its forced dependence upon existential experience.

Hans Arp, one of the original Dadaist spokesmen, wrote: 'The Renaissance taught men the haughty exaltation of their reason. Modern times, with their science and technology, turned men towards megalomania. The confusion of our epoch results from this overestimation of reason.'

And elsewhere: 'The law of chance, which embraces all other laws and is as unfathomable to us as the depths from which all life arises, can only be comprehended by complete surrender to the Unconscious.'[18]

Arp's statements are repeated today with a slightly modified vocabulary by all contemporary apologists of outrageous art. (I use the word 'outrageous' descriptively and not in a pejorative sense.)

During the intervening years, the Surrealists, Picasso, de Chirico, Miró, Klee, Dubuffet, the Abstract Expressionists and many others can be drafted into the same tradition: the tradition whose aim is to cheat the world of its hollow triumphs, and disclose its pain.

The example of Cubism forces us to recognize that this is a one-sided interpretation of history. Outrageous art has many earlier precedents. In periods of doubt and transition the majority of artists have always tended to be preoccupied with the fantastic, the uncontrollable and the horrific. The greater extremism of contemporary artists is the result of their having no fixed social role; to some degree they can create their own. But there are precedents for the spirit of it in the history of other activities: heretical religions, alchemy, witchcraft, etc.

The real break with tradition, or the real reformation of that tradition, occurred with Cubism itself. The modern tradition, based on a qualitatively different relationship being established between man and the world, began, not in despair, but in affirmation.

The proof that this was the objective role of Cubism lies in the fact that, however much its spirit was rejected, it supplied to all later movements the primary means of their own liberation. That is to say, it re-created the syntax of art so that it could accommodate modern experience. The proposition that a work of art is a new object and not simply the expression of its subject, the structuring of a picture to admit the coexistence of different modes of space and time, the inclusion in a work of art of extraneous objects, the dislocation of forms to reveal movement or change, the combining of hitherto separate and distinct media, the diagrammatic use of appearances – these were the revolutionary innovations of Cubism.

It would be foolish to underestimate the achievements of post-Cubist art. Nevertheless it is fair to say that in general the art of the post-Cubist period has been anxious and highly subjective. What the evidence of Cubism should prevent us doing is concluding from this that anxiety and extreme subjectivity constitute the nature of modern art. They constitute the nature of art in a period of extreme ideological confusion and inverted political frustration.

During the first decade of this century a transformed world became theoretically possible and the necessary forces of change could already be recognized as existing. Cubism was the art which reflected the possibility of this transformed world and the confidence it inspired. Thus, in a certain sense, it was the most modern art – as it was also the most philosophically complex – which has yet existed.

The vision of the Cubist moment still coincides with what is technologically possible. Yet three-quarters of the world remain undernourished and the foreseeable growth of the world's population is outstripping the production of food. Meanwhile millions of the privileged are the prisoners of their own sense of increasing powerlessness.

The political struggle will be gigantic in its range and duration. The transformed world will not arrive as the Cubists imagined it. It will be born of a longer and more terrible history. We cannot see the end of the present period of political inversion, famine and exploitation. But the moment of Cubism reminds us that, if we are to be representative of our century – and not merely its passive creatures – the aim of achieving that end must constantly inform our consciousness and decisions.

The moment at which a piece of music begins provides a clue to the nature of all art. The incongruity of that moment, compared to the uncounted, unperceived silence which preceded it, is the secret of art. What is the meaning of that incongruity and the shock which accompanies it? It is to be found in the distinction between the actual and the desirable. All art is an attempt to define and make *unnatural* this distinction.

For a long time it was thought that art was the imitation and celebration of nature. The confusion arose because the concept of nature itself was a projection of the desired. Now that we have cleansed our view of nature, we see that art is an expression of our sense of the inadequacy of the given – which we are not obliged to accept with gratitude. Art mediates between our good fortune and our disappointment. Sometimes it mounts to a pitch of horror. Sometimes it gives permanent value and meaning to the ephemeral. Sometimes it describes the desired.

Thus art, however free or anarchic its mode of expression, is always a plea for greater control and an example, within the artificial limits of a 'medium', of the advantages of such control. Theories about the artist's inspiration are all projections back on to the artist of the effect which his work has upon us. The only inspiration which exists is the intimation of our own potential. Inspiration is the mirror image of history: by means of it we can see our past, while turning our back upon it. And it is precisely this which happens at the instant when a piece of music begins. We suddenly become aware of the previous silence at the same moment as our attention is concentrated upon following sequences and resolutions which will contain the desired.

The Cubist moment was such a beginning, defining desires which are still unmet.

1969

Notes

1 See John Golding, *Cubism*, London, Faber & Faber, 1959; New York, Harper & Row, 1971.

2 D. H. Kahnweiler, *Cubism*, Paris, Editions Braun, 1950.

3 In the Penguin translation of Apollinaire a misreading of these lines unfortunately reverses the meaning of the poem.

4 *El Lissitzky*, Dresden, Verlag der Kunst, 1967, p. 325 (trans. Anya Bostock).

5 E. M. Remarque, *All Quiet on the Western Front*, trans. A. W. Wheen, London, Putnam & Co., 1929; New York, Mayflower/Dell Paperbacks, 1963.

6 Quoted in Anthony Blunt, *Artistic Theory in Italy, 1450–1600*, London and New York, Oxford University Press, 1956; OUP paperback edn, 1962.

7 See Arnold Hauser, *Mannerism*, London, Routledge, 1965; New York, Knopf, 1965; an essential book for anybody concerned with the problematic nature of contemporary art, and its historical roots.

8 Quoted in Anthony Blunt, *op. cit.*

9 *Artists on Art*, ed. R. J. Goldwate and M. Treves, New York, Pantheon Books, 1945; London, John Murray, 1976.

10 Ibid.

11 Ibid.

12 Werner Heisenberg, *Physics and Philosophy*, London, Allen & Unwin, 1959, p. 75; New York, Harper & Row/Torch, 1959.

13 For a similar analysis of Cubism, written thirty years earlier but unknown to the author at the time of writing, see Max Raphael's great work, *The Demands of Art*, London, Routledge, 1968, p. 162. Princeton, Princeton University Press, 1968.

14 Eddie Wolfram, in *Art and Artists*, London, September 1966.

15 Werner Heisenberg, *op. cit.*, p. 172.

16 W. Grey Walter, *The Living Brain*, London, Duckworth, 1953; Harmondsworth, Penguin, 1961, p. 69; New York, Norton, 1963.

17 Marshall McLuhan, *Understanding Media*, London, Routledge & Kegan Paul, 1964; New York, McGraw-Hill, 1964; pp. 4, 5.

18 Quoted in Hans Richter, *Dada*, London, Thames & Hudson, 1966, p. 55; New York, Oxford University Press, 1978.

The eyes of Claude Monet

Too much has been made of Cézanne's famous remark that, if Monet was only an eye, what an eye! More important now, perhaps, to acknowledge and question the sadness in Monet's eyes, a sadness which emerges from photograph after photograph.

Little attention has been paid to this sadness because there is no place for it in the usual art-historical version of the meaning of Impressionism. Monet was the leader of the Impressionists – the most consistent and the most intransigent – and Impressionism was the beginning of Modernism, a kind of triumphal arch through which European art passed to enter the twentieth century.

There is some truth in this version. Impressionism *did* mark a break with the previous history of European painting and a great deal of what followed – Post-Impressionism, Expressionism, Abstraction – can be thought of as being partly engendered by this first modern movement. It is equally true that today, after half a century, Monet's later works – and particularly the water lilies – appear now to have prefigured the work of artists such as Pollock, Tobey, Sam Francis, Rothko.

It is possible to argue, as Malevich did, that the twenty paintings which Monet made in the early 1890s of the façade of Rouen Cathedral, as seen at different times of day and under different weather conditions, were the final systematic proof that the history of painting would never be the same again. This history had henceforward to admit that every appearance could be thought of as a mutation and that visibility itself should be considered flux.

Furthermore, if one thinks of the claustrophobia of mid-nineteenth-century bourgeois culture, it is impossible not to see how

Impressionism appeared as a liberation. To paint out of doors in front of the motif; to observe directly, to accord to light its proper hegemony in the domain of the visible; to relativize all colours (so that everything sparkles); to abandon the painting of dusty legends and all direct ideology; to speak of everyday appearances within the experience of a wide urban public (a day off, a trip to the country, boats, smiling women in sunlight, flags, trees in flower – the Impressionist vocabulary of images is that of a popular dream, the awaited, beloved, secular Sunday); the innocence of Impressionism – innocence in the sense that it did away with the secrets of painting, everything was there in the full light of day, there was nothing more to hide, and amateur painting followed easily – how could all this not be thought of as a liberation?

Why can't we forget the sadness in Monet's eyes, or simply acknowledge it as something personal to him, the result of his early poverty, the death of his first wife when so young, his failing eyesight when old? And in any case, are we not running the risk of explaining the history of Egypt as the consequence of Cleopatra's smile? Let us run the risk.

Twenty years before painting the façade of Rouen Cathedral, Monet painted (he was thirty-two years old) 'Impression Soleil Levant', and from this the critic Castagnary coined the term *Impressionist*. The painting is a view of the port of Le Havre where Monet was brought up as a child. In the foreground is the tiny silhouette of a man standing and rowing with another figure in a dinghy. Across the water, masts and derricks are dimly visible in the morning twilight. Above, but low in the sky, is a small orange sun and, below, its inflamed reflection in the water. It is not an image of dawn (Aurora), but of a day slipping in, as yesterday slipped out. The mood is reminiscent of Baudelaire's 'Le Crépuscule de Matin', in which the coming day is compared to the sobbing of somebody who has just been woken.

Yet what is it that exactly constitutes the melancholy of this painting? Why, for example, don't comparable scenes, as painted by

Turner, evoke a similar mood? The answer is the painting method, precisely that practice which was to be called Impressionist. The transparency of the thin pigment representing the water – the thread of the canvas showing through it, the swift broken-straw-like brush strokes suggesting ripples of spars, the scrubbed-in areas of shadow, the reflections staining the water, the optical truthfulness and the *object*ive vagueness, all this renders the scene makeshift, threadbare, decrepit. It is an image of homelessness. Its very insubstantiality makes shelter in it impossible. Looking at it, the idea occurs to you of a man trying to find his road home through a theatre décor. Baudelaire's lines in 'La Cygne', published in 1860, belong to the slow intake of breath before the accuracy and the refusal of this scene.

> . . . La forme d'une ville
> Change plus vite, hélas, que le coeur d'un
> mortel.

If Impressionism was about 'impressions', what change did this imply in the relation between seen and seer? (Seer here meaning both painter and viewer.) You do not have an *impression* of a scene with which you feel yourself to be longstandingly familiar. An impression is more or less fleeting; it is what is *left behind* because the scene has disappeared or changed. Knowledge can coexist with the known; an impression, by contrast, survives alone. However intensely and empirically observed at the moment, an impression later becomes, like a memory, impossible to verify. (Throughout his life Monet complained, in letter after letter, about not being able to complete a painting already begun, because the weather and therefore the subject, the motif, had irredeemably changed.) The new relation between scene and seer was such that now the scene was more fugitive, more chimerical than the seer. And there we find ourselves returned to the same lines by Baudelaire: 'La forme d'une ville . . .'

Suppose we examine the experience offered by a more typical Impressionist painting. In the spring of the same year as 'Le Soleil

Levant' (1872) Monet painted two pictures of a lilac tree in his garden at Argenteuil. One shows the tree on a cloudy day and the other on a sunny day. Lying on the lawn beneath the tree in both pictures are three barely distinguishable figures. (They are thought to be Camille, Monet's first wife, Sisley and Sisley's wife.)

In the overcast picture these figures resemble moths in the lilac shade; in the second, dappled with sunlight, they become almost as invisible as lizards. (What betrays their presence is in fact the viewer's past experience; somehow the viewer distinguishes the mark of a profile with a tiny ear from the other almost identical marks which are only leaves.)

In the overcast picture the flowers of the lilac glow like mauve copper; in the second picture the whole scene is alight, like a newly lit fire: both are animated by a different kind of light energy, there is apparently no longer a trace of decrepitude, everything radiates. Purely optically? Monet would have nodded his head. He was a man of few words. Yet it goes much further.

Before the painted lilac tree you experience something unlike anything felt in front of any earlier painting. The difference is not a question of new optical elements, but of a new relation between what you are seeing and what you have seen. Every spectator can recognize this after a moment's introspection; all that may differ is the personal choice of which paintings reveal the new relation most vividly. There are hundreds of Impressionist paintings, painted during the 1870s, to choose from.

The painted lilac tree is both more precise and more vague than any painting you have seen before. Everything has been more or less sacrificed to the optical precision of its colours and tones. Space, measurement, action (history), identity, all are submerged within the play of light. One must remember here that *painted* light, unlike the real thing, is *not* transparent. The painted light covers, buries, the painted objects, a little like snow covering a landscape. (And the attraction of snow to Monet, the attraction of things being lost without a loss of first-degree reality, probably corresponded to a deep psychological need.) So the new energy *is* optical? Monet was right to nod his head? The painted light dominates everything? No, because all this ignores how the painting actually works on the viewer.

Given the precision and the vagueness, you are forced to re-see the lilacs of your own experience. The precision triggers your visual memory, while the vagueness welcomes and accommodates your memory when it comes. More than that, the uncovered memory of your sense of sight is so acutely evoked, that other appropriate memories of other senses – scent, warmth, dampness, the texture of a dress, the length of an afternoon – are also extracted from the past. (One cannot help but think again of Baudelaire's *Correspondances*.) You fall through a kind of whirlpool of sense memories towards an ever receding moment of pleasure, which is a moment of total re-cognition.

The intensity of this experience can be hallucinating. The fall into and towards the past with its mounting excitement, which, at the same time, is the mirror-opposite of expectation for it is a return, a withdrawal, has something about it which is comparable with an orgasm. Finally everything is simultaneous with and indivisible from the mauve fire of the lilac.

And all this follows – surprisingly – from Monet's affirmation, with slightly different words on several occasions, that 'the motif is for me altogether secondary; what I want to represent is what exists between the motif and me' (1895). What *he* had in mind were colours; what is bound to come into the viewer's mind are memories. If, in a generalized way, Impressionism lends itself to nostalgia (obviously in particular cases the intensity of the memories precludes nostalgia) it is not because we are living a century later, but simply because of the way the paintings always demanded to be read.

What then has changed? Previously the viewer entered into a painting. The frame or its edges were a threshold. A painting created its own time and space which were like an alcove to the world, and their experience, made clearer than it usually is in life, endured changeless and could be visited. This had little to do with the use of

any systematic perspective. It is equally true, say, of a Sung Chinese
landscape. It is more a question of permanence than space. Even
when the scene depicted was momentary – for example, Caravaggio's
'Crucifixion of St Peter' – the momentariness is held within a
continuity: the arduous pulling up of the cross constitutes part of the
permanent assembly point of the painting. Viewers passed one
another in Pierro della Francesca's 'Tent of Solomon' or on
Grunewald's 'Golgotha' or in the bedroom of Rembrandt. But not
in Monet's 'Gare de St Lazare'.

Impressionism closed that time and that space. What an Impressionist painting shows is painted in such a way that *you are compelled to
recognize that it is no longer there*. It is here and here only that
Impressionism is close to photography. You cannot enter an Impressionist painting; instead it extracts your memories. In a sense it is
more active than you – the passive viewer is being born; what you
receive is taken from what happens *between* you and it. No more
within it. The memories extracted are often pleasurable – sunlight,
river banks, poppy fields – yet they are also anguished, because each
viewer remains alone. The viewers are as separate as the brush
strokes. There is no longer a common meeting place.

Let us now return to the sadness in Monet's eyes. Monet believed
that his art was forward-looking and based on a scientific study of
nature. Or at least this is what he began by believing and never
renounced. The degree of sublimation involved in such a belief is
poignantly demonstrated by the story of the painting he made of
Camille on her death bed. She died in 1879, aged thirty-two. Many
years later Monet confessed to his friend Clemenceau that his need
to analyse colours was both the joy and torment of his life. To the
point where, he went on to say, I one day found myself looking at my
beloved wife's dead face and just systematically noting the colours,
according to an automatic reflex!

Without doubt the confession was sincere, yet the evidence of the
painting is quite otherwise. A blizzard of white, grey, purplish paint
blows across the pillows of the bed, a terrible blizzard of loss which

will for ever efface her features. In fact there can be very few death-bed paintings which have been so intensely felt or subjectively expressive.

And yet to this – the consequence of his own act of painting – Monet was apparently blind. The positivistic and scientific claims he made for his art never accorded with its true nature. The same was equally true of his friend Zola. Zola believed that his novels were as objective as laboratory reports. Their real power (as is so evident in *Germinal*) comes from deep – and dark – unconscious feeling. At this period the mantle of progressive positivist enquiry sometimes hid the very same premonition of loss, the same fears, of which, earlier, Baudelaire had been the prophet.

And this explains why *memory* is the unacknowledged axis of all Monet's work. His famous love of the sea (in which he wanted to be buried when he died), of rivers, of water, was perhaps a symbolic way of speaking of tides, sources, recurrence.

In 1896 he returned to paint again one of the cliffs near Dieppe which he had painted on several occasions fourteen years earlier. ('Falaise à Vavengeville', 'Gorge du Petit-Ailly'.) The painting, like many of his works of the same period, is heavily worked, encrusted, and with the minimum of tonal contrast. It reminds you of thick honey. Its concern is no longer the instantaneous scene, as revealed in the light, but rather the slower dissolution of the scene by the light, a development which led towards a more decorative art. Or at least this is the usual 'explanation' based on Monet's own premises.

It seems to me that this painting is about something quite different. Monet worked on it, day after day, believing that he was interpreting the effect of sunlight as it dissolved every detail of grass and shrub into a cloth of honey hung by the sea. But he wasn't, and the painting has really very little to do with sunlight. What he himself was dissolving into the honey cloth were all his previous memories of that cliff, so that it should absorb and contain them all. It is this almost desperate wish to save *all*, which makes it such an amorphous, flat (and yet, if one recognizes it for what it is, touching) image.

And something very similar is happening in Monet's paintings of the water lilies in his garden during the last period of his life (1900–26) at Giverny. In these paintings, endlessly reworked in face of the optically impossible task of combining flowers, reflections, sunlight, underwater reeds, refractions, ripples, surface, depths, the real aim was neither decorative nor optical; it was to preserve everything essential about the garden, which he had made, and which now as an old man he loved more than anything else in the world. The painted lily pond was to be a pond that remembered all.

And here is the crux of the contradiction which Monet as a painter lived. Impressionism closed the time and space in which previously painting had been able to preserve experience. And, as a result of this closure, which of course paralleled and was finally determined by other developments in late-nineteenth-century society, both painter and viewer found themselves more alone than even before, more ridden by the anxiety that their own experience was ephemeral and meaningless. Not even all the charm and beauty of the Ile de France, a Sunday dream of paradise, was a consolation for this.

Only Cézanne understood what was happening. Single-handed, impatient, but sustained by a faith that none of the other Impressionists had, he set himself the monumental task of creating a new form of time and space within the painting, so that finally experience might again be shared.

1980

The *work* of art

———

It has taken me a long time to come to terms with my reactions to Nicos Hadjinicolaou's book *Art History and Class Consciousness*.[1] These reactions are complex for both theoretical reasons and personal ones. Nicos Hadjinicolaou sets out to define the possible practice of a scientific Marxist art history. How necessary it is to produce this initiative, first proposed by Max Raphael nearly fifty years ago!

The exemplary figure of the book, one could almost say its chosen father, is the late Frederick Antal. To see at last this great art historian's work being recognized is a heartening experience; the more so for me personally because I was once an unofficial student of Antal's. He was my teacher, he encouraged me, and a great deal of what I understand by art history I owe to him. Two pupils of the same exemplary master might be likely to make common cause.

Yet I am obliged to argue against this book as a matter of principle. Hadjinicolaou's scholarship is impressive and well used; his arguments are courageously clear. In France, where he lives, he has helped to form with other Marxist colleagues the Association Histoire et Critiques des Arts, which has held several notable and important conferences. My argument will, I hope, be fierce but not dismissive.

Let me first try to summarize the book as fairly as I can. 'The history of all hitherto existing society is the history of class struggles.' Opening with this quotation from the Communist Manifesto, Hadjinicolaou asks: how should this apply to the discipline of art history? He dismisses as over-simple the answers of 'vulgar' Marxism which seek direct evidence of the class struggle in the class origins and political opinions of the painter or, alternatively, in the story the painting tells. He recognizes the relative autonomy of the production-of-pictures (a term which he prefers to *art* because implicit in the latter is a value judgment deriving from bourgeois aesthetics). He argues that pictures have their own ideology – a visual one, which must not be confused with political, economic, colonial and other ideologies.

For him an ideology is the systematic way in which a class or a section of a class projects, disguises and justifies its relations to the world. Ideology is a social/historical element – encompassing like water – from which it is impossible to emerge until classes have been abolished. The most one can do is identify an ideology and relate it to its precise class function.

By *visual ideology* he means the way that a picture makes you see the scene it represents. In some ways it is similar to the category of *style*, yet it is more comprehensive. He regrets totally the ordinary connotations of style. There is no such thing as the style of an artist. Rembrandt has no style, everything depends upon which picture Rembrandt was producing under what circumstances. The way each picture renders experience visible constitutes its visual ideology.

Yet in considering the visible – and this is my gloss, not his – one must remember that according to such a theory of ideology (which owes a lot to Althusser and Poulantzas) we are, in some ways, like blind men who have to learn to allow for and overcome our blindness, but to whom sight itself, whilst class societies continue, cannot be accorded. The negative implication of this becomes crucial as I shall try to show later.

The task of a scientific art history is to examine any picture, to identify its visual ideology and to relate it to the class history of its time, a complex history because classes are never homogeneous and consist of many conflicting groups and interests.

The traditional schools of art history are unscientific. He examines each in turn. The first treats art history as if it were no more than a history of great painters and then explains them in psychological, psychoanalytical or environmental terms. To treat art history as if it were a relay race of geniuses is an individualist illusion, whose origins in the Renaissance corresponded with the phase of the primitive accumulation of private capital. I argue something similar in *Ways of Seeing*. The immense theoretical weakness of my own book is that I do not make clear what relation exists between what I call 'the exception' (the genius) and the normative tradition. It is at this point that work needs to be done. It could well be the theme of a conference.

A second school sees art history as part of the history of ideas (Jacob Burckhardt, Aby Warburg, Panofsky, Saxl). The weakness of this school is to avoid the specificity of the language of painting and to treat it as if it were a hieroglyphic text of ideas. As for the ideas themselves, they tend to be thought of as emanating from a *Zeitgeist* who, in class terms, is immaculate and virgin. I find the criticisms valid.

The third school is that of formalism (Wölfflin, Riegl) which sees art as a history of formal structures. Art, independent of both artists and society, has its own life coiled in its forms. This life develops through stages of youthfulness, maturity, decadence. A painter inherits a style at a certain stage of its spiral development. Like all organic theories applied to highly socialized activities – mistaking *history* for *nature* – the formalist school leads to reactionary conclusions.

Against each of these schools Hadjinicolaou fights as valiantly as David, armed with his sling of *visual ideology*. The proper subject matter of 'art history as an autonomous science' is 'the analysis and explanation of the visual ideologies which have appeared in history'. Only such ideologies can explain art. 'Aesthetic effect' – the enhancement that a work of art offers – 'is none other than the pleasure felt by the observer when he recognizes himself in a picture's visual ideology.' The 'disinterested' emotion of classical aesthetics turns out to be a precise class interest.

Now, within the logic of Althusserian Marxism and its field of ideological formulations, this is an elegant if abstract formula. And it has the advantage of cutting the interminable knotting of the obsolete discourse of bourgeois aesthetics. It may also go some way to explaining the dramatic fluctuations which have occurred in the history of taste: for example, the neglect during centuries after their original fame of painters as different as Franz Hals and El Greco.

The formula would seem to cover retrospectively Antal's practice as an art historian. In his formidable study on Florentine painting – as well as in other works – Antal set out to show in detail how sensitive painting was to economic and ideological developments. Single-handed he disclosed, with all the rigour of a European scholar, a new seam of content in pictures, and through this seam ran the class struggle. But I do not think that he believed that this explained the phenomenon of art. His respect for art was such that he could not forgive, as Marx could not forgive, the history he studied.

And Marx himself posed the question which the formula of visual ideology cannot answer. If art is bound up with certain phases of social historical development, how is it that we still find, for example, classical Greek sculpture beautiful? Hadjinicolaou replies by arguing that what is seen as 'art' changes all the while, that the sculptures seen by the nineteenth century were no longer the same *art* as seen by the third century BC. Yet the question remains: what then is it, about certain works which allows them to 'receive' different interpretations and continue to offer a mystery? (Hadjinicolaou would consider the last word unscientific, but I do not.)

Max Raphael, in his two essays, *The Struggle to Understand Art* and *Towards an Empirical Theory of Art* (1941), began with the same question posed by Marx and proceeded in exactly the opposite direction. Whereas Hadjinicolaou begins with the work as an object and looks for explanations prior to its production and following its production, Raphael believed that the explanation had to be sought in the process of production itself: the power of paintings lay in their *painting*. 'Art and the study of art lead from the work to the process of creation.'

For Raphael, 'The work of art holds man's creative powers in a crystalline suspension from which they can again be transformed into living energies.' Everything therefore depends upon this crystalline suspension, which occurs in history, subject to its conditions, and yet at another level defies those conditions. Raphael shared Marx's doubt; he recognized that historical materialism and its categories as so far developed could only explain certain aspects of art. They could not explain why art is capable of defying the flow of historical process and time. Yet Raphael proposed an empirical – not an idealist – answer.

'Art is an interplay, an equation of three factors – the artist, the world and the means of figuration.' A work of art cannot be considered as either a simple object or simple ideology. 'It is always a synthesis between nature (or history) and the mind, and as such it acquires a certain autonomy vis-à-vis both these elements. This independence seems to be created by man and hence to possess a psychic reality; but in point of fact the process of creation can become an existent only because it is embedded in some concrete material.' Wood, pigment, canvas and so on. When this material has been worked by the artist it becomes like no other existing material: what the image represents (a head and shoulders, say) is pressed, embedded into this material, whilst the material by being worked into a representational image acquires a certain immaterial character. And it is this which gives works of art their incomparable energy. They exist in the same sense that a current exists: it cannot exist without substances and yet it is not in itself a simple substance.

None of this precludes 'visual ideologies'. But Raphael's theory is bound to situate them as one factor amongst others within the act of painting; they cannot form the simple grid through which the artist sees and the spectator looks. Hadjinicolaou wants to avoid the reductionism of vulgar Marxism, yet he replaces it with another because he has no theory about *the act* of painting or *the act* of looking at pictures.

The lack becomes obvious as soon as he considers the visual

ideology of particular pictures. There is nothing in common, he says, between a Louis David portrait painted in 1781, the David painting of 'The Death of Marat' of 1793, and his painting of 'Madame Récamier' of 1800. He has to say this because, if a painting consists of nothing but visual ideology, and these three paintings clearly have different visual ideologies reflecting the history of the Revolution, they cannot have anything in common. David's experience as a painter is irrelevant, and our experience as spectators of David's experience is also irrelevant. And there's the rub. The real experience of looking at paintings has been eliminated.

When Hadjinicolaou goes further and equates the visual ideology of 'Madame Récamier' with that of a portrait by Girodet, one realizes that the visual content to which he is referring goes no deeper than the *mise-en-scène*. The correspondence is at the level of clothes, furniture, hair-style, gesture, pose: at the level, if you wish, of manners and appearances!

Of course, there are paintings which do only function at this level, and his theory may help to fit some of these paintings into history. But no painting of value is about appearances: it is about a totality of which the visible is no more than a code. And in face of such paintings the theory of visual ideology is helpless.

To this Hadjinicolaou would reply that the term 'painting of value' is meaningless. And in a sense I cannot answer his objection because my own theory is weak about the relation existing between the exceptional work and the average. Nevertheless I would beg Hadjinicolaou and his colleagues to consider the possibility that their approach is self-defeating and retrograde, leading back to a reductionism not dissimilar in degree to Zhdanov's and Stalin's.

The refusal of comparative judgments about art ultimately derives from a lack of belief in the purpose of art. One can only qualify X as better than Y if one believes that X achieves more, and this achievement has to be measured in relation to a goal. If paintings have no purpose, have no value other than their promotion of a visual ideology, there is little reason for looking at old pictures except as specialist historians. They become no more than a text for experts to decipher.

The culture of capitalism has reduced paintings, as it reduces everything which is alive, to market commodities, and to an advertisement for other commodities. The new reductionism of revolutionary theory, which we are considering, is in danger of doing something similar. What the one uses as an advertisement (for a prestige, a way of life and the commodities that go with it), the other sees as only a visual ideology of a class. Both eliminate art as a potential model of freedom, which is how artists and the masses have always treated art when it spoke to their needs.

When a painter is working he is aware of the means which are available to him – these include his materials, the style he inherits, the conventions he must obey, his prescribed or freely chosen subject matter – as constituting both an opportunity and a restraint. By working and using the opportunity he becomes conscious of some of its limits. These limits challenge him, at either an artisanal, a magical or an imaginative level. He pushes against one or several of them. According to his character and historical situation, the result of his pushing varies from a barely discernible variation of a convention – changing no more than the individual voice of a singer changes a melody – to a fully original discovery, a breakthrough. Except in the case of the pure hack, who, needless to say, is a modern invention of the market, every painter from palaeolithic times onwards has experienced this will to push. It is intrinsic to the activity of rendering the absent present, of cheating the visible, of making images.

Ideology partly determines the finished result, but it does not determine the energy flowing through the current. And it is with this energy that the spectator identifies. Every image used by a spectator is a *going further* than he could have achieved alone, towards a prey, a Madonna, a sexual pleasure, a landscape, a face, a different world.

'On the margin of what man can do,' wrote Max Raphael, 'there appears that which he cannot or cannot yet do – but which lies at the root of all creativeness.' A revolutionary scientific history of art has to come to terms with such creativeness.

1978

Notes

1 Nicos Hadjinicolaou, *Art History and Class Consciousness*, London, Pluto Press, 1978; Atlantic Highlands, New Jersey, Humanities Press, 1978.

Painting and time

———

Paintings are static. The uniqueness of the experience of looking at a painting repeatedly – over a period of days or years – is that, in the midst of flux, the image remains changeless. Of course the significance of the image may change, as a result of either historical or personal developments, but what is depicted is unchanging: the same milk flowing from the same jug, the waves on the sea with exactly the same formation unbroken, the smile and the face which have not altered.

One might be tempted to say that paintings preserve a moment. Yet on reflection this is obviously untrue. For the moment of a painting, unlike a moment photographed, never existed as such. And so a painting cannot be said to preserve it.

If a painting 'stops' time, it is not, like a photograph, preserving a moment of the past from the supersession of succeeding moments. I am thinking of the image within the frame, the scene which is depicted. Clearly if one considers an artist's life-work or the history of art, one is treating paintings as being, partly, records of the past, evidence of what has been. Yet this historical view, whether used within a Marxist or idealist tradition, has prevented most art experts from considering – or even noticing – the problem of how time exists (or does not) *within* painting.

In early Renaissance art, in paintings from non-European cultures, in certain modern works, the image implies a passage of time. Looking at it, the spectator sees *before*, *during* and *after*. The Chinese sage takes a walk from one tree to another, the carriage runs over the child, the nude descends the staircase. And this of course has been analysed and commented upon. Yet the ensuing image is still static whilst referring to the dynamic world beyond its edges, and this poses the problem of what is the meaning of that strange contrast between static and dynamic. Strange because it is both so flagrant and so taken for granted.

Painters themselves practise a partial answer, even if it remains unformulated in words. When is a painting finished? Not when it finally corresponds to something already existing – like the second shoe of a pair – but when the *foreseen* ideal moment of it being looked at is filled as the painter feels or calculates it should be filled. The long or short process of painting a picture is the process of constructing the future moments when it will be looked at. In reality, despite the painter's ideal, these moments cannot be entirely determined. They can never be entirely filled by the painting. Nevertheless the painting is entirely addressed to these moments.

Whether the painter is a hack or a master makes no difference to the 'address' of the painting. The difference is in what a painting delivers: in how closely the moment of its being looked at, as foreseen by the painter, corresponds to the interests of the actual moments of its being looked at later by other people, when the circumstances surrounding its production (patronage, fashion, ideology) have changed.

Some painters when working have a habit of studying their painting, when it has reached a certain stage, in a mirror. What they then see is the image reversed. If questioned about why this helps, they say that it allows them to see the painting anew, with a fresher eye. What they glimpse in the mirror is something like the content of the future moment to which the painting is being addressed. The mirror allows them to half-forget their own present vision as a painter, and to borrow something of the vision of a future spectator.

What I am saying can perhaps be made sharper by again making a comparison with photographs. Photographs are records of the past. (The importance of the role of the photographer and his subjectivity in this recording does not change the fact that photographs are records.) Paintings are prophecies received from the past, prophecies

about *what the spectator is seeing in front of the painting at that moment.*
Some prophecies are quickly exhausted – the painting loses its
address; others continue.

Cannot the same be said about other art forms? Are not poems,
stories, music addressed to the future in a similar way? Often in their
written forms they are. Nevertheless painting and sculpture are
distinct.

First because, even in their origin, they were not spontaneous
performances. There is a sense in which a poem or story being
spoken, or music being played, emphasizes the *presence* of the speaker
or player. Whereas a visual image, so long as it is not being used as a
mask or disguise, is always a comment on an *absence*. The depiction
comments on the absence of what is being depicted. Visual images,
based on appearances, always speak of *dis*appearance.

Secondly because, whereas verbal and musical language have a
symbolic relation to what they signify, painting and sculpture have a
mimetic one, and this means that their static character is all the more
flagrant.

Stories, poetry, music, belong to time and play within it. The static
visual image denies time within itself. Hence its prophecies across
and through time are the more startling.

We can now ask what would have seemed at first an arbitrary
question. Why is it that the still imagery of painting interests us? What
prevents painting being patently inadequate – just because it is static?

To say that paintings prophesy the experience of their being
looked at, does not answer the question. Rather one has to say that
such prophecy assumes a continuing interest in the static image.
Why, at least until recently, was such an assumption justified? The
conventional answer has been that, because painting is static, it has
the power to establish a visually 'palpable' harmony. Only something
which is still can be so instantaneously composed, and therefore so
complete. A musical composition, since it uses time, is obliged to
have a beginning and an end. A painting only has a beginning and an
end in so far as it is a physical object: within its imagery there is

neither beginning nor end. All this is what was meant by composition, pictorial harmony, significant form and so on.

The terms of this explanation are both too restrictive and too aesthetic. There has to be a virtue in that flagrant contrast: the contrast between the unchanging painted form and the dynamic living model.

What I have so far argued can now help us to locate this virtue. The stillness of the image was symbolic of timelessness. The fact that paintings were prophecies of themselves being looked at had nothing to do with the perspective of modern avant-gardism whereby the future vindicates the misunderstood prophet. What the present and the future had in common, and to which painting through its very stillness referred, was a substratum, a ground of timelessness.

Until the nineteenth century all world cosmologies – even including that of the European Enlightenment – conceived of time as being in one way or another surrounded or infiltrated by timelessness. This timelessness constituted a realm of refuge and appeal. It was prayed to. It was where the dead went. It was intimately but invisibly related to the living world of time through ritual, stories and ethics.

Only during the last hundred years – since the acceptance of the Darwinian theory of evolution – have people lived in a time that contains everything and sweeps everything away, and for which there is no realm of timelessness. In the galactic perspective proposed by such a cosmology, a hundred years are less than an instant. Even in the perspective of the history of man they cannot yet be considered more than an aberration.

When we consider this history of man we are faced by change and recurrence. History *is* change. What recurs are the subjects (and objects) of history: the lives of conscious women and men. What such consciousness works upon is subject to change and is part of the material of history. The character of such consciousness also changes. Yet some of its structures since the birth of language have probably not changed. Consciousness is pegged to certain constants of the human condition: birth, sexual attraction, social cooperation, death. The list is by no means exhaustive: one could add contingencies such as hunger, pleasure, fear.

The nineteenth-century discovery of history as the terrain of human freedom inevitably led to an underestimation of the ineluctable and the continuous. It deposited the continuous within the flow of history – i.e. the continuous was that which had a longer duration than the ephemeral. Previously, the continuous was thought of as the unchanging or timeless existing outside the flow of history.

The language of pictorial art, because it was static, became the language of such timelessness. Yet what it spoke about – unlike geometry – was the sensuous, the particular and the ephemeral. Its mediation between the realm of the timeless and the visible and tangible was more total and poignant than that of any other art. Hence its iconic function, and special power.

We can all still discover through introspection a vestige of this power. Consider a photograph. I have emphasized that photographs, unlike paintings, are records. This is why they only work iconically if the record is personal and there is a continuity within that personal life which reanimates the photograph. But, having said that, photographs *are* static images and they do refer to the ephemeral. Take an old family photograph. And you will find your imagination bifurcating: reconstructing the occasion, finding the date; and, at the same time, grappling with the question: where is that moment now? This bifurcation is a vestige of the response to the iconic power of painting when, cosmologically and philosophically, a realm of timelessness was acceptable.

Needless to say the iconic power of pictorial art was used for diverse social and historical purposes, and the ideological function of art in a class society is part of that class history. Needless to say, too, that during the secularization of art its iconic power was often forgotten. Yet whenever a painting provoked deep emotion, something of this power reasserted itself. Indeed had pictorial art not possessed this power – the power to speak with the language of timelessness about the ephemeral – neither priesthoods nor ruling classes would have had any use for it.

During the second half of the nineteenth century, as the Darwinian proposal about time became more and more dominant in all fields, the mediation of painting between the timeless and the ephemeral became more and more problematic, more and more difficult to sustain. On one hand, the represented moment of the ephemeral became briefer and briefer; the Impressionists set out to represent one hour, the Expressionists an instant of subjective feeling; on the other hand, the Pointillists and Futurists tried to abolish the static and timeless. Other artists like Mondrian insisted upon a geometry from which the ephemeral was banished altogether. Only the Cubists, as painters, sketched out a new cosmology in which relativity might have accorded the timeless a new place. But the Cubist sketch was destroyed by the First World War.

After the war, the Surrealists made the unresolved problematic of time the constant theme of all their work; all Surrealist paintings conjure up the time of dreams; dreams being by then the only realm of the timeless left intact.

During the last forty years transatlantic painting has demonstrated how there is no longer anything left to mediate and therefore anything left to paint. The timeless–as Rothko so intensely showed us – had been emptied. The ephemeral has become the sole category of time. Banalized by pragmatism and consumerism, the ephemeral was excluded from abstract art, or fetishized as short-lived fashion in pop art and its derivatives. The ephemeral, no longer appealing to the timeless, becomes as trivial and instant as the fashionable. Without an acknowledged coexistence of the ephemeral and the timeless, there is nothing of consequence for pictorial art to do. Conceptual art is merely a discussion of this fact.

An acknowledgment of the coexistence of the timeless and the ephemeral need not necessarily imply a return to earlier religious forms. It does, however, presume a radical questioning of something which most recent European thinking, including revolutionary theory, has ignored: the view of time developed by, and inherited from the culture of nineteenth-century European capitalism.

This questioning becomes more urgent if one realizes that the problem of time has not been, and can never be, solved scientifically. On the question of time, science is bound to be solipsist. The problem of time is a problem of choice.

1979

The place of painting

To be visible is to be present: to be absent is to be invisible. A voice, a perfume or something microscopic may be present and yet invisible, not because of its whereabouts but because of its nature. The function of painting is to fill an absence with the simulacrum of a presence. Occasionally a portrait hangs in a room where the sitter is still to be found, but this is exceptional and, from the time of the palaeolithic cave paintings onwards, the main task of painting has been to contradict a law which governs the visible: to make what is not present 'seen'.

Absence is subtended by time and space. And so it is not surprising that painting, which contests absence, has a special relation to them. Thinking about time ['Painting and time', p. 205 above] I asked: why is a static painted image in a dynamic world not absurd? The related question now is: with what kind of space does a painting surround the 'presence' it depicts? To reply by talking about systems of perspective or non-perspective is inadequate. Something happens to space within and around a painted image prior to any perspective system. Every painting begins with the word 'here'. But where is this *here*?

Let us first consider the space surrounding the image, then later the space within it. During the Renaissance architecture was named the Mother of the Arts. This was because the principal visual arts have their being within architectural space. This space differs from natural space (that of the earth, the oceans, the sky) insofar as it encloses, and encloses in such a way as to make a formal distinction between inside and outside.

A hollow tree or a cave can enclose and offer shelter, but they have not been created with this in mind: the shelter they offer is contingent. The tree has died, the waters have subsided and, as a result, man can make use of a *vacated* interior. No alternative space has been proposed to nature's. By contrast, the humblest building makes such a proposal. It proposes a humanly created space which is not only a shelter, but a vantage point from which to break the otherwise endless, regardless extension of natural space. To break it by making the formal distinction: interior/exterior.

Something painted or carved may be placed in a wilderness, far from any human habitation, but, when this happens, the image only works as an appeal to a superhuman power who exists outside time and space. No image can withstand natural or cosmic space alone: the draught extinguishes its flame. As soon as an image is addressed, at least partially to other people, it requires the mediation of the space proposed by a human habitation or a human tomb: it needs to be surrounded by other human work (this 'surrounding' was at the origin of architecture), it needs the assurance of an interior.

It is sufficient to imagine coming across a painted panel by Dürer floating face-up in the middle of the Baltic, or a sculpture by Phidias in the middle of the tundra. Quite apart from any concern one might feel about their physical survival, their meaning would be obliterated, dispersed by the empty space around them; they would speak only of their own abandonment.

Consider the visual arts of nomadic peoples. For obvious functional reasons their art is mostly applied to what they wear or carry. The human body (or occasionally the body of an animal) offers something of the permanence that architecture offers to the settled. The myths of nomads relate how people are *visited*, spirits entering the head and body of the hunter. The body becomes a kind of habitation. Yet without the actual physical space of architecture, the visual signs and symbols of nomadic art rarely become images in the figurative sense. They do not depict the absent. This may also be because the nomad has a different relation to space. Perhaps he has less need of images transporting the far to the near, for he himself lives mysteriously between the two.

The image, then, has its place. And it's not anywhere. If architecture is the Mother of the Arts, it is so because it protects them from endless space by introducing the distinction interior/exterior. The metaphor of *Mother* is well chosen for the body of a real mother does something similar for the imagination of her child.

Let us now look at the space within an image. As soon as a painting is addressed principally to other human beings (as perhaps the cave paintings were not) it is conceived of as a framed image. The picture frame is fairly recent but the regular format of a painted surface – be it rectangular, circular, oval – acts as a frame. The image has edges and, being geometric, they *contain* it.

And from this arises the need for composition. Composition begins with a simple question: where in the given format is it best to put this? And this, and this. The laws of composition change from epoch to epoch, but the act of composing is always the act of placing forms within a contained, separate space. To compose is to arrange an interior.

Yet what does it mean here to arrange an interior? Paintings depict the boundless world. Even when an event depicted occurs within an interior – as in one of Saenredam's churches – the people depicted have come from outside. A still life is what has been brought in, through the door. Most paintings depict women, the sky, the earth, the sun, wild animals, towns, rivers, the sea, flowers, heroes, the darkness of the night, gods, mountains, trees, grass. When painted, all are arranged as if they constituted an interior, as if they were side by side with the intimate. To paint is to bring inside – doubly: into the inhabited space around the image and into the frame. The paradox of painting is that it invites the spectator into its room to look at the world beyond.

Hence the terms of its fundamental dialectic. To paint is to bring inside: yet what is brought inside is what is far away. The terms of this contradiction are never settled once and for all. At different historical moments, in different cultures, the language of painting has favoured one term more than the other. For example, the language of the

Byzantine tradition from the fourth to the eighth century, or of the Italian Quattrocento, favoured the 'bringing inside'; and by contrast, the language of the Mannerist school of the sixteenth century, or of early Romanticism, favoured 'the boundless'.

During one period the given ideological explanations of the world seem largely convincing and then the *will* of paintings is to include; during another the given explanations seem to be lies, and then the will of painting is to search for the open truth in the boundless or cosmic. Yet whatever it wills, the act of painting necessarily brings about an inclusion.

In Turner's work, for instance, we can distinctly see how the will changed. In his landscapes painted under the influence of Claude Lorraine in the 1820s entire panoramas are brought inside. Ten, twenty years later – in pictures like 'Snow-Storm Steam-Boat off Harbour-Mouth' (even the title is revealing!) – Turner was to struggle more totally than any other painter before him, to make the image boundless, to destroy the home, the habitation.

So painting has its place. But it also has its reason. Its interiorization of the world – with more or less confidence – corresponds to a human need.

The visible was always and still remains our principal source of information about the world. Through the visible we orientate ourselves. Even perceptions coming from other senses, we translate into visual terms. (Vertigo is a pathological example: originating in the ear, we experience it as a visual, spatial confusion.) It is thanks to the visible that we recognize space as the precondition for physical existence. The visible brings the world to us. But at the same time it reminds us ceaselessly that it is a world in which we risk to be lost. The visible with its space also takes the world away from us. Nothing is more two-faced.

The visible implies an eye. It is the stuff of the relation between seen and seer. Yet the seer, when human, is conscious of what his eye cannot and will never see because of time and distance. The visible both includes him (because he sees) and excludes him (because he is not omnipresent). The visible consists for him of the seen which, even when it is threatening, confirms his existence, and of the unseen which defies that existence. The desire to *have seen* (the ocean, the desert, the aurora borealis) has a deep ontological basis.

To this human ambiguity of the visible one then has to add the visual experience of absence, whereby we no longer see what we saw. We face a *dis*-appearance. And a struggle ensues to prevent what has disappeared falling into the negation of the unseen, defying our existence.

Thus the visible produces faith in the reality of the invisible, and provokes the development of an inner eye which retains, and assembles and arranges as if an interior, as if what has been seen will be forever partly protected against the ambush of space, which is absence. Thus a phenomenological experience of space supports the special nature of the painted image. But if this were its sole support, the determination of painting would be nostalgic and this is only partly true. There is also revelation.

Both life itself and the visible owe their existence to light. Before there was life, nothing was seen – unless by God. Neither the optical explanation of visual perception nor the evolutionist theory of the slow, hazardous development of the eye in response to the stimulus of light – neither of these dissolves the enigma which surrounds the fact that, at a certain moment, the visible was born, at a certain moment appearances were revealed as appearances. As a response to this enigma, the first faculty accredited to the most important gods was that of sight: an eye, often an all-seeing eye. Then it could be said: *the visible exists because it has already been seen.*

The Genesis story is consistent with this. The first thing God created was light. After every subsequent act of creation, the light allowed him to see that what he had created was good. At the end of the sixth day he saw everything that he had made and, behold, it was very good. One does not need to get involved here with the argument between Darwinists and Creationists. What is profound about the

Genesis story is that it acknowledges the mystery of the visible's coming into being. This mystery is sustained and repeated in the almost universal experience of what is now called natural beauty. Whatever normative categories are employed, such beauty is always experienced as a form of revelation. It speaks.

What happens when it speaks? The Sung masters, Ovid, Meister Eckhart, Izaak Walton, Rimbaud, Tolstoi . . . what artist or thinker has not testified to these moments? The testimony varies according to the character and the historical time. But the mechanism of the moment remains the same.

A rose is a rose is a rose. What happens is that appearance and significance, look and meaning, become identical, whereas usually they are separate and have to be brought together by the one who is looking and questioning. A revelation is this fusion.

And the fusion changes one's spatial sense or, rather, changes one's sense of Being in space. The boundlessly visible, as we have noted, includes but also excludes man. He sees, and he sees that he is being continually abandoned. Appearances belong to the boundless space of the visible. With his inner eye man also experiences the space of his own imagination and reflection. (The relation between the two spaces, whether they are not perhaps different forms of the same thing, is another subject.) Normally it is within the protection of his inner space that man places, retains, cultivates, lets run wild or constructs *meaning*. At the moment of revelation when appearance and meaning become identical, the space of physics and the seer's inner space coincide: momentarily and exceptionally she or he *achieves an equality with the visible*. To lose all sense of exclusion; to be at the centre.

The way that all painting, irrespective of its epoch or tradition, interiorizes, brings inside, arranges as a home the visible, is far more than a simple complement to the enclosing act of architecture; it is a way of safeguarding the experiences of memory and revelation which are man's only defences against that boundless space which otherwise continually threatens to separate and marginalize him.

What is painted survives within the shelter of the painting, within the shelter of the having-been-seen. The *home* of a true painting is this shelter.

1982

On visibility

——

To look:
at everything which overflows the outline, the contour, the category, the name of what it is.

All appearances are continually changing one another: visually everything is interdependent. Looking is submitting the sense of sight to the experience of that interdependence. To look *for* something (a pin that has dropped) is the opposite of this looking. Visibility is a quality of light. Colours are the faces of light. This is why looking is to recognize, enter a whole. Identity of an object or colour or form is what visibility *reveals*: it is a conclusion of visibility; but it has nothing to do with the *process* of visibility which is as uncontainable, which is as much a form of energy as light itself. Light which is the source of all life. The visible is a feature of that life; it cannot exist without it. In a dead universe nothing is visible.

Visibility is a form of growth.

Aim: to see the appearance of a thing (even an inanimate thing) as a stage in its growth – or as a stage in a growth of which it is part. To see its visibility as a kind of flowering.

Clouds gather visibility, and then disperse into invisibility. All appearances are of the nature of clouds.

The hyacinth grows into visibility. But so does the garnet or sapphire.

Not to say that *behind* appearances is the truth, the Platonic way. It is very possible that visibility *is* the truth and that what lies outside visibility are only the 'traces' of what has been or will become visible.

To look at light.

To recognize that outlines are an invention.

To transcend scale: a few blades of grass as large as the sky looks: the ant visibly coexistent with the mountain: in its *visibility* comparable with the mountain. Perhaps that's the point. The fact is visibility (inseparable from light) is greater than its categories of measurement (small, big, distant, near, dark, light, blue, yellow, etc.).

To look is to rediscover, over and beyond these measurements, the primacy of visibility itself.

The eye receiving.

But also the eye intercepting. The eye intercepts the continual intercourse between light and the surfaces which reflect and absorb it. Separate objects are like isolated words. Meaning is only to be found in the relation between them. What is the meaning to be found in the visible? A form of energy, continually transforming itself.

Exercise.

Look:

White transparent curtains across the window.

Light coming from the right.

Shadows of folds, hanging folds, darker than clouds.

Suddenly sunlight.

The window frames now cast shadows across the curtains.

The shadows are convoluted following the folds: the window frames are straight and rectangular.

Between the curtains and the window: a space like the lines on which music is written: but three-dimensional, and the notes of light, rather than sound. The space between the rectangular window frames and their shadows convoluted because the curtains hang in folds half-transparently.

Looking through the curtain, a cloud crossing the sky, its upper edge yellowy silver and undulating – with almost exactly the same rhythm as the convolutions of the shadows (now disappeared because the sun

has gone in). The cloud is moving fast. Almost at gale speed.
On the houses opposite the wrought-iron balconies are absolutely still. For an instant the sun comes out again.

Snake shadow – gone.

Clouds moving.

Sea swelling.

Charlie's van comes back.

A heavy swell at sea.

A memory. Visual.

Tall cliffs. White. With straight horizontal lines of dark flashing grey flint. Between the lines centuries of chalk deposit.
The fringe of the cliffs against the sky, grass hanging over.
The thickness of the turf in relation to the height of the cliffs like the thickness of an animal's fur. At the height of the grass gulls wheeling. Figures of eight cut off by the cliff. The shadows of the cliffs on the sea (the tide is in, almost up to the cliffs.)
The shadow of the cliffs on the sea, lying on the sea, from the water's edge to eighty metres out: the length of the coast. In the shadow of the cliff the sea is almost brown.
Further out, just beyond the shadow of the grass fringe, the sea is a green mixed with a little white. The green that oxidized copper goes, but with sun. As I write this very sentence, the sun comes out above Noel Road, casts the shadow of the window frame on the curtains, the curtains stir in the window, my pen casts a shadow on this paper and the sun goes in.

To look:
at everything which overflows the outline, the contour, the category, the name of what it is.

1977

7

THE UNMADE ROAD

Redder every day

———

Redder every day
the leaves of the pear trees.
Tell me what is bleeding.
Not summer
for summer left early.
Not the village
for the village though drunk on its road
has not fallen.
Not my heart
for my heart bleeds no more
than the arnica flower.

Nobody has died this month
or been fortunate enough
to receive a foreign work-permit.
We fed with soup
let sleep in the barn
no more thoughts of suicide
than is normal in November.
Tell me what is bleeding
you who see in the dark.

Hands of the world
amputated by profit
bleed in
streets of bloodsheds.

1985

Mayakovsky: his language and his death
[*with Anya Bostock*]

———

Jackals used to creep right up to the house. They moved in large packs and howled terribly. Their howling was most unpleasant and frightening. It was there that I first heard those wild piercing howls. The children could not sleep at night and I used to reassure them, 'Don't be afraid, we have good dogs, they won't let them come near.'

Thus Mayakovsky's mother described the forest in Georgia, Russia, where Vladimir and his sisters were brought up. The description is a reminder at the start that the world into which Mayakovsky was born was very different from our own.

When a man in good health commits suicide it is, finally, because there is no one who understands him. After his death the incomprehension often continues because the living insist on interpreting and using his story to suit their own purposes. In this way the ultimate protest against incomprehension goes unheard after all.

If we wish to understand the meaning of Mayakovsky's example – and it is an example central to any thinking about the relation between revolutionary politics and poetry – we have to work on that meaning. A meaning embodied both in his poetry and in the destiny of his life, and death.

Let us begin simply. Outside Russia, Mayakovsky is known as a romantic political legend rather than as a poet. This is because his poetry has so far proved very hard to translate. This difficulty has encouraged readers to return to the old half-truth that great poetry is untranslatable. And so the story of Mayakovsky's life – his avant-garde Futurist youth, his commitment to the Revolution in 1917, his complete self-identification as poet with the Soviet state, his role during ten years as poetic orator and proselytizer, his apparently sudden despair and suicide at the age of 36 – all this becomes abstract because the stuff of his poetry, which, in Mayakovsky's case, *was* the stuff of his life, is missing. Everything began for Mayakovsky with the language he used, and we need to appreciate this even if we cannot read Russian. Mayakovsky's story and tragedy concern the special historical relation which existed between him and the Russian language. To say this is not to depoliticize his example but to recognize its specificity.

Three factors about the Russian language.

1. During the nineteenth century the distinction between spoken and written Russian was far less marked than in any Western European country. Although the majority were illiterate, the written Russian language had not yet been expropriated and transformed to express the exclusive interests and tastes of the ruling class. But by the end of the century a differentiation between the language of the people and the new urban middle class was beginning to become apparent. Mayakovsky was opposed to this 'emasculation of the language'. Nevertheless it was still possible and even natural for a Russian poet to believe that he could be the inheritor of a living popular language. It was not mere personal arrogance which made Mayakovsky believe that he could speak with the voice of Russia, and when he compared himself with Pushkin it was not to bracket two isolated geniuses but two poets of a language which might still belong to an entire nation.

2. Because Russian is an inflected and highly accented language, it is especially rich in rhymes and especially rhythmical. This helps to explain why Russian poetry is so widely known by heart. Russian poetry when read out loud, and particularly Mayakovsky's, is nearer to rock than to Milton. Listen to Mayakovsky himself:

Where this basic dull roar of a rhythm comes from is a mystery. In my case it's all kinds of repetitions in my mind of noises, rocking motions, or in fact of any phenomenon with which I can associate a sound. The sound of the sea, endlessly repeated, can provide my rhythm, or a servant who slams the door every morning, recurring and intertwining with itself, trailing through my consciousness; or even the rotation of the earth, which in my case, as in a shop full of visual aids, gives way to, and inextricably connects with the whistle of a high wind.[1]

These rhythmic and mnemonic qualities of Mayakovsky's Russian are not, however, at the expense of content. The rhythmic sounds combine whilst their sense separates with extraordinary precision. The regularity of the sound reassures whilst the sharp, unexpected sense shocks. Russian is also a language which lends itself easily, through the addition of prefixes and suffixes, to the invention of new words whose meaning is nevertheless quite clear. All this offers opportunities to the poet as virtuoso: the poet as musician, or the poet as acrobat or juggler. A trapeze artist can bring tears to the eyes more directly than a tragedian.

3. After the Revolution, as a result of the extensive government literacy campaign, every Soviet writer was more or less aware that a vast new reading public was being created. Industrialization was to enlarge the proletariat and the new proletarians would be 'virgin' readers, in the sense that they had not previously been corrupted by purely commercial reading matter. It was possible to think, without unnecessary rhetoric, of the revolutionary class claiming and using the written word as a revolutionary right. Thus the advent of a literate proletariat might enrich and extend written language in the USSR instead of impoverishing it as had happened under capitalism in the West. For Mayakovsky after 1917 this was a fundamental article of faith. Consequently he could believe that the formal innovations of his poetry were a form of political action. When he worked inventing slogans for the government's propaganda agency, ROSTA, when he toured the Soviet Union giving unprecedented public poetry readings to large audiences of workers, he believed that by way of his words he would actually introduce new turns of phrase, and thus new concepts, into the workers' language. These public readings (although as the years went by he found them more and more exhausting) were probably among the few occasions when life really

appeared to confirm the justice of his own self-appointed role. His words were understood by his audiences. Perhaps the underlying sense sometimes escaped them, but there in the context of his reading and their listening this did not seem to matter as it seemed to matter in the interminable arguments he was forced to have with editors and literary officials: there the audience, or a large part of it, seemed to sense that his originality belonged to the originality of the Revolution itself. Most Russians read poetry like a litany; Mayakovsky read like a sailor shouting through a megaphone to another ship in a heavy sea.

Thus the Russian language at that moment in history. If we call it a language *demanding poetry* it is not an exaggerated figure of speech, but an attempt to synthesize in a few words a precise historical situation. But what of the other term of the relation, Mayakovsky the poet? What kind of poet was he? He remains too original to be easily defined by comparison with other poets, but perhaps, however crudely, we can begin to define him as a poet by examining his own view of poetry, always remembering that such a definition is made without the pressures to which he was subject throughout his life: pressures in which subjective and historical elements were inseparable.

This is how, in his autobiographical notes, he describes becoming a poet:

Today I wrote a poem. Or to be exact: fragments of one. Not good. Unprintable. 'Night'. Sretensky Boulevard. I read the poem to Burlyuk. I added: written by a friend. David stopped and looked at me. 'You wrote it yourself!' he exclaimed. 'You're a genius!' I was happy at this marvellous and undeserved praise. And so I steeped myself in poetry. That evening, quite unexpectedly, I became a poet.

The tone is laconic. Nevertheless he is saying that he became a poet because he was called upon to become one. Obviously the potential of his genius already existed. And would probably have been released in any case. But his temperament insisted that the release should come *through a demand*.

Later, he continually refers to poetry as something which must meet 'a social command'. The poem is a direct response to that command. One of the things which his early, marvellously flamboyant Futurist poetry has in common with his later political poetry is its form of address. By which we mean the poet's stance towards the *you* being addressed. The *you* may be a woman, God, a party official, but the way of presenting the poet's life to the power being addressed remains similar. The *you* is not to be found in the life of the *I*. Poetry is the making of poetic sense of the poet's life for the use of another. One might say that this is more or less true of all poetry. But in Mayakovsky's case the notion that poetry is a kind of exchange *acting between* the poet's life and the demands of other lives is specially developed. In this idea is implanted the principle that the poetry will be justified or not by its reception. And here we touch upon one of the important conflicts in Mayakovsky's life as a poet. Its starting point is the existence of language as the primary fact; its finishing point is the judgment of others towards his use of that language in a set of particular circumstances. He took language upon himself as though it were his own body, but he depended upon others to decide whether or not that body had the right to exist.

One of Mayakovsky's favourite comparisons is between the production of poetry and industrial factory production. To explain this metaphor just in terms of a Futurist admiration for modern technology would be to miss the point. Poetry for Mayakovsky was a question of processing or transforming experience. He speaks of the poet's experience as the *raw material* for poetry, the finished product being the poem which will answer the social command.

Only the presence of rigorously thought-out preliminary work gives me the time to finish anything, since my normal output of work in progress is eight to ten lines a day.

A poet regards every meeting, every signpost, every event in whatever circumstances simply as material to be shaped into words.

What he means there by preliminary work is the inventing and storing of rhymes, images, lines which will later be useful. The 'manufacture' of the poem, as he explains with unique frankness in *How Are Verses Made?*, goes through several stages. First there is the preliminary work: the casting into words of experience and the storing of these relatively short word-units.

In about 1913, when I was returning from Saratov to Moscow, so as to prove my devotion to a certain female companion, I told her that I was 'not a man, but a cloud in trousers'. When I'd said it, I immediately thought it could be used in a poem . . . Two years later I needed 'a cloud in trousers' for the title of a whole long poem.

Then comes the realization that there is 'a social command' for a poem on a particular theme. The need behind the command must be fully understood by the poet. Finally comes the composition of the poem in accordance with the need. Some of what has been cast into words can now be used to its ideal maximum. But this requires trial and retrial. When it is at last right, it acquires explosive power.

> Comrade tax inspector,
>   on my honour,
> A rhyme
>   costs the poet
>   a sou or two.
> If you'll allow the metaphor,
>   a rhyme is
>   a barrel.
> A barrel of dynamite.
>   The line is the fuse.
> When the fuse burns up
>   the barrel explodes.
> And the city blows into the air:
>   that's the stanza.
> What is the price tariff
>   for rhymes
> Which aim straight
>   and kill outright?
> It could be that
>   only five undiscovered rhymes
>   are left

In all the world
      and those perhaps in Venezuela.
The trail leads me
      into cold and hot climates.
I plunge,
     entangled in advances and loans.
Citizen,
     make allowance for the cost of the
     fare!
Poetry – all of it! –
      is a voyage into the unknown.
Poetry
     is like mining for radium.
The output an ounce
     the labour a year.
For the sake of a single word
       you must process
Thousands of tons
     of verbal ore.
Compare the flash-to-ashes
      of such a word
With the slow combustion
     of the ones left in their natural
     state!
Such a word
     sets in motion
Thousands of years
     and the hearts of millions.[2]

When the poem is written, it needs to be read. By readers themselves, but also by the poet out loud. At his public readings Mayakovsky was a man showing what the things he had made could do: he was like a driver or test pilot – except that his performance with the poems took place, not on the ground or in the air, but in the minds of his listeners.

We should not, however, be deceived, by Mayakovsky's desire to rationalize the making of verses, into believing that there was no mystery in the process for him. His poetic vision was passionate, and continually rocked by his own astonishment.

> The universe sleeps
> And its gigantic ear
> Full of ticks
> That are stars
> Is now laid on its paw.

Yet he saw poetry as an act of exchange, an act of translation whose purpose was to make the poet's experience usable by others. He believed in an alchemy of language; in the act of writing the miraculous transformation occurred. When he wrote about Yessenin's suicide in 1925 he was unable to give any convincing reason why Yessenin should have gone on living – although he judged that this was what the social command required. It is early in the poem that he makes his real point: if only there had been ink in the hotel bedroom where Yessenin cut his wrists and hanged himself, if only he had been able to *write*, he could have gone on living. To write was simultaneously to come into one's own and to join others.

In the same poem Mayakovsky speaks of the Russian people 'in whom our language lives and breathes', and he castigates all timid, academic usage of this language. (Yessenin, he says, would have told the conformist orators at his funeral to stuff their funeral orations up their arse.) He admits that it is a difficult time for writers. But what time hasn't been? he asks. And then he writes:

> Words are
> > the commanders
> > > of mankind's forces.
> March!
> > and behind us
> > > time
> > > > explodes like a landmine.
> To the past
> > we offer
> > > only the streaming tresses
> Of our hair
> > tangled
> > > by the wind.[3]

To clarify what we are saying, it may be helpful to compare Mayakovsky with another writer. Yannis Ritsos, the contemporary Greek poet, is like Mayakovsky an essentially political poet: he is also a Communist. Yet despite their common political commitment, Ritsos is precisely the opposite kind of poet to Mayakovsky. It is not from the act of writing or processing words that Ritsos's poetry is born. His poetry appears as the *consequence* of a fundamental decision which in itself has nothing to do with poetry. Far from being the finished product of a complicated production process, Ritsos's poetry seems like a by-product. One has the impression that his poems exist for him *before* their accumulation of words: they are the precipitate of an attitude, a decision already taken. It is not by his poems that he proves his political solidarity, but the other way round: on account of his political attitude, certain events offer their poetic face.

> *Saturday 11 a.m.*
> The women gather the clothes from
>   the clothes line.
> The landlady stands in the doorway
>   of the yard.
> One holds a suitcase.
> The other has a black hat on.
> The dead pay no rent.
> They have disconnected Helen's
>   telephone.
> The doughnut man shouts on
>   purpose: 'Doughnuts,
> warm doughnuts.' The young
> violinist at the window –
> 'warm zero-round doughnuts,'
> he says.
> He throws his violin down on the
>   sidewalk.
> The parrot looks over the baker's
>   shoulder.
> The landlady tinkles her keys.
> The three women go in, shut the
>   door.[4]

234

There can be no question of quoting Ritsos against Mayakovsky, or vice versa. They are different kinds of poets writing in different circumstances. Ritsos's choice, of which his poetry (given his poetic genius) is the by-product, is a choice of opposition and resistance. Mayakovsky considered that it was his political duty to celebrate and affirm. One form of poetry is public, the other clandestine. Contrary, however, to what one may expect, the former may be the more solitary.

To return now to Mayakovsky. Before the Revolution and during its first years, one can say that the Russian language was *demanding* poetry on a mass scale; it was seeking its own national poets. It is impossible to know whether Mayakovsky's genius was actually formed by this demand or only developed by it. But the coincidence between his genius and the state of the language at that moment is crucial to his life's work, and perhaps to his death. It was a coincidence which lasted only for a certain time.

From the period of NEP onwards, the language of the Revolution began to change. At first the change must have been almost imperceptible – except to a poet-performer like Mayakovsky. Gradually words were ceasing to mean exactly what they said. (Lenin's will-to-truthfulness was exceptional and his death, in this respect as in others, now appears as a turning point.) Words began to hide as much as they signified. They became double-faced: one face referring to theory, the other to practice. For example the word *Soviet* became a designation of citizenship and a source of patriotic pride: only in theory did it still refer to a particular form of proletarian democracy. The 'virgin' reading public became, to a large degree, a reading public that was deceived.

Mayakovsky was dead before the devaluation of the Russian language had extended very far, but already in the last years of his life, in works like *Good*, *The Bedbug*, *The Bath-house* – all of which were badly received – his vision became increasingly satirical. Words were loaded with a meaning that was no longer just or true. Listen to the Producer in the third act of *The Bath-house*:

All right now, all the men on stage. Kneel down on one knee and hunch your shoulders, you've got to look enslaved, right? Hack away there with your imaginary picks at the imaginary coal. Gloomier there, gloomier, you're being oppressed by dark forces.

You there, you're Capital. Stand over here, Comrade Capital. You're going to do us a little dance impersonating Class Rule . . .

The women on stage now. You'll be Liberty, you've got the right manners for it. You can be Equality, doesn't matter who acts that does it? And you're Fraternity, dear, you're not likely to arouse any other feeling anyway. Ready? Go! Infect the imaginary masses with your imaginary enthusiasm! That's it! That's it!

Meanwhile, what was happening to Mayakovsky himself? A woman he was in love with had abandoned him. His work was being subjected to more and more severe criticism, on the grounds that its spirit was far from the working class. The doctors had told him that he had damaged his vocal chords irrevocably by straining his voice when reading. He had dissolved his own avant-garde group (LEF, renamed REF) and had joined the most official, 'majority' association of writers, which had always been highly critical of him (RAPP): as a result, he was snubbed by them and treated as a renegade by his former friends. A retrospective exhibition of his life's work – poems, plays, posters, films – failed to make the impact he had hoped. He was thirty-seven, the same age as Pushkin when Pushkin was killed. Pushkin had incontestably been the founder of the language of modern Russian poetry. Yet what was happening to the language of revolutionary poetry which Mayakovsky had once believed in?

If a writer sees his life as raw material waiting to enter language, if he is continually involved in processing his own experience, if he sees poetry primarily as a form of exchange, there is a danger that, when he is deprived of an immediate audience, he will conclude that his life *has been used up*. He will see only its fragments strewn across the years – as if, after all, he had been torn to pieces by the jackals. 'Don't be afraid, we have good dogs, they won't let them come near.' The promise was broken. They came.   1975

Notes

1   V. V. Mayakovsky, *How Are Verses Made?*, London, Cape, 1970; New York Grossman, 1970.
2   This is a literal translation by the authors.
3   Mayakovsky, *op. cit.*
4   Yannis Ritsos, *Gestures*, trans. Nikos Stangos, London, Cape Goliard, 1971; New York, Grossman, 1970.

The secretary of Death

The day before yesterday a close friend of mine killed himself by blowing his brains out. Today in my head his death assembles a thousand memories of his life, which I now see, not perhaps more clearly, but more truthfully than before. Life being lived always tends to simplify; hence one of the reasons why a certain kind of story is told to contest the opportunism of these simplifications. In one sense a story does not go anywhere, it just *is* – as my departed friend now *is* in my imagination.

These simple thoughts are relevant to García Márquez's new book, *Chronicle of a Death Foretold*, whether one considers its story or its form of storytelling. I want principally to consider the latter because García Márquez is an exemplary storyteller in a tradition which to us in our NATO culture has become rare. By understanding better García Márquez's storytelling we can perhaps learn more about most people in the world and even about our own future, when our culture falls apart.

Like his others, this story is set somewhere roundabout Colombia, the country where García Márquez was born. It is short, a mere 120 pages. Like *The Autumn of the Patriarch*, this one is about a death, a violent one.

The narrative, told with the hindsight of today, describes what happened between 5.30 and 6.30 one morning, in February a quarter of a century ago, when Santiago Nasar, of Arab descent, is knifed to death while hung over after the previous night's wedding revels and after the bride had been discovered by the sad groom not to have been a virgin; knifed to death against one of the two doors of his own house which inadvertently his mother, usually so clairvoyant about her son's dreams, had ordered to be bolted, thus cutting off his only means of escape from the two brothers Vicario with their pig-slaughtering knives who had been forced by honour (notwithstanding all their attempts to let their victim be forewarned and thus to escape) to kill the man whom in a moment of truthfulness or aberration – who knows? – their sister Angela, the bride, had just named that night as the one who had deflowered her.

The story is more austere than any of his others. It is written as though by an investigator who is anxious to find out the simplest truth. But because it is not a Protestant Western book the model for the investigator is not that of a detective but rather that of a hieroglyphist. The lines of enquiry are centred, like the petals of a daisy, round their capitulum, which is the moment of the assassination against the door. Everything is centred on that instant when Santiago Nasar, twenty-one years old, ranch-owner, falconer, cries out for his mother for the last terrible time.

And with all his short, slender petals of enquiry, what is it that García Márquez hopes to find out? Never psychological motivation. Never legal guilt or innocence. Never a process of cause and effect. Never the pathology of drunkenness or sexuality. Never a story of success or failure. He simply wants to establish what *may* have happened that early morning in the public square when the town was already awake and out in the streets: because if he establishes this and if he allows us, his listeners, to grasp what may have happened, it is possible that the destiny of all those involved – Nasar, his fiancée, his mother, the two brothers reluctantly avenging the honour of their sister, the bride and bridegroom – will be mounted (like a stone in a ring) in all its mystery. Detective stories set out to solve mysteries. The *Chronicle of a Death Foretold* sets out to preserve one.

For years we couldn't talk about anything else. Our daily conduct, dominated then by so many linear habits, had suddenly begun to spin around a single common anxiety. The cocks of dawn would catch us trying to give order to the chain of many chance events that had made absurdity possible, and it was obvious that we weren't doing it from an urge to clear up mysteries but because none of us could go on living without an exact knowledge of the place and the mission assigned to us by fate.

Of my contemporaries, García Márquez is the one I admire the most. Perhaps this is not disinterested. In some countries critics have compared my own recent fiction with his and it is true that I see him, not as a critic but as a colleague in an art of storytelling.

But which art? García Márquez sets out to preserve a mystery. Does this mean that he is an obscurantist, profiting from, or enjoying, mystification for its own sake? Such an accusation would be absurd; he is also a highly professional journalist committed to exposing ideological myths and to the struggle for the democratic right to know. He speaks of 'the mission assigned to us by fate'. Yet undoubtedly his sense of history is Marxist. What is the form and tradition of storytelling which reconciles what we have been taught to think of as such irreconcilable contradictions?

A moment's reflection shows that any story drawn from life begins, for the storyteller, with its end. The story of Dick Whittington becomes that story when he has at last become mayor of London. The story of Romeo and Juliet first begins as a story after they are dead. Most, if not all, stories begin with the death of the principal protagonist. It is in this sense that one can say that storytellers are Death's secretaries. It is Death who hands them the file. The file is full of sheets of uniformly black paper but they have eyes for reading them and from this file they construct a story for the living. Here the question of invention, so much insisted upon by certain schools of modern critics and professors, becomes patently absurd. All that the storyteller needs or has is the capacity to read what is written in black.

I think of Rembrandt's painting in The Hague of the blind Homer; it is the supreme image of such a secretary. And I like to think of a photograph of Gabriel García Márquez, with his bon vivant's face and scurrilous energy, beside it. There is nothing pretentious in this comparison: we Death's secretaries all carry the same sense of duty, the same oblique shame (we have survived, the best have departed) and the same obscure pride which belongs to us personally no more than do the stories we tell. Yes, I like to think of that photo beside that painting.

It is significant that this book is called a chronicle. The tradition of storytelling of which I am speaking has little to do with that of the *novel*. The chronicle is public and the novel is private. The chronicle, like the epic poem, retells more memorably what is already generally known; the novel, by contrast, reveals what is secret in a family of private lives. The novelist surreptitiously beckons the reader into the private home and there, their fingers to their lips, they watch together. The chronicler tells his story in the market-place and competes with the clamour of all the other vendors: his occasional triumph is to create a silence around his words.

Thus novelist and storyteller are distinct and it is obvious that they both belong to different historical periods, confronting or collaborating with different ruling classes. Yet there is an internal distinction too which concerns the tense of the narrative. Novels begin with the drama of hope: their protagonists' hopes for their lives. The novel as a form does not lend itself to the telling of the lives of the absolutely underprivileged. (Dickens *rescues* the most destitute of his characters so that they can become characters in a novel.) And so the tenses of the novel, or, rather, the tenses of the reader's heart as he reads a novel, are those of the future or the conditional. Novels are about Becoming.

The tense of the chronicle, the narrative of the storyteller, is the historic present. The story refers insistently to what is over but it refers to it in such a way that, although it is over, it can be retained. This retaining is not so much a question of recollection as of coexistence, the past with the present. Epic chronicles are about Being. The capitulum of Santiago Nasar's assassination, that moment at 6.30 a.m. twenty-five years ago, is still present.

Perhaps this makes the story sound portentous. Those who know García Márquez's writings will find this hard to believe and they are right. Indeed, of all his books, this one is the most everyday, the most ordinary. All the characters are small-town petit-bourgeois. Their daily preoccupations are short-sighted and trivial. There is not a single noble appeal in the book. When he goes to meet his death, Santiago Nasar (who in my opinion did not seduce Angela and was to die absurdly for an act that he never committed) is still calculating with a kind of idle curiosity – in a few seconds' time this idleness will acquire the quality of a paradise – is still calculating exactly how much the previous night's wedding celebrations have cost the bridegroom.

Nevertheless everyone in the story (in life was it different?) has another dimension, a dignity which has nothing to do with power, but with the way they live their fate. This implies neither passivity nor the abnegation of choice. The notion of fate confuses the western novelist only because he conceives of it as existing in the same time as free will. It exists in a different time where, quite literally, all has been said and done.

To put it now very simply: this is a story about people and told to people who still believe that life is a story. Nobody chooses their story. Yet, by definition, a story whether lived or heard has a meaning. To ask whether this meaning is objective or subjective is already to move outside the circle of listeners. To ask what the meaning is is to ask for the unsayable. Nevertheless the faith in meaning promises one thing: meaning has to be shareable. Such stories begin with mortality but they never end with solitude. When Santiago Nasar cries for the last time for his mother he is suffering a terrible loneliness. For more than twenty years Angela will live alone with her secret and her memories. Finally her wronged and unhappy husband who has received from her thousands of letters, not one of which he opened, comes back to live with her – such was their loneliness during those years. There is bitter loneliness but there is no solitude, for all are engaged in an unending common struggle to glimpse through and beyond the absurd. Everyone is reading, but not a book. As I am reading the life of my friend who killed himself, I think, when he was happiest.

1982

The hour of poetry

We all know the number of steps,
compañero, from the cell
to that room.

If it's twenty
they're not taking you to the bathroom.
If it's forty-five
they can't be taking you out
for exercise

If you get past eighty
and begin
to stumble blindly
up a staircase
oh if you get past eighty
there's only one place
they can take you
there's only one place
there's only one place
now there's only one place left
they can take you.

There is a hotel by a lake, near where I live. During the last war it was the local headquarters of the Gestapo. Many people were interrogated and tortured there. Today it is a hotel again. From the bar you look out across the water to the mountains on the far side; you look out on a scene that would have appealed to hundreds of romantic painters in the nineteenth century as sublime. And it was on to this scene that, before and after their interrogations, the tortured looked out. It was before this scene that loved ones and friends of the tortured stopped, powerless, to stare at the building, in which their own was being subjected to unspeakable pain or a lingering and

243

agonizing death. Between the sublime and their present reality, what did they see in those mountains and that lake?

Of all experiences, systematic human torture is probably the most indescribable. Not simply because of the intensity of the suffering involved, but also because the initiative of such torture is opposed to the assumption on which all languages are based: the assumption of mutual understanding across what differentiates. Torture smashes language: its purpose is to tear language from the voice and words from the truth. The one being tortured knows: they are breaking me. His or her resistance consists in trying to limit the *me* being broken. Torture tears apart.

> Don't believe them when they show you
> the photo of my body,
> don't believe them.
> Don't believe them when they tell you
> the moon is the moon,
> if they tell you the moon is the moon,
> that this is my voice on tape,
> that this is my signature on a confession,
> if they say a tree is a tree
> don't believe them,
> don't believe
> anything they tell you
> anything they swear to
> anything they show you,
> don't believe them.

Torture has a very long and widespread history. If people today are surprised by the scale of its reappearance (did it ever disappear?), it is perhaps because they have ceased believing in evil. Torture is not shocking because it is rare or because it belongs to the past: it is shocking because of what it does. The opposite of torture is not *progress* but *charity*. (The subject is so close to the New Testament that its terms are usable.)

The majority of torturers are neither sadists – in the clinical sense of the word – nor incarnations of pure evil. They are men and women who have been conditioned to accept and then use a certain practice. There are formal and informal schools for torturers, mostly state-financed. But the first conditioning begins, before the school, with ideological propositions that a certain category of people are fundamentally different and that their difference constitutes a supreme threat. The tearing apart of the third person, *them*, from *us* and *you*. The next lesson, now in the schools for torture, is that *their* bodies are lies because, as bodies, they claim *not* to be so different: torture is a punishment for this lie. When and if the torturers begin to question what they have learnt, they still continue, out of fear of what they have already done; they torture now to save their own untortured skins.

The fascist regimes of Latin America – Pinochet's Chile, for example – have recently and systematically extended the logic of torture. Not only do they tear apart the bodies of their victims, but they also try to tear up – so that they cannot be read – their very names. It would be wrong to suppose that these regimes do this out of shame or embarrassment: they do it in the hope of eliminating martyrs and heroes, and in order to produce the maximum intimidation among the population.

A woman or man is openly arrested, taken away in a car from his home at night, or from his workplace during the day. The arresters, the abductors, wear plain clothes. After this it is impossible to have any news of the one who has disappeared. Police, ministers, courts, deny all knowledge of the missing person. Yet the missing persons are in the hands of the military intelligence services. Months, years, pass. To believe that the missing are dead is to betray those who have thus been torn away; yet to believe that they are alive is to dream of them being tortured and then, often later, to be forced to admit their death. No letter, no sign, no whereabouts, no one responsible, no one to appeal to, no imaginable end to the sentence, because no sentence. Normally silence means a lack of sound. Here silence is active and has been turned, once again systematically, into an instrument, this time for torturing the heart. Occasionally carcasses are washed up on the beaches and identified as belonging to the list of the missing.

Occasionally one or two return with some news of the others who are
still missing: released intentionally perhaps, so as to sow again hopes
which will torture thousands of hearts.

> My son has been
> missing
> since May 8
> of last year.

>> They took him
>> just for a few hours
>> they said
>> just for some routine
>> questioning.

> After the car left,
> the car with no licence plate,
> we couldn't

>> find out

> anything else
> about him.

> But now things have changed.
> We heard from a compañero
> who just got out
> that five months later
> they were torturing him
> in Villa Grimaldi,
> at the end of September
> they were questioning him
> in the red house
> that belonged to the Grimaldis.

>> They say they recognized
>> his voice his screams
>> they say.

> Somebody tell me frankly
> what times are these
> what kind of world
> what country?

What I'm asking is
how can it be
that a father's
joy
a mother's
joy
is knowing
that they
that they are still
torturing
their son?
Which means
that he was alive
five months later
and our greatest
hope
will be to find out
next year
                 that they're still torturing him
eight months later

and he may   might   could
still be alive.

Physical torture often concentrates upon the genitalia because of their sensitivity, because of the humiliation involved, and because thus the victim is threatened with sterility. In the emotional torture of the women and men who love those who have been made to disappear, their hopes are chosen as the point of application for pain, so as to produce – at another level – a comparable threat of sterility.

If he were dead
I'd know it.
Don't ask me how.
I'd know.

I have no proof,
no clues, no answer,
nothing that proves
or disproves.

247

> There's the sky,
> the same blue
> it always was.

> But that's no proof.
> Atrocities go on
> and the sky never changes.

> There are the children.
> They've finished playing.
> Now they'll start to drink
> like a herd of wild
> horses.
> Tonight they'll be asleep
> as soon as their heads
> touch the pillow.

> But who would accept that
> as proof
> that their father
> is not dead?

In the face of such practices and their increasing frequency and the involvement of US agencies in their preparation, if not their daily routine, every sort of active protest and resistance needs to be mounted. (Amnesty International is coordinating some of them.) In addition, poets – such as the Chilean Ariel Dorfman – will write poems (all the above quotations are from Dorfman's *Missing*, published by Amnesty International). In face of the monstrous machinery of modern totalitarian power, so often now compared to that of the Inferno, poems will increasingly be written.

During the eighteenth and nineteenth centuries many protests against social injustice were written in prose. They were reasoned arguments written in the belief that, given time, people would come to see reason; and that, finally, history was on the side of reason. Today this is by no means so clear. The outcome is by no means guaranteed. The suffering of the present and the past is unlikely to be redeemed by a future era of universal happiness. And evil is a

constantly ineradicable reality. All this means that the resolution –
the coming to terms with the sense to be given to life – cannot be
deferred. The future cannot be trusted. The moment of truth is now.
And more and more it will be poetry, rather than prose, that receives
this truth. Prose is far more trusting than poetry: poetry speaks to the
immediate wound.

The boon of language is not tenderness. All that it holds, it holds
with exactitude and without pity. Even a term of endearment: the
term is impartial; the context is all. The boon of language is that
potentially it is complete, it has the potentiality of holding with words
the totality of human experience. Everything that has occurred and
everything that may occur. It even allows space for the unspeakable.
In this sense one can say of language that it is potentially the only
human home, the only dwelling place that cannot be hostile to man.
For prose this home is a vast territory, a country which it crosses
through a network of tracks, paths, highways; for poetry this home is
concentrated on a single centre, a single voice.

One can say anything to language. This is why it is a listener, closer
to us than any silence or any god. Yet its very openness often signifies
indifference. (The indifference of language is continually solicited
and employed in bulletins, legal records, communiqués, files.) Poetry
addresses language in such a way as to close this indifference and to
incite a caring. How does poetry incite this caring? What is the labour
of poetry?

By this I do not mean the work involved in writing a poem, but the
work of the written poem itself. Every authentic poem contributes to
the labour of poetry. And the task of this unceasing labour is to bring
together what life has separated or violence has torn apart. Physical
pain can usually be lessened or stopped by action. All other human
pain, however, is caused by one form or another of separation. And
here the act of assuagement is less direct. Poetry can repair no loss,
but it defies the space which separates. And it does this by its
continual labour of reassembling what has been scattered.

O my beloved
how sweet it is
to go down
and bathe in the pool
before your eyes
letting you see how
my drenched linen dress
marries
the beauty of my body.
Come, look at me

Poem inscribed on an Egyptian statue, 1500 BC

Poetry's impulse to use metaphor, to discover resemblance, is not for the sake of making comparisons (all comparisons as such are hierarchical), nor is it to diminish the particularity of any event; it is to discover those correspondences of which the sum total would be proof of the indivisible totality of existence. To this totality poetry appeals, and its appeal is the opposite of a sentimental one; sentimentality always pleads for an exemption, for something which *is* divisible.

Apart from reassembling by metaphor, poetry reunites by its *reach*. It equates the reach of a feeling with the reach of the universe; after a certain point the type of extremity involved becomes unimportant and all that matters is its degree; by their degree alone extremities are joined.

I bear equally with you
the black permanent separation.
Why are you crying? Rather give me
    your hand,
promise to come again in a dream.
You and I are a mountain of grief.
You and I will never meet on this earth.
If only you could send me at midnight
a greeting through the stars

Anna Akhmatova

To argue here that the subjective and objective are confused is to return to an empirical view which the extent of present suffering challenges; strangely enough it is to claim an unjustified privilege.

Poetry makes language care because it renders everything intimate. This intimacy is the result of the poem's labour, the result of the bringing-together-into-intimacy of every act and noun and event and perspective to which the poem refers. There is often nothing more substantial to place against the cruelty and indifference of the world than this caring.

> From where does Pain come to us?
> From where does he come?
> He has been the brother of our visions
>   from time immemorial
> And the guide of our rhymes

writes the Iraqi poet Nazik al-Mil'-ika.

To break the silence of events, to speak of experience however bitter or lacerating, to put into words, is to discover the hope that these words may be heard, and that when heard, the events will be judged. This hope is, of course, at the origin of prayer, and prayer – as well as labour – was probably at the origin of speech itself. Of all uses of language, it is poetry that preserves most purely the memory of this origin.

Every poem that works as a poem is original. And *original* has two meanings: it means a return to the origin, the first which engendered everything that followed; and it means that which has never occurred before. In poetry, and in poetry alone, the two senses are united in such a way that they are no longer contradictory.

Nevertheless poems are not simple prayers. Even a religious poem is not exclusively and uniquely addressed to God. Poetry is addressed to language itself. If that sounds obscure, think of a lamentation – there words lament loss to their language. Poetry is addressed to language in a comparable but wider way.

To put into words is to find the hope that the words will be heard and the events they describe judged. Judged by God or judged by history. Either way the judgment is distant. Yet the language – which is immediate, and which is sometimes wrongly thought of as being only a means – offers, obstinately and mysteriously, its own judgment when it is addressed by poetry. This judgment is distinct from that of any moral code, yet it promises, within its acknowledgment of what it has heard, a distinction between good and evil – as though language itself had been created to preserve just that distinction!

This is why poetry opposes more *absolutely* than any other force in the world the monstrous cruelties by which the rich today defend their ill-gotten riches. This is why the hour of the furnaces is also the hour of poetry.

1982

The Screen and *The Spike*

———

The Spike became an American bestseller, with over a million copies sold. It has appeared in paperback in England and in translation in other areas of the world. The book[1] and its success deserve to be examined more closely. Not from the point of view of literature (for nobody claims literary status for the book), but from the point of view of world politics or, more precisely, of world ideologies. In this respect the book's success may well be original and significant.

It is, I believe, the first book of its kind to achieve such a success. Although its narrative imitates that of a spy story or thriller, at this level the book is so weakly conventional that one has to ask: what is its other appeal? *The Spike* purports to explain the ongoing ideological struggle for world power. It is not a book that encourages the reader to escape from the world or to pursue her or his own quirks and fantasies within it; rather it promises to expose to its readers the global but hidden and institutional forces of which they are victims. As a book among bestsellers it has little glamour and little talent. If it has sold so well, it has been sold as an ideological explanation of the world.

Which brings us to the second reason for examining what this book is really about. Its explanation of the world coincides almost exactly with that of the new Reagan administration's rhetoric. Both proclaim that the Free World, in which wealth is beautiful, is being threatened by international terrorism, which is Moscow's secret arm for achieving world domination. The moment has come to recognize this truth and to protect the Free World. In these circumstances to hesitate to shoot is to betray a moral responsibility. *The Spike* is perhaps the first purely ideological bestseller. Reagan is probably the first purely ideological President of the United States.

The action begins in 1967 and continues into the future, with a Democrat President who succeeds Carter. The action takes place in Washington, New York, Paris, Moscow, Saigon, Rome. The story concerns Bob Hockney, an ambitious radical student who wants to be a journalist and win a Pulitzer prize. He launches his career of investigative journalism by exposing the illegal activities of the CIA and the hidden facts about the war in Vietnam. With this he achieves his ambition, becomes famous. But gradually he begins to suspect the disinterestedness of the sources of much of his 'unpatriotic' information and, by the middle of the book, he is convinced that the KGB has been for years, and is still, engaged in a global plan to 'disinform' and disastrously confuse western opinion about what is really happening.

This plan involves, among other things, infiltrating the western news media and *spiking* (not publishing) any story that might reveal what the KGB is really doing. Once more determined, despite the spiking, to expose the naked truth, Hockney eventually discovers that nobody less than the US Vice-President is (unwittingly) working for the KGB.

The book, like Hockney's journalism, is also itself an exposé. Such a Vice-President doesn't yet exist. But many of the characters and institutions do exist, and though the authors have changed some of the names to protect themselves against libel, the book hopes to accuse with the same 'fearlessness' as the reader is supposed to accredit to Hockney.

Should these false accusations be contested? When once one begins to see *covers* everywhere, who knows? Perhaps Haig is a KGB agent, with the long-term plan of taking de facto power out of Reagan's hands for all that concerns foreign affairs? Perhaps the assassination attempt was not intended . . . ?

It may be more important to look at what the book tells us about the accusers: Arnaud de Borchgrave and Robert Moss. Messrs M. and B. are high-powered journalists (*Newsweek* and *Foreign Report*). They interpret the world. They are not, however, front-line reporters. They are desk and jet men. Thanks to modern means of communication and of transmitting and storing information, journalists of their type and generation have a wider view of the world than was ever possible before. They are strategists, their picture is global, and in this book they are arguing that there is a global KGB plan of 'disinformation'.

*Dis*information is to information something like what the lie is to the truth. But these last terms would be too simplistic for Messrs M. and B., who are concerned, not with direct single statements, but with media systems, cumulative effects and ideological war. Besides which – and this is of crucial importance – a truth or a lie needs to be checked against facts or experience, whereas *dis*information can simply be checked against its rival system which is termed 'information'.

Messrs M. and B. have a global view, yet they live nowhere. They monitor the world, yet they have no idea of what actually happens in houses and streets. Between them and reality there is always a reading and its technology. They only know what is happening in a heart when they look at a cardiogram.

As one proceeds with their book, one is gradually forced to realize to what degree this buffer, this screen – in every sense of the word – has isolated them from experience. I say *almost* because there is a certain amount of evidence of certain experiences of being successful, male, international journalists. Airports, bars, hotels, nightclubs.

In such a context inexperience should not be confused with naïvety or innocence. On the contrary, it can well be accompanied by sophistication and ruthlessness. Perhaps it should be compared with, or checked against, experience – as disinformation is checked against information.

'I don't even remember what you said your name was,' he reflected aloud.

'I never liked my name anyway.'

Hockney didn't pursue it. 'You know,' he said solemnly, 'we're not going to be students forever.'

'I don't know about that.' She stubbed out her cigarette and put her hand on his penis, feeling it harden again under her touch. 'I don't think I'll ever pass my exams. What are you going to do – I mean, after you graduate?'

Hockney closed his eyes, thinking of another girl, back on the East Coast. He was instantly rigid. Then he felt lips and teeth moving gently along him. Julia had never done that.

'I want to see things and write about them,' he said without opening his eyes. The statement sounded astonishingly mild. Tom Flack would call him a shit ass spectator. 'Tom Flack,' he continued, 'has got it all wrong. You don't stop the war or beat the police state by pissing on the National Guard or trashing Telegraph Avenue. You do it by *explaining* things to people – the things the government doesn't want us to know.'

The girl hauled herself up the bed and straddled him.

'I'm going to be a reporter,' Hockney announced, gasping slightly, but still intent on the idea he wanted to get across.

'I'm going to be . . . ah . . . the greatest reporter in America,' he emphasized.

'Mmmm.' The girl's groan had nothing to do with Hockney's declaration of intent.

In this passage, which occurs at the very beginning of the book, the way Messrs M. and B. describe the scene is as far from any experience of it as Hockney is, in his mind, from the girl in bed with him. All three, M., B. and H., are so obsessed with what they believe people don't want them to know, that they ignore what is already there to be known. They are persistently elsewhere.

Hockney makes his first reputation as a journalist by exposing a French CIA agent in Paris who works as a news editor. As a result of the exposé the Frenchman commits suicide. High drama. Yet we never see *how* Hockney works as a sleuth, takes photos, amasses his evidence. M. and B. are never, as the French say, *dans la mille*, never in the centre where things are at. In Paris there is also a lot of talk and innuendo about high-class orgies – where agents and spies are recruited. But the orgy itself is persistently off scene, only observed through two-way mirrors.

'I'm new to Paris and I got stuck on the wrong metro line,' says Hockney, 'I should have changed at Réaumur-Sebastopol.'

That rings true. M. and B. never, however, go beyond the new arrival's first impressions, which are mostly hearsay, presented and boasted of as if there were experience and knowledge. There is another French journalist who lasts the length of the book: his wife's voracious (a hearsay?) sexual appetites cause him to become a pawn of the KGB. Inevitably – because it is a new arrival's stereotype – but fairly improbably given his lifestyle – this Frenchman always has 'a perennial Gauloise drooping' from his lower lip.

Such unimportant but telltale details betray the truth. Anyway they make clear that M. and B. are unremittingly elsewhere – in the cities of the strategic maps where nobody lives. Not even a black cat.

Saigon apart, I am familiar with all the sites of this book. And everywhere the same sophisticated gloss, covering ignorance of reality at the first degree, is evident. The unhappy wife of a Russian bureaucrat in Moscow – and the gloss naturally permits us a description of how she is fucked – would not be likely to greet her husband, after a six months' absence, in the way that M. and B. imagine.

Amsterdam – I am a member of the institute there which in the book is the centre of a KGB network – is not a city 'where you can get away with murder'. But you might get this impression from taxi rides.

M. and B.'s addiction to a screen, which divides what appears to be happening from the truth, is not only revealed by mistakes and isolated phrases, it is also explicitly *inwritten* into the story they tell.

In Vietnam, Hockney falls into the hands of the Vietcong and is sentenced to death as an American spy. Afterwards it turns out that this 'terrifying experience' was not real but was deliberately enacted in order to brainwash him.

A film-star friend of Hockney's is kidnapped by a German terrorist group because they estimate that pictures of her apparent participation in their actions will impress the media. In fact she is a drugged puppet.

When Hockney has to decide whether his oldest and best friend is lying to him, he does so by cross-questioning him over the telephone and attaching a voice-stress analysing gadget to the receiver. All eight red lights start flashing, so Hockney knows that his best friend must be telling lies.

In each of these examples what appears to be real is proven by outside knowledge (this *outside* is the *elsewhere*) to be false.

At other times, Hockney and M. and B. try to break through the screen. Hockney gets himself flown in Vietnam to a Marine unit under heavy attack.

'You press guys don't have to be up here.' The captain sounded puzzled. 'Tell me,' he said, 'why do you do it?'

Hockney searched for an adequate answer. 'I had to find the real war,' he tried to explain.

'The real war?' The captain's brow was still furrowed. 'Hell, you don't have to go up to Hill 383 to find that. Who's going to remember Hill 383 anyway?'

'That's just the point.' Hockney thought of the cynical Saigon press corps, breakfasting in the Givral on Tu Do Street, or heckling the floundering briefers at the Five O'Clock Follies. 'I bet,' he shouted against the squall of the chopper blades, 'I bet they won't even mention the fight for Hill 383 at the Five O'Clock Follies. But I'm going to make sure people know about Hill 383 at home.'

Circumstantially he breaks through. The Marines recognize 'Newsy' as a real man. But this does not solve the problem, because 'Newsy' has brought the screen with him, and what he writes as a journalist will be no more than another scenario.

Not because it isn't great literature, but because what Hockney lives or sees is *unconvincing to him*. He doesn't trust it. He only trusts readings.

This is how M. and B. describe the film star's escape from captivity. She has by now lost everything. They do not watch her as she might *be*; they watch her as she might appear in a television play. Note how the camera lingers a moment 'glued to her breasts':

The crisp fall breeze cut through her as she struggled along the pier and up a broad flight of stone steps to reach street level. Her thin, sodden blouse, glued to her breasts, offered no protection. She found herself in a district of seedy bars with names like OK and Oklahoma. The word Reeperbahn floated out of her dulled memory. Drunken sailors lurched out of a bar where the jukebox was blaring the hit tunes of a decade before and called out to her. She had surfaced in the lowest quarter of Hamburg's red-light district. She sensed the need to hurry up the badly lit street toward the brighter lights at the other end.

The sailors, who looked Asian, were walking behind her. She quickened her step until she was half running, half stumbling up the narrow street. She heard thudding footsteps behind her, advancing on her.

Beyond the screen there is nothing. And beyond the screen is where experience begins.

If we take the two pairs of terms experience/inexperience and information/disinformation, we can now see how they may be linked. They operate on very different levels. The first pair refers to the way an individual does or does not make sense of what happens to him or her. The second pair refers to a systematic social process of ordering facts in which the question of *meaning* does not, strictly speaking, arise. (This is the unique and unprecedented feature of the modern category of *information*.) Yet information is finally addressed to people who use it or judge it, according to their own experience.

' "I'm prepared to take the risk." Hockney was conscious that his inexperience was showing.' An unrecognized fear of one's own inexperience can lead to an excessive fear about being misinformed. The less one has learnt from experience, the more gullible one is. This doesn't worry children because the idea of being fooled doesn't worry them: they can fool the world back. But it can worry adults, especially highly competitive ones.

It can even lead to paranoia: the belief that one is being threatened behind one's back, and hence the compulsion continually to turn round and set up controls, the anxiety which prevents one ever staying put. Persistently *being elsewhere* is a paranoiac symptom. The pathology starts with inexperience. This triggers a suppressed fear that one is peculiarly open to being 'disinformed'. This then leads to never accepting *what is* and therefore prolonging, even absolutizing, the state of inexperience.

The Spike is a document of how this vicious circle turns.

There is no need to consider the personal case histories of M. and B., for the two are very representative, and such a paranoiac process is as much cultural as personal.

It might be appropriately named *screening*. Not just because the term reminds us of all the modern bureaucratic security systems, but because it points to the fundamental character of such a way of looking at the world. The screen replaces reality. And the replacement is a double one. For reality is born of the encounter of consciousness and events. To deny reality is not simply to deny what is objective. It is also to amputate an essential part of the subjective.

Nevertheless the screen protects and has its own easily available set of controls. (It is issued with instructions.) It lacks authority, however. Neither life nor death occurs there. The screen has no gravity. It is never incontestable. There is no reality.

Screening permits a ruthlessness, an indifference to life such as has probably never occurred before in history. But ultimately it ensures helplessness. The days of beautiful wealth are numbered.

Many developments have contributed to this phenomenon of screening, which is one of the most extreme forms of modern alienation: technological, organizational and economic developments. But above all, screening is the mark of privilege. Scarcity, necessity, poverty dismantle the screens. Only the rich can survive with inexperience. And perhaps it is their ill-gotten wealth – for all wealth is ill-gotten in a world of poverty like ours – their wealth which sows the first fear, the first refusal.

1981

Notes

1   Arnaud de Borchgrave and Robert Moss, *The Spike*, New York, Crown, 1980; Avon paperback, 1981; London, Futura, 1981.

Sicilian lives

————

I have never met Danilo Dolci. I would count it a great honour to do so. He is a man who believes in poetry and action, a man who has devoted his life to an uncompromising struggle against injustice and poverty, yet who is tolerant. Perhaps most important of all, he does not believe in saviours, only in catalysts.

Without Dolci this book[1] would not exist. Yet it is not his voice which speaks through it. It is a book of voices that he has assembled and encouraged to speak: the voices of impoverished peasants and fishermen from around the village of Trappeto and of the urban poor from the Sicilian capital of Palermo.

In recent years there have been many books which, using a tape recorder, have recorded and collected popular voices. Such a way of recording has become part of sociological research. Some of these books are valuable. But this one is in an altogether different category. Dolci, who kept a record of these conversations over a period of thirty years, had no sociological ambitions. And the women and men who talked with him were not talking to an investigator, not even to a well-meaning one. The quality of Dolci's life's work in Sicily is reflected in the stories of this book without a word being said by him. What are these stories like?

The few interviews with the rich and powerful, although forming an invaluable point of comparison, are of course different. I am talking of the poor, those exploited by the rich and powerful, telling the stories of *their* lives. They are graphic storytellers. This has nothing to do with literary ability. Many of them are illiterate. It has to do with a practice which predates literature.

In all pre-industrial societies people have believed that living is a way of living a story. In this story one is always the protagonist and occasionally the teller, but the inventor of the story, the designer of the plot, is elsewhere. People who believe this, and who lead the story of their life in this way, are often natural storytellers. Just as, if they happen to be shepherds who spend a great deal of time alone, companioned only by animals and the spirit of the landscape, they are often natural poets: poetry being that form of language which addresses itself to that which is beyond speaking.

In many of the stories told in this book there is little or no hope. That is to say, there is no ground for hope in the events narrated. And yet they are never recitals of despair. Of bitterness, tragedy, injustice, hopelessness, yes. But of despair, no. How can one explain such a paradox? There is the inventor of the story and there is also the judge of the story. It is by no means clear that the two are the same. The distinction between them may be somewhat like that between the Devil and God.

This idea of an inventor and a judge of the story of one's life is closely connected with religion. Yet no religious formulation completely covers this belief. The belief arises in the face of an enigma, not in the face of a set of answers.

The stories are not recitals of despair because, despite all, the telling of them is an appeal for judgment. The judgment for which the appeal is made is a multiform one: it is human, social, moral, metaphysical. Ultimately it is an appeal for a judgment made by a being who is comparable to the teller, but who is more powerful, who has more opportunities, more time, more peace within which to judge. Who or what is this being? God, you will say. Perhaps. It can also be history, other people, the dead parents who brought one into the world, the children who may survive one, the co-existence of everything on the other side of time, the listener to the story. I cannot give the ontological answer. I want only to describe the spirit in which these stories have been told, and hence their essential character.

Dolci's role in the telling of these stories was a very special one. He was at the beginning of each story, in that he prompted it and then listened to it. And he was at the end of each story – the very end – in that in some way he was, not the judge, but an agent, a trustworthy, understanding agent, of that which would judge.

Last year I and my family drove in our small Citroën 2CV to Genoa. Just after the war the port area of this city had inspired me to make several paintings. Paintings made very much in the spirit of the early neo-realist Italian films, such as *Open City*, *Bicycle Thieves*. 'Let's go and see if we can find a pizzeria that I used to know,' I said. We left the car and went on foot through the narrow streets which are still like ravines, and in which you can still buy and be sold just about anything. The pizzeria had disappeared, but we ate in another, rather more modern one.

We returned to the car and drove off. When we arrived at the house of the friends we were visiting, I unlocked the luggage compartment of the car to take out our suitcase. And it was then that I saw that my haversack had disappeared. It had been stolen whilst we were eating our pizza. It had contained an electric razor, a camera, a pair of binoculars and a notebook. It was only the loss of the latter which really affected me. It was full of jottings for a story I was writing, and of theoretical notes about different forms of narrative. About the difference between bourgeois and popular narration, about how privilege or the lack of privilege gives a very different perspective to the narrating of events. Within half an hour the absurdity of either anger or regret became obvious to me. Occasionally the poor levy their own taxes in their own locale. And against this I was in no position to complain.

As you will learn from one of the stories here, it is quite possible that the band of two or three kids who opened the locked compartment of my car, skilfully, silently, and in full daylight, came from Palermo, on one of their professional tours of the mainland. As a result my notes on how *they* might tell the story of their sojourn in Genoa are no longer at hand!

Nevertheless I want to say something about their storytelling. First, however, I want to emphasize that what I have to say is not the most important thing to be said. Dolci himself describes what the telling of such stories can to do the consciousness of those who have lived them. And this is more important. Nobody reading this book can fail to be struck by what the stories reveal about the intolerable conditions, flagrant injustice and endemic violence imposed upon the lives of the tellers. What remains is the question how we, the relatively privileged, read such a book. The question how we translate these stories into our experience. For if we do not translate them, we shall read them only as exotica.

The annals of the poor. I choose the word 'poor' deliberately. I might say: of landless peasants and of the lumpenproletariat. The word 'poor' has a very long tradition to it, and it is necessary to recognize this tradition. And already we are hard up against the first problem. We have to recognize and respect this tradition, without, for one moment, falling into the revolting complacency which accepts poverty as an ordained component of the human condition. Personally I believe that Marxism, with its precise social and historical analysis, is an apprenticeship which the poor have already undergone or will undergo. Such an apprenticeship helps to train them to face the world as it is, and to contest it. Yet Marxism cannot draw a line under the centuries' experience of the poor and thus close the account, as if thereafter this experience were no more than an anomaly.

With modern means of production, and given a radical transformation of existing social relations, a world of plenty is today possible. Yet what we actually see, for the most part, is a world of unprecedentedly violent poverty. Everyone talks of this, but this talk does not usually even begin to eliminate the poverty. When it does – as in Mao's China or in the non-European republics of the Soviet Union – the improvement is hidden, at least in the minds of the West, under a barrage of political debate about other issues.

One could say that we are living the crisis of utopianism. The utopian vision of a just world of plenty nowhere accords with reality. It is not my task here to lay out what conclusions should be drawn from this impasse. What does need to be pointed out is that the crisis of utopianism has absolutely nothing to do with the poor as they live their own lives.

Their crises are much more immediate and material. There is no need to list them. Likewise their hopes are both smaller and tougher, that is to say more persistent and longer-lasting. There have been educators, including revolutionary ones, who have explained this paradox of desperation and hope among the poor as the consequence of superstition and ignorance. But there are many systems of knowledge, and each one calls the other ignorant. The poor's overall view of life is very evident in the pages of *Sicilian Lives*, but it is so far removed from the view that most of us have inherited that we risk not seeing its logic and coherence. And failing to see its logic and coherence, we risk being blind to its intellectual and moral courage.

First and foremost, life for the poor is an arena of struggle. Ceaseless, unremitting struggle in which only partial victories can ever be foreseen, and of those foreseen, only a fraction gained. Life is the arena, the stage, of this struggle; but not the struggle itself. That life is only a struggle for survival is a notion of nineteenth-century social and biological science. The poor could never allow themselves the luxury of such cynicism.

If life appears to them to be nothing but a struggle for survival, because they are living it and not merely investigating it, they conclude that life is a trial which, obscurely and terribly, must nevertheless have some other purpose. At the very least this purpose may be the grateful acceptance of repose at the end of the struggle. At the most, it may be that the eventual role of the poor will be to cleanse the world – at least temporarily – of evil.

And here it is worth remembering that this last occasional yet recurrent revolutionary vision was never utopian, for it was based, not upon a detailed vision of what would follow, but on a sense of the overwhelming justice of retrospective revenge!

The poor estimate that life is a trial: that pleasure is a gift and a mystery, perhaps the deepest mystery of all; that there are no final solutions; that all men are fallible; that events are more powerful than choices. The idea that life bestows a *right* to satisfaction and happiness is to them naïve, and furthermore, because somewhere such an idea implies an unrealizable promise, profoundly dishonest.

Such a view accords with many thousands of years of varied human experience, but it is in direct opposition to the life view of the privileged today in modern Europe and North America. And this opposition is part of the content of the most profound drama of our time.

It can be put very simply. On one hand an essentially tragic view of life; on the other hand a technocratic and optimistic view of life, which precludes the category of the tragic. And then, if we pass from theory to practice, the systematic oppression of those who have a tragic view by those who have a technocratic and optimistic one. Only the term 'systematic oppression' is inadequate. For this oppression *is* tragedy.

It is necessary to say this, for it is not what the poor themselves are in a position to say. But once it is said, it is to their evidence that we should listen, and in listening something different will also become apparent.

To say that the poor are closer to reality than the rich is a cliché. And a somewhat patronizing one, in that it suggests that reality is coarse, material, brutal, physical. And it suggests that reality is thus opposed to the spiritual, from which the poor are mostly excluded. Yet the true antithesis of the real is the abstract.

What is remarkable in the stories and reflections that follow is their lack of abstraction. And in the interviews with the rich and the Mafiosi, what is remarkable is the opposite. In poor societies abstraction and tyranny go together; in rich societies it is indifference which usually goes with abstraction. Abstraction's capacity to ignore what is real (and the heart can abstract as well as the mind: unjustified

266

learn so much, that even the tone of the commentary owes the master a debt. It is surely important that Creagh is a poet in his own right. This new book deserves to be read far beyond the academic readership for which it was principally designed. Anybody, from fourteen to eighty years old, interested in the primary questions posed by the human condition, will find pages to mark, distract and frighten him.

FASHION. Madame Death!

DEATH. Go to the devil. I'll come when you don't want me.

FASHION. As if I weren't immortal!

DEATH. Immortal? Already now the thousandth year hath passed since the times of the immortals.

FASHION. So even Madame can quote Petrarch like an Italian poet of the sixteenth or the nineteenth century.

DEATH. I like Petrarch's poems, because among them I find my Triumph, and because nearly all of them talk about me. But anyway, be off with you.

FASHION. Come on, by the love you bear the Seven Deadly Sins, stand still for once and look at me.

DEATH. Well? I'm looking.

FASHION. Don't you recognize me?

DEATH. You must know I'm short-sighted, and that I can't use spectacles because the English don't make any that suit me, and even if they did, I haven't got a nose to stick them on.

FASHION. I am Fashion, your sister.

DEATH. My sister?

FASHION. Yes: don't you remember that both of us are daughters of Decay?

DEATH. What do you expect me to remember, I who am the mortal foe of memory?

FASHION. But I remember it well; and I know that both of us equally aim continually to destroy and change all things here below, although you achieve this by one road and I by another.

In the *Moral Tales* wit often takes the place of the lyricism to be found in Leopardi's poetry, but the same approach to life, the same way of thinking, is present in both. Leopardi was a prodigy of the Enlightenment. He saw the world through the eyes of its materialism. He accepted the place that its philosophers gave to Pleasure. He was in agreement with their dismantling of religion and their exposure of the reactionary power of the Church. In his own way he was a populist. But he rejected absolutely the Enlightenment's belief in Progress. The basis of human equality, as he saw it, could never be a promise of happiness, but always a present suffering.

Writing as he was during the aftermath of Napoleon, his prognosis for the coming century, in which he foresaw money and the new means of communication and demagogy finally distorting everything, was catastrophic. Every historical period, he said, was a period of transition and every transition involved unhappiness. Once, however, there had been consolations – faith, a belief in destiny or redemption; such consolations had now been shown to be illusory, and the modern truth was starker and more hopeless than ever before.

Man was constructed in such a way that, above all, he loved his own life. This love made him believe that his life promised him happiness. This belief was incorrigible, and therefore most of the time he suffered. All this was the work of nature, in whose scheme of things man was an insignificant, marginal detail. (The *Tales* abound in ideas related to current science fiction.) The only possible deliverance from the human condition was the eternal sleep of death. He wrote often about the 'logic' of suicide, but he always refused it out of a curious but very deep solidarity with the living.

There is a paradox buried in Leopardi's work: a paradox which he himself was aware of. In the following quotation he was not so much claiming genius for himself, as describing what he felt to be the potentiality of the written word:

Works of genius have this intrinsic property, that even when they give a perfect likeness of the nullity of things, even when they clearly demonstrate and make us feel the inevitable unhappiness of life, even when they express the most terrible despair; nevertheless to a great soul, that may even find itself in a state of utter prostration, disillusionment, futility, boredom and discouragement with life, or in the harshest and most death-dealing adversities (whether these appertain to the strong and lofty emotions, or to any other thing), they always serve as a consolation, rekindling enthusiasm, and though speaking of and portraying nothing but death, restore to it, at least for a while, the life that it had lost.

Zibaldone, 259–60

A Marxist interpretation of Leopardi would place him historically and remind us of all that he leaves out of account: the class struggle, the suffering directly caused by the economic law of capitalism, the historical destiny of man. At the limit, Leopardi, as a thinker, might even be dismissed as representing the despair of the aristocracy whose days were being numbered. Anyone attempting this would nevertheless have to contend with the Italian Marxist Sebastiano Timpanaro, who has written brilliantly on his behalf.

A year or two ago, at a meeting of the Transnational Institute in Amsterdam, I was asked to speak about Hopes for the Future. Somewhat mischievously, I played a recording of Beethoven's Thirty-first Piano Sonata (*Opus* 110) and then made the following proposal: political disillusion is born of political impatience and we have all been conditioned to live this impatience because of the overall promises repeatedly made in the name of Progress.

Suppose, I said, that we change the scenario, suppose we say that we are not living in a world in which it is possible to construct something approaching heaven-on-earth, but, on the contrary, are living in a world whose nature is far closer to that of hell; what difference would this make to any single one of our political or moral choices? We would be obliged to accept the same obligations and participate in the same struggle as we are already engaged in; perhaps even our sense of solidarity with the exploited and suffering would be more singleminded. All that would have changed would be the enormity of our hopes and finally the bitterness of our disappoint-ments. My argument was, if you like, a Leopardian one, and it seems to me to be unanswerable.

And yet we cannot stop there. By force of circumstance, or (and how he would have appreciated the irony of the word!) by privilege, Leopardi was essentially a passive observer. And the unrelieved consistency of his pessimism was connected with this fact. The connection is named Ennui, bordom.

As soon as one is engaged in a productive process, however circumscribed, total pessimism becomes improbable. This has nothing to do with the dignity of labour or any other such crap; it has to do with the nature of physical and psychic human energy. Expenditure of this energy creates a need for food, sleep and brief moments of respite. This need is so acute that, when it is satisfied or partly satisfied, the satisfaction, however fleeting, produces a hope for the next break. It is thus that the fatigued survive; fatigue plus total pessimism condemns to extinction.

Something similar happens at the level of imagination. The act of participating in the production of the world, even if the particular act in itself seems absurd, creates the imaginative perspective of a potential, more desired production. When in the old (halcyon?) days, a worker on an assembly line, tied to meaningless repetition, dreamt of a colour television or a new fishing-rod, it was wrong to explain this only in terms of consumerism or misplaced hopes. Inexorably, work, because it is productive, produces in man a productive hope. Hence one of the reasons why unemployment is so inhuman.

Leopardi, solitary, childless, incapable of physical work, was condemned to be a spectator of production. His personal condition cannot be used to explain his philosophical position. Yet, because of this condition, there was one thing which he, who knew so much and had such a respect for knowledge, did not know. He did not know how the body, with its terrible mortality, nevertheless comes to the rescue.

'Those whom the gods love, die young,' he used to quote as a confirmation of the sombre wisdom of the past. Probably that is still true. Yet what it excludes is the love of one or of both parents, and the hope that the infant – perhaps one of those whom the gods were to love – sometimes inspired in them.

Leopardi would, of course, have dismissed these hopes and the small rescue operations of the body as illusory. And indeed they do not, in themselves, undermine his argument. They coexist with it. Just as affirmation coexists with anguish in Beethoven's Thirty-first Sonata.

I want now to return to the paradox: how is it that Leopardi's black pages still encourage? When I said that Leopardi's life was that of a passive spectator, I was deliberately leaving aside one outstanding fact: the heroic, solitary production of his writings. If, for all their bleakness, these writings inspire, it is because, in their own way, they participate in the production of the world. And by now it should be clear that this term needs to cover, not only production in the classical economic sense of the word, but also the never-completed, always-being-produced state of existence: the production of the world as reality. It is highly significant that in the *Moral Tales* Leopardi continually refers to, and speculates about, the creation of the universe and the forces, never entirely omnipotent, which lay behind it.

Which lay or which lie? His preoccupations were not retrospective but actual. The production of reality has never been finished, its outcome has never been made decisive. Something is always in the balance. *Reality is always in need.* Even of us, damned and marginal as we may be. This is why what Leopardi called Intensity and Schopenhauer called The Will – as man experiences them – are part of the continuous act of creation, part of the interminable production of meaning in face of 'the nullity of things'. And this is why his pessimism transcends itself.

1983

Notes

1   Giacomo Leopardi, *Moral Tales*, trans. Patrick Creagh, Manchester, Carcanet, 1983; New York, Columbia University Press, 1983.

The production of the world

——

I no longer know how many times I have arrived at the Central Station in Amsterdam, nor how many times I have been to the Rijksmuseum to look at Vermeer or Fabritius or van Gogh. The first time must have been nearly thirty years ago, and during the last seven years I have been to Amsterdam systematically every six months to attend meetings of the Transnational Institute, of which I am a fellow.

I come away from each meeting where twenty or so fellows from the Third World, the United States, Latin America, Britain and the Continent discuss aspects of the world situation within a socialist perspective – I come away each time a little less ignorant and more determined. By now we all know each other well and when we reassemble it is like a team coming together; sometimes we win, sometimes we are beaten. Each time we find ourselves battling against false representations of the world – either those of ruling-class propaganda or those we carry within ourselves.

I owe this Institute a great deal, yet the last time I was due to go to Amsterdam I almost decided not to go. I felt too exhausted. My exhaustion, if I may so put it, was as much metaphysical as physical. I could no longer hold meanings together. The mere thought of making connections filled me with anguish. The only hope was to stay put. Nevertheless at the last minute I went.

It was a mistake. I could scarcely follow anything. The connection between words and what they signified had been broken. It seemed to me that I was lost; the first human power – the power to name – was failing, or had always been an illusion. All was dissolution. I tried joking, lying down, taking a cold shower, drinking coffee, not drinking coffee, talking to myself, imagining faraway places – none of it helped.

I left the building, crossed the street and entered the van Gogh museum, not in order to look at the paintings but because I thought that the one person who could take me home might be there; she was, but before I found her I had to run the gauntlet of the paintings. At this moment, I told myself, you need van Gogh like you need a hole in the head.

'It seems to me not impossible that cholera, gravel, consumption may be celestial means of transport just as steamships, buses, railways, are means of transport on this earth. To die quietly of old age would be like going on foot . . .' van Gogh wrote in a letter to his brother, Theo.

Still I found myself glancing at the paintings and then looking at them. 'The Potato Eaters'. 'The Cornfield with a Lark'. 'The Ploughed Field at Auvers'. 'The Pear Tree'. Within two minutes – and for the first time in three weeks – I was calm, reassured. Reality had been confirmed. The transformation was as quick and thorough-going as one of those sensational changes that can sometimes come about after an intravenous injection. And yet these paintings, already very familiar to me, had never before manifested anything like this therapeutic power.

What, if anything, does such a subjective experience reveal? What is the connection, if any, between my experience in the van Gogh museum and the life work of van Gogh the painter? I would have been tempted to reply: none or very little, were it not for a strange correspondence. Sometime after my return from Amsterdam I happened to take up a book of stories and essays by Hugo von Hoffmannsthal. Among them is a story entitled 'Letters of a Traveller Come Home'. The 'letters' are dated 1901. The supposed letter-writer is a German businessman who has lived most of his life outside Europe; now that he has returned to his homeland, he increasingly suffers from a sense of unreality; Europeans are not as he remembered them, their lives mean nothing because they systematically compromise.

'As I told you, I cannot grasp them, not by their faces, not by their gestures, not by their words; for their Being is no longer anywhere, indeed they *are* no longer anywhere.'

His disappointment leads him on to question his own memories and finally the credibility of anything. In many respects these thirty pages are a kind of prophesy of Sartre's *Nausea*, written thirty years later. This is from the last letter:

Or again – some trees, those scraggy but well-kept trees which, here and there, have been left in the squares, emerging from the asphalt, protected by railings. I would look at them and I would know that they reminded me of trees – and yet were not trees – and then a shudder, seizing me, would break my breast in two, as though it were the breath, the indescribable breath of everlasting nothingness, of the everlasting nowhere, something which comes, not from death, from non-being.

The final letter also relates how he had to attend a business meeting in Amsterdam. He was feeling spineless, lost, indecisive. On his way there he passed a small art gallery, paused, and decided to go inside.

How am I to tell you half of what these paintings said to me? They were a total justification of my strange and yet profound feelings. Here suddenly I was in front of something, a mere glimpse of which had previously, in my state of torpor, been too much for me. I had been haunted by that glimpse. Now a total stranger was offering me – with incredible authority – a reply – an entire world in the form of a reply.

The ending of the story is unexpected. Rehabilitated, confirmed, he went on to his meeting and pulled off the best business coup of his entire career.

A PS to the final letter gives the name of the artist in question as being a certain Vincent van Gogh.

What is the nature of this 'entire world' which van Gogh offers 'in the form of a reply' to a particular kind of anguish?

For an animal its natural environment and habitat are a given; for a man – despite the faith of the empiricists – reality is not a given: it has to be continually sought out, held – I am tempted to say *salvaged*. We are taught to oppose the real to the imaginary, as though one were always at hand and the other distant, far away. And this opposition is false. Events are always to hand. But the coherence of these events – which is what we mean by reality – is an imaginative construction. Reality always *lies beyond*, and this is as true for materialists as for idealists, for Plato and for Marx. Reality, however one interprets it, lies beyond a screen of clichés. Every culture produces such a screen, partly to facilitate its own practices (to establish habits) and partly to consolidate its own power. Reality is inimical to those with power.

All modern artists have thought of their innovations as offering a closer approach to reality, as a way of making reality more evident. It is here, and only here, that the modern artist and the revolutionary have sometimes found themselves side by side, both inspired by the idea of pulling down the screen of clichés, clichés which in the modern period have become unprecedentedly trivial and egotistical.

Yet many such artists have reduced what they found beyond the screen, to suit their own talent and social position as artists. When this has happened they have justified themselves with one of the dozen variants of the theory of art for art's sake. They say: reality is art. They hope to extract an artistic profit from reality. Of no one is this less true than van Gogh.

We know from his letters how intensely he was aware of the screen. His whole life story is one of an endless yearning for reality. Colours, the Mediterranean climate, the sun, were for him vehicles going towards this reality; they were never objects of longing in themselves. This yearning was intensified by the crises he suffered when he felt that he was failing to salvage any reality at all. Whether these crises are today diagnosed as being schizophrenic or epileptic changes nothing; their content, as distinct from their pathology, was a vision of reality consuming itself like a phoenix.

We also know from his letters that nothing appeared more sacred to him than work. He saw the physical reality of labour as being, simultaneously, a necessity, an injustice and the essence of humanity to date. The artist's creative act was for him only one among many. He believed that reality could best be approached through work, precisely because reality itself was a form of production.

The paintings speak of this more clearly than words. Their so-called clumsiness, the gestures with which he drew with pigment upon the canvas, the gestures (invisible to us but imaginable) with which he chose and mixed his colours on the palette, all the gestures with which he handled and manufactured the stuff of the painted image, are analogous to the *activity* of the existence of what he is painting. His paintings imitate the active existence – the labour of being – of what they depict.

Take a chair, a bed, a pair of boots. His act of painting them was far nearer than that of any other painter to the carpenter's or the shoemaker's act of making them. He brings together the elements of the product – legs, cross bars, back, seat; sole, uppers tongue, heel – as though he too were fitting them together, *joining* them, and as if this *being joined* constituted their reality.

Before a landscape the process required was far more complicated and mysterious, yet it followed the same principle. If one imagines God creating the world from earth and water, from clay, his way of handling it to make a tree or a cornfield might well resemble the way that van Gogh handled paint when he painted that tree or cornfield. I am not suggesting that there was something quasi-divine about van Gogh: this would be to fall into the worst kind of hagiography. If, however, we think of the creation of the world, we can imagine the act only through the visual evidence, before our eyes here and now, of the energy of the forces in play. And to these energies, van Gogh was terribly – and I choose the adverb carefully – attuned.

When he painted a small pear tree in flower, the act of the sap rising, of the bud forming, the bud breaking, the flower forming, the styles thrusting out, the stigmas becoming sticky, these acts were present for him in the act of painting. When he painted a road, the roadmakers were there in his imagination. When he painted the turned earth of a ploughed field, the gesture of the blade turning the earth was included in his own act. Wherever he looked he saw the labour of existence; and this labour, recognized as such, for him constituted reality.

If he painted his own face, he painted the construction of his destiny, past and future, rather as palmists believe they can read this construction in the hand. His contemporaries who considered him abnormal were not all as stupid as is now assumed. He painted compulsively – no other painter was ever compelled in a comparable way.

His compulsion? It was to bring the two acts of production, that of the canvas and that of the reality depicted, ever closer and closer. This compulsion derived not from an idea about art – this is why it never occurred to him to profit from reality – but from an over-whelming feeling of empathy.

'I admire the bull, the eagle, and man with such an intense adoration, that it will certainly prevent me from ever becoming an ambitious person.'

He was compelled to go ever closer, to approach and approach and approach. *In extremis* he approaches so close that the stars in the night sky became maelstroms of light, the cypress trees ganglions of living wood responding to the energy of wind and sun. There are canvases where reality dissolves him, the painter. But in hundreds of others he takes us as close as any man can, while remaining intact, to that permanent process by which reality is being produced.

Once, long ago, paintings were compared with mirrors. Van Gogh's might be compared with lasers. They do not wait to receive, they go out to meet, and what they traverse is, not so much empty space, as the act of production. The 'entire world' that van Gogh offers as a reply to the vertigo of nothingness is the production of the world. Painting after painting is a way of saying, with awe but little comfort: it works.

1983

Mother tongue

Mother let me cry
not letterpress
nor telex
nor stainless speech
bulletins
announce disaster
with impunity –
but the pages of the wound.

Mother let me speak
not adjectives
to colour
their maps of wretchedness
nor nouns to classify
the families of pain –
but the verb of suffering.

My mother tongue taps
the sentence
on the prison wall
Mother let me write
the voices
howling in the falls.

In a pocket of earth
I buried all the accents
of my mother tongue

there they lie

like needles of pine
assembled by ants

one day the stumbling cry
of another wanderer
may set them alight

then warm and comforted
he will hear all night
a lullaby as truth

1985

8

THE SIXTH OF AUGUST 1945

———

Hiroshima

The whole incredible problem begins with the need to reinsert those events of 6 August 1945 back into living consciousness.

I was shown a book last year at the Frankfurt Book Fair. The editor asked me some question about what I thought of its format. I glanced at it quickly and gave some reply. Three months ago I was sent a finished copy of the book. It lay on my desk unopened. Occasionally its title and cover picture caught my eye, but I did not respond. I didn't consider the book urgent, for I believed that I already knew about what I would find within it.

Did I not clearly remember the day – I was in the army in Belfast – when we first heard the news of the bomb dropped on Hiroshima? At how many meetings during the first nuclear disarmament movement had I and others not recalled the meaning of that bomb?

And then, one morning last week, I received a letter from America, accompanying an article written by a friend. This friend is a doctor of philosophy and a Marxist. Furthermore, she is a very generous and warm-hearted woman. The article was about the possibilities of a third world war. Vis-à-vis the Soviet Union she took, I was surprised to read, a position very close to Reagan's. She concluded by evoking the likely scale of destruction which would be caused by nuclear weapons, and then welcomed the positive possibilities that this would offer the socialist revolution in the United States.

It was on that morning that I opened and read the book on my desk. It is called *Unforgettable Fire*.[1]

The book consists of drawings and paintings made by people who were in Hiroshima on the day that the bomb was dropped, thirty-six years ago today. Often the pictures are accompanied by a verbal record of what the image represents. None of them is by a professional artist. In 1974, an old man went to the television centre in Hiroshima to show to whoever was interested a picture he had painted, entitled 'At about 4 pm, 6th August 1945, near Yurozuyo bridge'.

This prompted an idea of launching a television appeal to other survivors of that day to paint or draw their memories of it. Nearly a thousand pictures were sent in, and these were made into an exhibition. The appeal was worded: 'Let us leave for posterity pictures about the atomic bomb, drawn by citizens.'

Clearly, my interest in these pictures cannot be an art-critical one. One does not musically analyse screams. But after repeatedly looking at them, what began as an impression became a certainty. These were images of hell.

I am not using the word as hyperbole. Between these paintings by women and men who have never painted anything else since leaving school, and who have surely, for the most part, never travelled outside Japan, between these traced memories which had to be exorcised, and the numerous representations of hell in European medieval art, there is a very close affinity.

This affinity is both stylistic and fundamental. And fundamentally it is to do with the situations depicted. The affinity lies in the degree of the multiplication of pain, in the lack of appeal or aid, in the pitilessness, in the equality of wretchedness, and in the disappearance of time.

I am 78 years old. I was living at Midorimachi on the day of the A-bomb blast. Around 9 am that morning, when I looked out of my window, I saw several women coming along the street one after another towards the Hiroshima prefectural hospital. I realized for the first time, as it is sometimes said, that when people are very much frightened hair really does stand on end. The women's hair was, in fact, standing straight up and the skin of their arms was peeled off. I suppose they were around 30 years old.

Time and again, the sober eyewitness accounts recall the surprise and horror of Dante's verses about the Inferno. The temperature at

How survivors saw it. A painting by Kazuhiro Ishizu, aged 68

At the Aioi bridge, by Sawami Katagiri, aged 76

the centre of the Hiroshima fireball was 300,000 degrees centigrade. The survivors are called in Japanese *hibakuska* – 'those who have seen hell'.

Suddenly, one man who was stark naked came up to me and said in a quavering voice, 'Please help me!' He was burned and swollen all over from the effects of the A-bomb. Since I did not recognize him as my neighbour, I asked who he was. He answered that he was Mr Sasaki, the son of Mr Ennosuke Sasaki, who had a lumber shop in Funairi town. That morning he had been doing volunteer labour service, evacuating the houses near the prefectural office in Kato town. He had been burned black all over and had started back to his home in Funairi. He looked miserable – burned and sore, and naked with only pieces of his gaiters trailing behind as he walked. Only the part of his hair covered by his soldier's hat was left, as if he was wearing a bowl. When I touched him, his burned skin slipped off. I did not know what to do, so I asked a passing driver to take him to Eba hospital.

Does not this evocation of hell make it easier to forget that these scenes belonged to life? Is there not something conveniently unreal about hell? The whole history of the twentieth century proves otherwise.

Very systematically in Europe the conditions of hells have been constructed. It is not even necessary to list the sites. It is not even necessary to repeat the calculations of the organizers. We know this, and we choose to forget it.

We find it ridiculous or shocking that most of the pages concerning, for example, Trotsky were torn out of official Soviet history. What has been torn out of our history are the pages concerning the experience of the two atom bombs dropped on Japan.

Of course, the facts are there in the textbooks. I may even be that school children learn the dates. But what these facts mean – and originally their meaning was so clear, so monstrously vivid, that every commentator in the world was shocked, and every politician was obliged to say (whilst planning differently), 'Never again' – what these facts mean has now been torn out. It has been a systematic, slow and thorough process of suppression and elimination. This process has been hidden within the reality of politics.

Do not misunderstand me. I am not here using the word 'reality' ironically, I am not politically naïve. I have the greatest respect for political reality, and I believe that the innocence of political idealists is often very dangerous. What we are considering is how in this case in the West – not in Japan for obvious reasons and not in the Soviet Union for different reasons – political and military realities have eliminated another reality.

The eliminated reality is both physical –

Yokogawa bridge above Tenma river, 6th August 1945, 8.30 am.
People crying and moaning were running towards the city. I did not know why. Steam engines were burning at Yokogawa station.
Skin of cow tied to wire.
Skin of girl's hip was hanging down.
'My baby is dead, isn't she?'

and moral.

The political and military arguments have concerned such isues as deterrence, defence systems, relative strike parity, tactical nuclear weapons and – pathetically – so-called civil defence. Any movement for nuclear disarmament today has to contend with those considerations and dispute their false interpretation. To lose sight of them is to become as apocalyptic as the Bomb and all utopias. (The construction of hells on earth was accompanied in Europe by plans for heavens on earth.)

What has to be redeemed, reinserted, disclosed and never be allowed to be forgotten, is the other reality. Most of the mass means of communication are close to what has been suppressed.

These paintings were shown on Japanese television. Is it conceivable that the BBC would show these pictures on channel one at a peak hour? Without any reference to 'political' and 'military' realities, under the straight title, *This is How It Was, 6th August 1945?* I challenge them to do so.

What happened on that day was, of course, neither the beginning nor the end of the act. It began months, years before, with the planning of the action, and the eventual final decision to drop two

bombs on Japan. However much the world was shocked and surprised by the bomb dropped on Hiroshima, it has to be emphasized
that it was not a miscalculation, an error, or the result (as can happen
in war) of a situation deteriorating so rapidly that it gets out of hand.
What happened was consciously and precisely planned. Small scenes
like this were part of the plan:

> I was walking along the Hihiyama bridge about 3 pm on 7th August. A
> woman, who looked like an expectant mother, was dead. At her side, a girl of
> about three years of age brought some water in an empty can she had found.
> She was trying to let her mother drink from it.
>
> As soon as I saw this miserable scene with the pitiful child, I embraced
> the girl close to me and cried with her, telling her that her mother was
> dead.

There was a preparation. And there was an aftermath. The latter
included long, lingering deaths, radiation sickness, many fatal
illnesses which developed later as a result of exposure to the bomb,
and tragic genetical effects on generations yet to be born.

I refrain from giving the statistics: how many hundreds of
thousands of dead, how many injured, how many deformed children.
Just as I refrain from pointing out how comparatively 'small' were the
atomic bombs dropped on Japan. Such statistics tend to distract. We
consider numbers instead of pain. We calculate instead of judging.
We relativize instead of refusing.

It is possible today to arouse popular indignation or anger by
speaking of the threat and immorality of terrorism. Indeed, this
appears to be the central plank of the rhetoric of the new American
foreign policy ('Moscow is the world-base of all terrorism') and of
British policy towards Ireland. What is able to shock people about
terrorist acts is that often their targets are unselected and innocent – a
crowd in a railway station, people waiting for a bus to go home after
work. The victims are chosen indiscriminately in the hope of producing a shock effect on political decision-making by their government.

The two bombs dropped on Japan were terrorist actions. The
calculation was terrorist. The indiscriminacy was terrorist. The small

groups of terrorists operating today are, by comparison, humane killers.

Another comparison needs to be made. Today terrorist groups mostly represent small nations or groupings, who are disputing large powers in a position of strength. Whereas Hiroshima was perpetrated by the most powerful alliance in the world against an enemy who was already prepared to negotiate, and was admitting defeat.

To apply the epithet 'terrorist' to the acts of bombing Hiroshima and Nagasaki is logically justifiable, and I do so because it may help to re-insert that act into living consciousness today. Yet the word changes nothing in itself.

The first-hand evidence of the victims, the reading of the pages which have been torn out, provokes a sense of outrage. This outrage has two natural faces. One is a sense of horror and pity at what happened; the other face is self-defensive and declares: *this should not happen again (here).* For some the *here* is in brackets, for others it is not.

The face of horror, the reaction which has now been mostly suppressed, forces us to comprehend the reality of what happened. The second reaction, unfortunately, distances us from that reality. Although it begins as a straight declaration, it quickly leads into the labyrinth of defence policies, military arguments and global strategies. Finally it leads to the sordid commercial absurdity of private fall-out shelters.

This split of the sense of outrage into, on one hand, horror and, on the other hand, expediency occurs because the concept of evil has been abandoned. Every culture, except our own in recent times, has had such a concept.

That its religious or philosophical bases vary is unimportant. The concept of evil implies a force or forces which have to be continually struggled against so that they do not triumph over life and destroy it. One of the very first written texts from Mesopotamia, 1,500 years before Homer, speaks of this struggle, which was the first condition of human life. In public thinking nowadays, the concept of evil has been reduced to a little adjective to support an opinion or hypothesis (abortions, terrorism, ayatollahs).

Nobody can confront the reality of 6th August 1945 without being forced to acknowledge that what happened was evil. It is not a question of opinion or interpretation, but of events.

The memory of these events should be continually before our eyes. This is why the thousand citizens of Hiroshima started to draw on their little scraps of paper. We need to show their drawings everywhere. These terrible images can now release an energy for opposing evil and for the life-long struggle of that opposition.

And from this a very old lesson may be drawn. My friend in the United States is, in a sense, innocent. She looks beyond a nuclear holocaust without considering its reality. This reality includes not only its victims but also its planners and those who support them. Evil from time immemorial has often worn a mask of innocence. One of evil's principal modes of being is *looking beyond* (with indifference) that which is before the eyes.

August 9th: On the west embankment of a military training field was a young boy four or five years old. He was burned black, lying on his back, with his arms pointing towards heaven.

Only by looking beyond or away can one come to believe that such evil is relative, and therefore under certain conditions justifiable. In reality – the reality to which the survivors and the dead bear witness – it can never be justified.

1981

Notes

1   Edited by Japan Broadcasting Corporation, London, Wildwood House, 1981; New York, Pantheon, 1981.

Of all the colours

—

Green
fills
the earth's two breasts
day and night
trees of the forest
suckle green.
of all the colours
green is the last.

Wind
dries the soil
powdery and light
in the deepest clay
stains
the brown of blood
repeatedly dried
die again
as the wind drops
under the rain.

Green
unlike silver or red
I say to you Nella
is never still
green who waited
mineral ages

for the leaf
is the colour of their souls
and comes as gift.

1985

Sources and acknowledgments

'Rembrandt self-portrait': previously unpublished.

'Self-portrait 1914–1918': previously unpublished.

'The white bird': previously unpublished.

'The storyteller': first published in *New Society*, 30 March 1978.

'On the edge of a foreign city': first published in *The Look of Things*, London, Penguin, 1972.

'The eaters and the eaten': first published in the *Guardian*, 3 January 1976.

'Dürer: a portrait of the artist': first published in *Realities*, 1971.

'One night in Strasbourg': first published in *The Nation*, 21 December 1974.

'On the banks of the Sava': first published in *New Society*, 1 June 1972.

Four 'postcard poems': first published in the *New Statesman*, 21 December 1979.

'On the Bosphorus': first published in *New Society*, 1 February 1979.

'Manhattan': first published in *New Society*, 6 February 1975.

'The theatre of indifference': first published in *New Society*, 26 June 1975.

'The city of Sodom': first published in *Realities*, January 1972.

'The deluge': first published in *Realities*, June 1972.

'Kerchief': previously unpublished.

'Goya: the Maja, dressed and undressed': first published in *The Moment of Cubism*, London, Weidenfeld & Nicholson, 1969; New York, Pantheon, 1969.

'Bonnard': first published in *The Moment of Cubism*, op. cit.

'Modigliani's alphabet of love': first published in *Village Voice*, May/June 1981.

'The Hals mystery': first published in *New Society*, 20 December 1979.

'In a Moscow cemetery': first published in *New Society*, 22 December 1983.

'Ernst Fischer: a philosopher and death': first published as an introduction to his autobiography *An Opposing Man*, London, Allen Lane, 1974; New York, Liveright, 1974.

'François, Georges and Amélie: a requiem in three parts': first published in *New Society*, 12 June 1980.

'Drawn to that moment': first published in *New Society*, 8 July 1976.

'The unsaid': previously unpublished.

'On a Degas bronze of a dancer': first published in *Permanent Red*, London, Methuen, 1960.

'The moment of Cubism': first published in *The Moment of Cubism*, *op. cit.*

'The eyes of Claude Monet': first published in *New Society*, 17 April 1980.

'The *work* of art': first published in *New Society*, 28 September 1978.

'Painting and time': first published in *New Society*, 27 September 1979.

'The place of painting' first published in *New Society*, 7 October 1982.

'On visibility': first published in *The Structurist*, 17/18, 1977–78.

'Redder every day': previously unpublished.

'Mayakovsky: his language and his death': first published in *7 Days*, 15 March 1972.

'The secretary of Death': first published in *New Society*, 2 September 1982.

'The hour of poetry': first published in *New Society*, 20 May 1982.

'The screen and *The Spike*: first published in *New Society*, 21 May 1981.

'Sicilian lives': first published as a foreword to Danilo Dolci, *Sicilian Lives*, trans. J. Vitiello, London, Writers & Readers, 1981; New York, Pantheon, 1982.

'Leopardi': first published in *New Society*, 2 June 1983.

'The production of the world': first published in *New Society*, 5 August 1982.

'Mother tongue': previously unpublished.

'Hiroshima': first published in *New Society*, 6 August 1981.

'Of all the colours': previously unpublished.

Extracts from 'The place of painting', 'Painting and time', 'The production of the word' and 'The hour of poetry' were incorporated in the text of *And our faces, my heart, brief as photos*, Writer & Readers, London and New York, 1984.